STEWS, CASSEROLES, PIES & MASH

CONTENTS

Egg and bacon pie, page 137

Lentil bhujia stew, page 61

Tomato and potato stew, page 60

Beef in red wine, page 14

All recipes are double-tested by our team of home economists. When we test our recipes, we rate them for ease of preparation. The following cookery ratings are on the recipes in this book, making them easy to use and understand.

A single Cooking with Confidence symbol indicates a recipe that is simple and generally quick to make—perfect for beginners.

Two symbols indicate the need for just a little more care and a little more time.

Three symbols indicate special dishes that need more investment in time, care and patience—but the results are worth it.

Note: International conversions and a glossary containing unfamiliar terms can be found on page 208. Cooking times may vary slightly depending on the individual oven. We suggest you check the manufacturer's instructions to ensure proper temperature control.

STEWS & CASSEROLES

NAVARIN OF LAMB

Preparation time: 25 minutes
Total cooking time: 1 hour 35 minutes
Serves 4

8 lamb noisettes
plain flour, seasoned with salt
 and black pepper
2 tablespoons oil
2 sticks celery, sliced diagonally
 into 2 cm (³/4 inch) lengths
12 baby carrots, peeled
12 new potatoes, unpeeled
6 sprigs of thyme
¹/4 cup (15 g/¹/2 oz) chopped
 parsley, and extra to garnish
2 onions, chopped
2 cloves garlic, crushed
¹/3 cup (40 g/1¹/4 oz) plain flour
2¹/2 cups (625 ml/21 fl oz)
 chicken stock
1 cup (250 ml/8 fl oz) good red
 wine
¹/4 cup (60 g/2 oz) tomato
 paste

1 Toss the lamb in the seasoned flour, shaking off the excess. Preheat the oven to moderate 180°C (350°F/Gas 4).
2 Heat the oil in a heavy-based pan. In batches, brown the lamb well on both sides over medium-high heat.

Remove from the heat, drain well on paper towels, then transfer to a greased, 6 cup (3 litre) capacity ovenproof casserole dish. Top with the celery, carrots, potatoes, thyme and parsley.
3 Cook the onion and garlic in the same heavy-based pan, stirring over medium heat for about 5–10 minutes, or until the onion is soft.
4 Add the flour and stir for 1 minute, or until the onion is coated. Add the remaining ingredients and stir until the sauce boils and thickens. Pour the sauce over the lamb and vegetables. Bake, covered, for 1¹/4 hours, or until the lamb is tender. Carefully remove the string from the lamb; sprinkle with extra parsley to serve.

COOK'S FILE

Notes: A noisette is a round slice of meat, cut from a boned loin and tied with string to hold its shape. For this recipe you could also use a boned leg of lamb, cut into 3 cm (1¹/4 inch) cubes.
● If baby carrots are not available, use four sliced carrots instead.
Storage time: This dish keeps for up to 2 days. Cover and refrigerate, and reheat gently before serving.

Add the lightly floured lamb to the hot oil and brown well all over.

Add the stock, wine and tomato paste to the softened onion mixture.

7

BOSTON BAKED BEANS

Preparation time: 25 minutes +
    6–8 hours soaking
Total cooking time: 1 hour 35 minutes
Serves 4–6

1¾ cups (350 g/11 oz) dried
    cannellini beans
1 whole ham hock
2 onions, chopped
2 tablespoons tomato paste
1 tablespoon Worcestershire sauce
1 tablespoon molasses
1 teaspoon French mustard
¼ cup (45 g/1½ oz) soft
    brown sugar
½ cup (125 ml/4 fl oz) tomato
    juice

1 Cover the beans with cold water and soak for 6–8 hours, or overnight.
2 Drain the beans, rinse them well and place in a large pan. Add the ham hock and cover with cold water. Bring to the boil, then reduce the heat and simmer, covered, for 25 minutes, or until the beans are tender. Preheat the oven to warm 160°C (315°F/Gas 2–3).
3 Remove the ham hock from the pan and set aside to cool. Drain the beans, reserving 1 cup (250 ml/8 fl oz) of the cooking liquid. Trim the ham of all skin, fat and sinew, then roughly chop the meat and discard the bone.
4 Transfer the meat and beans to a 8 cup (2 litre) casserole dish. Add the reserved liquid and all remaining ingredients. Mix gently, then cover and bake for 1 hour. Serve with hot, buttered toast.

COOK'S FILE

Notes: Any type of dried bean can be used in this recipe.

● To quick-soak beans, place them in a pan, add hot water to cover, bring slowly to the boil, then remove from the heat. Leave to soak for 1 hour before draining and using.

● Cooked beans can be frozen in 1 cup quantities and thawed as required.

Place the drained beans in a large pan. Add the ham hock and cover with cold water.

Trim the ham of all fat, skin and sinew, then roughly chop the meat.

Add the reserved liquid and remaining ingredients to the meat and beans.

SPICY BEEF, POTATO AND CAPSICUM STEW

Preparation time: 35 minutes
Total cooking time: 2 hours 20 minutes
Serves 4–6

300 g (10 oz) French shallots
2 tablespoons olive oil
1 kg (2 lb) gravy beef, cut into
    4 cm (1¹/2 inch) cubes
4 cloves garlic, crushed
3 teaspoons paprika
1 teaspoon fennel seeds
¹/2 teaspoon ground cumin
1 tablespoon plain flour
¹/2 cup (125 ml/4 fl oz) red wine
2 tablespoons brandy
¹/2 teaspoon dried thyme

¹/2 teaspoon dried oregano
1 bay leaf
1¹/2 cups (375 ml/12 fl oz) beef
    stock
1 tablespoon honey
400 g (13 oz) potatoes, cut into
    large chunks
2 red capsicums, chopped
¹/2 cup (125 g/4 oz) sour cream
chopped chives, for serving

1 Preheat the oven to moderate 180°C (350°F/Gas 4). Place the shallots in a bowl, cover with boiling water and leave for 30 seconds. Drain and peel.
2 Heat the oil in a large, heavy-based pan, then brown the meat in batches over medium-high heat and transfer to a large casserole dish.
3 Add the shallots to the pan and cook over medium heat until soft and golden. Add the garlic, paprika, fennel seeds and cumin; cook until fragrant.
4 Add the flour, cook for 30 seconds, then remove from the heat. Stir in the red wine and brandy. Return to the heat and add the thyme, oregano, bay leaf and stock. Stir until the mixture bubbles, then add to the meat.
5 Cover and bake for 1¹/2 hours, then add the honey, potato and capsicum. Cook, uncovered, for 30 minutes, or until the potato is tender. Season to taste. Serve with a dollop of sour cream and a sprinkling of chives.

Remove the skin from the blanched and drained shallots.

Brown the meat in batches in the hot oil over medium-high heat.

Add the red wine and brandy to the spice mixture and stir well.

LAMB CHOP CASSEROLE

Preparation time: 15 minutes
Total cooking time: 1 hour 15 minutes
Serves 4

6–8 lamb chump chops
1 teaspoon oil
1 large onion, finely chopped
1/3 cup (160 g/5 1/2 oz) redcurrant
   jelly
1 teaspoon finely grated
   lemon rind
1 tablespoon lemon juice
1 tablespoon barbecue sauce
1 tablespoon tomato sauce
1/2 cup (125 ml/4 fl oz) chicken
   stock

1 Trim any fat from the lamb. Preheat the oven to warm 170°C (325°F/Gas 3). Heat the oil in a large heavy-based frying pan; add the chops and cook over medium-high heat for 2–3 minutes, turning once, until well browned. Remove from the pan and put in a casserole dish.
2 Add the onion to the frying pan and cook over medium heat, stirring frequently, for 5 minutes, or until the onion is softened. Add the jelly, lemon rind and juice, barbecue and tomato sauces and stock. Stir for 2–3 minutes until heated through. Pour over the chops and stir well, cover and place in the oven. Cook for 1 hour, or until the meat is tender, turning 2–3 times. Lift out the chops onto a side plate and leave them to keep warm.
3 Pour the sauce into a pan and boil rapidly for 5 minutes until the sauce has thickened and reduced. Return the chops to the sauce before serving.

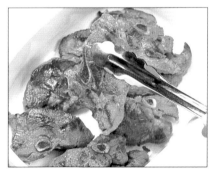

Once the chops have been well browned put them in a casserole dish.

Pour the sauce over the chops in the dish and stir to combine.

Use a pair of tongs to turn the chops a couple of times during cooking.

10

VEGETARIAN CHILLI

Preparation time: 15 minutes
Total cooking time: 40 minutes
Serves 6–8

3/4 cup (130 g/4¹/2 oz) burghul
2 tablespoons olive oil
1 large onion, finely
    chopped
2 cloves garlic,
    crushed
1 teaspoon chilli powder
2 teaspoons ground cumin
1 teaspoon cayenne pepper

¹/2 teaspoon ground cinnamon
3 cups (750 ml/24 fl oz)
    vegetable stock
2 x 400 g (13 oz) cans crushed
    tomatoes
440 g (14 oz) can red kidney
    beans, rinsed and drained
2 x 300 g (10 oz) cans
    chickpeas, rinsed and
    drained
300 g (10 oz) can corn kernels,
    drained
2 tablespoons tomato paste
corn chips and sour cream,
    for serving

1 Soak the burghul with 1 cup (250 ml/ 8 fl oz) boiling water for 10 minutes. Heat the oil in a large heavy-based pan and cook the onion for 10 minutes, stirring often, until it soft and golden.
2 Add the garlic, chilli powder, cumin, cayenne and cinnamon and cook, stirring, for a further minute.
3 Add the tomatoes, stock and burghul. Bring to the boil and simmer for 10 minutes. Stir in the beans, chickpeas, corn and tomato paste and simmer for 20 minutes, stirring often. Serve imediately with the corn chips and sour cream.

Stir the garlic and spices into the pan with the onion and cook for a minute.

Add the crushed tomatoes, stock and burghul to the pan.

Stir in the beans, chickpeas, corn kernels and tomato paste.

11

TAGINE OF LAMB WITH QUINCE AND LEMON

Preparation time: 25 minutes
Total cooking time: 2 hours 10 minutes
Serves 4

1.5 kg (3 lb) boned shoulder of
    lamb, cut into 12 even pieces
1 onion, finely chopped
2 cloves garlic, crushed
1 cinnamon stick
1 teaspoon ground ginger
1/2 teaspoon saffron threads
1 large quince, peeled, seeded
    and cut into 12 pieces
1/4 cup (60 ml/2 fl oz) honey
1 teaspoon ground cinnamon
1/2 preserved lemon
chopped parsley, for serving

1 Trim the lamb of excess fat and place in a large pan. Add the onion, garlic, cinnamon stick, ginger and saffron and enough cold water to cover. Slowly bring to the boil, stirring occasionally. Reduce the heat, cover and simmer for 45 minutes. Transfer the meat to a large casserole dish and set aside.
2 Add the quince, honey and ground cinnamon to the cooking liquid and simmer for 15 minutes, or until the quince is tender. Discard the cinnamon stick; remove the quince and add to the meat, reserving the liquid.

3 Preheat an oven to moderate 180°C (350°F/Gas 4). Boil the cooking liquid for 30 minutes, or until reduced by half, then pour over the meat and quince. Remove and discard the flesh from the lemon. Slice the rind thinly, then add to the meat. Cover and bake for 40 minutes, or until the meat is tender. Sprinkle with parsley to serve.

COOK'S FILE

Hint: As you work, place the peeled quince in water with a little lemon juice to prevent discolouring.

Add the onion, garlic, cinnamon stick, ginger, saffron and cold water to the lamb.

Add the quince, honey and ground cinnamon to the cooking liquid.

Remove and discard the flesh from the preserved lemon and slice the rind thinly.

VEAL, LEMON AND CASER STEW

VEAL, LEMON AND CAPER STEW

Preparation time: 30 minutes
Total cooking time: about 2 hours
Serves 4–6

1 tablespoon olive oil
50 g (1¾ oz) butter
1 kg (2 lb) stewing veal, cut into
    4 cm (1½ inch) chunks
300 g (10 oz) French shallots
3 leeks, cut into large chunks
2 cloves garlic, crushed
1 tablespoon plain flour
2 cups (500 ml/16 fl oz) chicken
    stock
1 teaspoon grated lemon rind
⅓ cup (80 ml/2¾ fl oz) lemon
    juice
2 bay leaves
2 tablespoons capers, drained
    and well rinsed
chopped parsley, for serving
caper berries, to garnish

1 Preheat the oven to moderate 180°C (350°F/Gas 4). Heat the oil and half the butter in a large, heavy-based pan. Brown the veal in batches over medium-high heat and transfer to a large casserole dish.
2 Blanch the shallots in boiling water for 30 seconds, then peel and add to the pan with the leeks. Gently cook for 5 minutes, or until soft and golden. Add the garlic, cook for 1 minute, then transfer to the casserole dish.
3 Melt the remaining butter in the pan, add the flour and cook for 30 seconds. Remove from the heat, add the stock and stir until well combined. Return to the heat and cook, stirring, until the sauce begins to bubble.
4 Pour the sauce into the casserole dish and stir in the lemon rind, lemon juice and bay leaves. Cover and bake for 1–1½ hours, or until the veal is tender. During the last 20 minutes of cooking, remove the lid to allow the sauces to reduce a little.
5 To serve, stir in the capers and season with salt and freshly ground black pepper. Sprinkle with parsley and garnish with caper berries.

COOK'S FILE

Notes: Caper berries are sold in jars of brine or vinegar in speciality stores.

• If possible, use tiny capers in this dish as they have a superb flavour. Regular capers can be used instead.

Add the leeks and peeled shallots to the pan and gently fry until soft and golden.

Remove the pan from the heat and stir in the stock, scraping up the brown bits.

BEEF IN RED WINE

Preparation time: 20 minutes
Total cooking time: 2 hours 15 minutes
Serves 4

2 tablespoons olive oil
1 kg (2 lb) trimmed chuck
   steak, cubed
12 baby onions, halved, with
   root base left intact
4 rashers bacon, rind removed,
   chopped
2 cloves garlic, finely chopped
3 tablespoons plain flour
1½ cups (375 ml/12 fl oz) red
   wine
2 tablespoons port
2 bay leaves
5 sprigs fresh parsley
3 sprigs fresh thyme
1 thin slice lemon rind
1½ cups (375 ml/12 fl oz) beef
   or chicken stock
500 g (1 lb) flat mushrooms,
   halved

1 Heat 1 tablespoon of oil in a large heavy-based pan, and cook the steak in small batches over high heat for 2 minutes, or until well browned. Remove from the pan.

2 Heat the remaining oil in the same pan, and add the onion, bacon and garlic. Stir over medium–high heat for 5 minutes, or until the onion is browned. Return the beef to the pan, add the flour, and stir for 1 minute. Remove the pan from the heat, and gradually stir in the wine and port, mixing the flour in well. Return the pan to the heat and bring to the boil, stirring, then reduce the heat and simmer for 3 minutes, or until the sauce boils and thickens slightly.

3 Make a bouquet garni by wrapping the bay leaves, parsley, thyme and lemon rind in a piece of muslin and tying with string. Add the bouquet garni, stock and mushrooms to the pan, bring to the boil, then reduce the heat to low and simmer, covered, for

2 hours, or until the beef is tender, stirring occasionally. Remove the bouquet garni, and season to taste. Serve with mashed potato or soft polenta and baby carrots.

Chop the baby onions in half, leaving the root base intact.

Cook the steak in batches until well browned all over.

Gradually add the wine and port, and stir to mix in the flour.

CHICKEN AND MUSHROOM CASSEROLE

Preparation time: 20 minutes
Total cooking time: 1 hour
Serves 4

20 g (³/4 oz) dried porcini
   mushrooms
plain flour, seasoned with salt
   and black pepper
1.5 kg (3 lb) chicken pieces
2 tablespoons oil
1 large onion, chopped
2 cloves garlic, crushed
¹/4 cup (60 ml/2 fl oz) chicken
   stock

1 tablespoon balsamic vinegar
¹/3 cup (80 ml/2³/4 fl oz) white
   wine
425 g (14 oz) can peeled whole
   tomatoes
3 sprigs fresh thyme
1 bay leaf
300 g (10 oz) field mushrooms,
   thickly sliced

1 Preheat the oven to moderate 180°C (350°F/Gas 4). Put the porcini mushrooms in a bowl and cover with ¹/4 cup (60 ml/2 fl oz) boiling water. Leave for 5 minutes, or until the mushrooms are rehydrated.
2 Lightly toss the chicken in flour to coat and shake off any excess.

3 Heat the oil in a flameproof casserole, and cook the chicken in batches until well browned all over. Set aside. Add the onion and garlic to the casserole and cook for 3–5 minutes, or until the onion softens. Stir in the chicken stock.
4 Return the chicken to the casserole with the porcini mushrooms (and any remaining liquid), vinegar, wine, tomatoes, thyme and bay leaf. Cover and cook in the oven for 30 minutes.
5 After 30 minutes, remove the lid and add the mushrooms. Return to the oven and cook, uncovered, for a further 15–20 minutes, or until the sauce thickens slightly. Serve immediately.

Cover the porcini mushrooms with boiling water and soak until rehydrated.

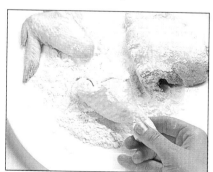

Lightly toss the chicken pieces in the flour and shake off any excess.

Add the chicken to the casserole and cook in batches until browned.

15

CREAMY TOMATO AND CHICKEN STEW

Preparation time: 35 minutes
Total cooking time: 50 minutes
Serves 4–6

4 rashers bacon
2 tablespoons oil
50 g (1¾ oz) butter
300 g (10 oz) small button
    mushrooms, halved
1.5 kg (3 lb) chicken pieces
2 onions, chopped
2 cloves garlic, crushed
400 g (13 oz) can tomatoes
1 cup (250 ml/8 fl oz) chicken
    stock
1 cup (250 ml/8 fl oz) cream
2 tablespoons chopped parsley
2 tablespoons lemon thyme
    leaves

1 Chop the bacon into large pieces. Place a large, heavy-based pan over medium heat. Brown the bacon, then remove and set aside on paper towels.
2 Heat half the oil and a third of the butter in the pan until foaming, then stir in the mushrooms and cook until softened and golden brown. Remove from the pan with a slotted spoon.
3 Add the remaining oil to the pan with a little more butter. When the oil is hot, brown the chicken pieces in batches over high heat until the skin is golden all over and a little crisp. Remove from the pan.
4 Heat the remaining butter in the pan. Add the onion and garlic and cook over medium-high heat for about 3 minutes, or until softened. Pour in the tomatoes, stock and cream. Return the bacon, mushrooms and chicken pieces to the pan and simmer over medium-low heat for 25 minutes. Stir in the herbs, season with salt and freshly ground pepper and simmer for another 5 minutes before serving.

When the oil and butter are foaming, add the mushrooms and cook until soft.

Brown the chicken pieces in batches over high heat until the skin is golden and crisp.

Add the tomatoes, stock and cream to the softened onion and garlic.

BRAISED CHICKEN WITH CHICKPEAS

Preparation time: 35 minutes
Total cooking time: 1 hour 35 minutes
Serves 4

50 g (1³/4 oz) butter
1 onion, roughly chopped
3 cloves garlic, crushed
1 carrot, finely chopped
¹/2 stick celery, finely chopped
1.5 kg (3 lb) chicken pieces
    (about 8 portions)
¹/3 cup (80 ml/2³/4 fl oz) Marsala
1 cup (250 ml/8 fl oz) chicken
    stock
2 tablespoons lemon juice

¹/2 cup (40 g/1¹/4 oz) fresh
    breadcrumbs
300 g (10 oz) can chickpeas,
    rinsed and drained
200 g (6¹/2 oz) button mushrooms,
    sliced
2 tablespoons shredded mint
2 tablespoons chopped parsley

1 Heat half the butter in a large, heavy-based pan and cook the onion over medium heat until soft and golden. Add the garlic, carrot and celery and cook over gentle heat for 5 minutes. Remove from the pan and set aside.
2 Melt the remaining butter in the pan and brown the chicken in batches over high heat. Return all the chicken to the pan with the carrot and celery mixture. Quickly add the Marsala and stir well, scraping the sides and base of the pan. Add the stock and lemon juice, bring to the boil, then reduce the heat and simmer gently for 1 hour, stirring occasionally.
3 Remove the chicken; keep warm. In a food processor, purée the contents of the pan, then add the breadcrumbs and blend for another 15 seconds.
4 Return the chicken to the pan, pour in the purée, add the chickpeas and mushrooms and simmer, covered, for 15 minutes. Season to taste, and scatter with mint and parsley to serve.

Gently fry the garlic, carrot and celery in the butter for 5 minutes.

Pour the Marsala over the vegetables and chicken, stirring well.

Add the fresh breadcrumbs to the puréed pan mixture and process until smooth.

17

KASHMIR LAMB WITH SPINACH

Preparation time: 20 minutes
Total cooking time: 1 hour 30 minutes
Serves 4

2 tablespoons oil
750 g (1¹/₂ lb) diced leg of lamb
2 large onions, chopped
3 cloves garlic, crushed
4 cm (1¹/₂ inch) fresh ginger, grated
2 teaspoons ground cumin
2 teaspoons ground coriander
2 teaspoons turmeric
¹/₄ teaspoon ground cardamom
¹/₄ teaspoon ground cloves
3 bay leaves
1¹/₂ cups (375 ml/12 fl oz) chicken stock
¹/₂ cup (125 ml/4 fl oz) cream
2 bunches English spinach leaves, washed and chopped

1 Heat the oil in a heavy-based pan and brown the lamb in batches, stirring regularly. Remove from the pan. Add the onions, garlic and ginger and cook for 3 minutes, stirring regularly. Add the cumin, coriander, turmeric, cardamom and cloves and cook, stirring, for 1–2 minutes, or until fragrant.

Return the lamb to the pan with any juices. Add the bay leaves and stock.
2 Bring to the boil and then reduce the heat, stir well, cover and simmer for 35 minutes. Add the cream and cook, covered, for a further 20 minutes, or until the lamb is very tender.
3 Add the spinach and cook until the spinach has softened. Season to taste and serve with steamed rice.

COOK'S FILE

Storage time: Curry is best cooked a day in advance and refrigerated. Do not add the spinach until reheating.

Return the browned lamb to the pan and add the bay leaves.

Stir in the cream and simmer until the lamb is very tender.

It will only take a few minutes for the spinach to soften and reduce.

ROMAN CHICKEN

Preparation time: 10 minutes
Total cooking time: 45 minutes
Serves 2–4

1 tablespoon olive oil
1 small onion, sliced
4 thick rashers bacon, diced
4 large or 8 small chicken legs
¹/₃ cup (20 g/³/₄ oz) chopped fresh parsley
1 clove garlic, crushed
1 cup (250 ml/8 fl oz) chicken stock
1 tablespoon chopped fresh marjoram
440 g (14 oz) can crushed tomatoes

1 Heat the oil in a large heavy-based pan and cook the onion and bacon over medium heat for 5 minutes. Increase the heat and add the chicken in batches. Brown the chicken on all sides, turning often and taking care not to overcook the onion and bacon, for about 5 minutes.
2 Reduce the heat, add the garlic and parsley and cook for 2–3 minutes. Add the stock and marjoram, stirring well. Add the tomatoes, stir well and season to taste.
3 Bring to the boil, cover the pan and simmer gently for 30 minutes, turning the chicken legs occasionally, until they are cooked through.

Brown the chicken well, taking care not to burn the onion.

Add the stock and marjoram. Stir well to prevent anything sticking to the pan base.

Turn the chicken legs occasionally to ensure even cooking on all sides.

CREAMY CHICKEN WITH MUSHROOMS

Preparation time: 20 minutes
Total cooking time: 40 minutes
Serves: 6

2 tablespoons olive oil
200 g (6½ oz) button
    mushrooms, halved
200 g (6½ oz) field mushrooms,
    chopped
1 small red capsicum, sliced
4 chicken breast fillets, cut into
    bite-sized pieces
2 tablespoons plain flour

1 cup (250 ml/8 fl oz) chicken
    stock
½ cup (125 ml/4 fl oz) red wine
3 spring onions, finely chopped
1¼ cups (315 ml/10 fl oz) cream
1 tablespoon chopped chives
1 tablespoon finely chopped
    fresh parsley
¼ teaspoon turmeric

1 Heat the oil in a large heavy-based pan and add the button and field mushrooms and capsicum. Cook over medium heat for 4 minutes, or until soft. Remove and set aside.

2 Brown the chicken quickly in batches over a medium-high heat. Sprinkle with flour in the pan and cook for a further 2 minutes until the flour is golden. Add the stock and wine and bring to the boil. Cover and simmer for 10 minutes, or until the chicken is tender.

3 Add the spring onion and cream, return to the boil and simmer for 10–15 minutes, or until the cream has reduced and thickened. Return the mushrooms and capsicum to the pan and add the chives, parsley and turmeric. Stir, season and simmer for a further 5 minutes to heat through.

Choose large field mushrooms and wipe them with a damp cloth before chopping.

Add the spring onions and cream and return to the boil.

Add the mushrooms, capsicum, chives, parsley and turmeric.

COUNTRY BEEF STEW

Preparation time: 40 minutes
Total cooking time: 2 hours 10 minutes
Serves 8

1 small eggplant, cubed
2–3 tablespoons olive oil
2 red onions, sliced
2 cloves garlic, crushed
1 kg (2 lb) chuck steak, cubed
1 teaspoon ground coriander
1/2 teaspoon allspice
3/4 teaspoon sweet paprika
6 ripe tomatoes, chopped
1 cup (250 ml/8 fl oz) red wine

3 cups (750 ml/12 fl oz) beef
  stock
2 tablespoons tomato paste
250 g (8 oz) baby new potatoes,
  halved
2 sticks celery, sliced
3 carrots, chopped
2 bay leaves
1/4 cup (7 g/1/4 oz) fresh parsley,
  chopped

1 Put the eggplant in a colander, sprinkle generously with salt and leave for 20 minutes. Rinse, pat dry with paper towels and set aside.
2 Heat the oil in a large heavy-based pan and cook the onion for 5 minutes until soft; add the garlic and cook for 1 minute. Remove and set aside. Add the eggplant and brown for 5 minutes. Remove and set aside. Brown the meat in batches over medium heat, sprinkle with the spices, season and cook for 1–2 minutes. Add the tomato, onion, wine, stock and tomato paste and bring to the boil. Reduce the heat and simmer, covered, for 25 minutes.
3 Add the potato, celery, carrot and bay leaves, bring to the boil, reduce the heat, cover and simmer for 1 hour. Add the eggplant and simmer for 30 minutes, uncovered. Lift out the bay leaves and stir in the parsley.

Put the eggplant in a colander and sprinkle with salt to draw out any bitterness.

Add the tomato, onion, wine, stock and tomato paste to the pan.

Add the potato, celery, carrot and bay leaves to the pan.

21

RICH STEAK AND KIDNEY STEW

Preparation time: 35 minutes
Total cooking time: 2 hours 30 minutes
Serves 4–6

1 kg (2 lb) chuck steak
2–3 tablespoons oil
1 thick rasher bacon, rind
    removed and thinly sliced
40 g (1¼ oz) butter
1 large onion, chopped
300 g (10 oz) button mushrooms
1 cup (250 ml/8 fl oz) brown
    muscat
2–3 cloves garlic, crushed
¼ teaspoon ground allspice
½ teaspoon paprika
2 teaspoons coriander seeds,
    lightly crushed
8 lamb kidneys (about 425 g/
    14 oz), quartered, cores
    removed
1 tablespoon wholegrain mustard
1 cup (250 ml/8 fl oz) beef or
    vegetable stock
2–3 tablespoons soft
    brown sugar
1–2 teaspoons fresh thyme
1–2 teaspoons fresh rosemary

1 Trim the steak of any excess fat and sinew and cut into 2–3 cm (¾–1¼ inch) cubes. Heat 1 teaspoon of the oil in a large, heavy-based pan. Add the bacon and cook for 2–3 minutes until just crisp; remove from the pan. Add 2 tablespoons oil and 30 g (1 oz) butter to the pan. Brown the steak in batches then remove from the pan and set aside.

2 Add the onion to the pan and cook for 2–3 minutes until just soft and golden. Add the mushrooms and cook, stirring, for 3 minutes, until starting to brown. Stir in half the muscat and simmer for 3–4 minutes. Remove the mixture from the pan and set aside.

3 Add the remaining oil and butter to the pan. Stir in the garlic, allspice, paprika and coriander seeds and cook for 1 minute. Add the kidneys and cook, stirring, over medium heat until just beginning to brown. Stir in the remaining muscat and mustard and simmer for 2 minutes. Return the mushroom and onion mixture to the pan, with the steak and bacon. Stir until combined. Stir in the stock. Bring to the boil, reduce the heat, cover and simmer for 1 hour. Stir in the sugar (the amount depends on the sweetness of the muscat), cover and simmer for 40 minutes. Uncover and simmer for 20 minutes. Stir in the thyme and rosemary during the last 10 minutes.

Cut under and up to remove the attached inner cores from the kidneys.

When the mushrooms start to brown stir in half the muscat.

Return the browned steak and bacon to the pan and stir in the stock.

MEXICAN BEEF STEW

Preparation time: 30 minutes
Total cooking time: 1 hour 30 minutes
Serves 6

500 g (1 lb) plum tomatoes, halved
6 flour tortillas
1–2 red chillies, finely chopped
1 tablespoon olive oil
1 kg (2 lb) stewing beef, cubed
1/2 teaspoon black pepper
2 onions, thinly sliced
1/4 cup (60 g/2 oz) tomato paste

11/2 cups (375 ml/12 fl oz) beef stock
375 g (12 oz) can kidney beans, drained
1 teaspoon chilli powder
1/2 cup (125 g/4 oz) sour cream

1 Preheat the oven to moderate 180°C (350°F/Gas 4). Put the tomato halves, skin-side-up, under a hot grill for 6–8 minutes, or until the skin is black and blistered. Cool, remove the skin and roughly chop the flesh.

2 Bake 2 of the tortillas in the oven for 4 minutes, or until crisp. Break into pieces and put in a food processor

with the tomato and chilli. Process for 30 seconds until almost smooth.

3 Heat the oil in a large heavy-based pan. Brown the beef in batches, season with pepper, then remove. Add the onion to the pan and cook for 5 minutes. Return the meat to the pan. Stir in the processed mixture, stock and tomato paste and bring to the boil. Reduce the heat, cover and simmer for 11/4 hours. Add the beans and chilli powder and heat through.

4 Grill the remaining tortillas for 2–3 minutes on each side, cool and cut into wedges. Serve the stew with sour cream and toasted tortilla wedges.

Grill the tomatoes until the skin is black and blistered and it will peel away easily.

Once the tortillas are crisp, break into pieces and put in the food processor.

Stir in the processed mixture, stock and tomato paste.

POACHER'S RABBIT

Preparation time: 30 minutes
Total cooking time: 2 hours 15 minutes
Serves 4

1 tablespoon vinegar
1 tablespoon salt
1 rabbit, about 1 kg (2 lb), cut
    into 12 portions (ask your
    butcher to do this)
plain flour, seasoned with salt
    and black pepper
1/3 cup (80 ml/2¾ fl oz) olive oil
2 rashers bacon, roughly
    chopped
8 bulb spring onions, trimmed
2 medium carrots, finely sliced
1½ cups (375 ml/12 fl oz) cider
2 teaspoons French mustard
1/2 teaspoon dried rosemary
1/2 teaspoon dried thyme
1 bay leaf
1/3 cup (10 g/¼ oz) finely
    chopped parsley

1 Add the vinegar and salt to a bowl of water and leave the rabbit portions to soak overnight. Drain, rinse well and dry on paper towels. Toss the rabbit in the seasoned flour, shaking off any excess. Preheat the oven to moderate 180°C (350°F/Gas 4).
2 Heat ¼ cup (60 ml/2 fl oz) oil in a large heavy-based frying pan and brown the rabbit quickly in batches over medium heat. Transfer to a 8 cup (2 litre) casserole dish.
3 Add the remaining oil to the pan; add the bacon, onions and carrot and fry over medium heat for 5 minutes, or until lightly browned. Add to the casserole dish.
4 Pour the cider into the frying pan and stir in the mustard, herbs and bay leaf. Bring to the boil and then pour over the rabbit. Cover with a tight-fitting lid and bake for 2 hours, or until tender. Remove the bay leaf and stir in the parsley.

COOK'S FILE

Storage time: Refrigerate for up to 2 days. Freeze for up to 1 month.
Hint: For more sauce, add more cider or water towards the end of cooking.

Use paper towels to dry the drained and rinsed rabbit portions.

Cut the tops and tails from the bulb spring onions.

Fry the bacon, onions and carrot until lightly browned.

Add the mustard, herbs and bay leaf to the cider in the frying pan.

BEEF STEW WITH PECANS

Preparation time: 15 minutes
Total cooking time: 2 hours
Serves 4

1/4 cup (60 ml/2 fl oz) olive oil
1 onion, sliced
125 g (4 oz) mushrooms, sliced
1–2 cloves garlic, crushed
1 1/2 tablespoons plain flour
1 teaspoon ground cinnamon
1/2 teaspoon black pepper
1/2 teaspoon ground nutmeg
1/2 teaspoon ground coriander
1 1/2 teaspoons salt
pinch cayenne pepper
1 teaspoon grated ginger

750 g (1 1/2 lb) lean stewing
   beef, cubed
3/4 cup (185 ml/6 fl oz) beef
   stock
1/4 cup (60 ml/2 fl oz) red wine
1 tablespoon soy sauce
12 prunes, pitted, soaking in
   1/2 cup (125 ml/4 fl oz) extra
   beef stock
1 tablespoon soft brown sugar
60 g (2 oz) pecan nuts

1 Heat half the oil in a large, heavy-based pan. Fry the onion for 3 minutes until soft, add the mushrooms and garlic and cook for 2 minutes. Remove from the pan. Mix together the flour, 1/2 teaspoon cinnamon, pepper, nutmeg, coriander, 1 teaspoon salt, cayenne and ginger and use to coat the meat. Add the remaining oil to the pan and brown the meat in batches. Remove from the pan.

2 Add the stock, wine, soy sauce and extra stock (from soaking the prunes) to the pan. Bring to the boil, return the onions, mushrooms, garlic and meat to the pan. Simmer for 2 hours. Add the sugar and cook for 10 minutes, or until the meat is tender.

3 Heat the remaining oil in a small pan and fry the pecans for 4 minutes, or until golden brown. Add the rest of the cinnamon and salt and toss to coat the pecans. Add these to the stew with the prunes 5 minutes before serving.

To coat the meat toss it in a plastic bag with the seasoned flour.

Return the onions, mushrooms, garlic and meat to the pan.

Make sure the pecans are well coated with the cinnamon and salt.

FAMOUS IRISH STEW

Preparation time: 20 minutes
Total cooking time: 1 hour 15 minutes
Serves 4

8 lamb neck chops
4 thick rashers bacon
30 g (1 oz) dripping or butter
1 kg (2 lb) potatoes, thickly
    sliced
3 carrots, sliced
3 medium onions, thickly
    sliced
2 cups (500 ml/16 fl oz) beef or
    vegetable stock
sprigs of thyme, to taste

1 Trim the chops, removing any excess fat, and cut the bacon into short strips. Heat the dripping or butter in a pan and cook the chops until brown on both sides; remove from the pan. Add the bacon and cook until crisp. Remove from the pan and leave to drain on paper towels.
2 Arrange half the potato, carrot and onion in the base of a deep, heavy-based pan. Season with freshly ground black pepper and add half the bacon. Layer the chops over this and cover with the rest of the potato, carrot, onion and bacon.
3 Add the stock and thyme. Cover, bring to the boil, reduce the heat and simmer for 1 hour, or until the lamb is very tender.

COOK'S FILE

Note: Traditionally, Irish Stew was made from mutton with no potatoes or carrots. The addition of vegetables makes the dish a very satisfying one-pot meal.

Use a sharp knife to remove any excess fat from the chops.

Spread the chops in one layer over the vegetables and bacon.

Once all the ingredients are layered, pour the stock and thyme over them.

VEAL BRAISED WITH LEMON THYME

Preparation time: 15 minutes
Total cooking time: 1 hour 30 minutes
Serves 4

2 tablespoons olive oil
one 6 cutlet rack of veal,
    trimmed to a neat shape
2 medium leeks, finely sliced
30 g (1 oz) butter
1 tablespoon plain flour
1 tablespoon grated lemon rind
2 cups (500 ml/16 fl oz) chicken
    stock
1¹/₂ cups (375 ml/12 fl oz) dry
    white wine
2 tablespoons fresh lemon
    thyme leaves
¹/₂ cup (125 ml/4 fl oz) cream

1 Heat the oil in a deep heavy-based frying pan over medium heat and brown the veal rack well on all sides. Remove the veal from the pan and set aside on a plate. Add the leeks and butter to the pan, reduce the heat and cover. Gently simmer for 10 minutes, stirring occasionally. Be careful not to burn the leeks or they will be bitter.
2 Add the flour to the pan and cook for 2 minutes, stirring continuously. Add the lemon rind and season with freshly ground black pepper. Stir in the stock and wine and bring to the boil, stirring continously. Reduce the heat.
3 Return the veal to the pan, with any juices. Cover and simmer for 1 hour, or until the veal is tender. Cut the veal into cutlets. Add the lemon thyme, cream and salt to the sauce and stir until combined. Pour over the veal and serve.

Remove the fat and trim the veal rack into a neat shape.

Add the grated lemon rind to the leeks in the pan.

Put the browned veal back in the pan once you have braised the leeks.

TRADITIONAL LAMB SHANKS

Preparation time: 30 minutes
Total cooking time: 2 hours 25 minutes
Serves 4–6

8 lamb shanks
1 tablespoon olive oil
1 orange
1 large onion, sliced
4 cloves garlic
1 large carrot, cut into chunks
1 parsnip, cut into chunks
1 stick celery, cut into chunks
2 bay leaves
3 cups (750 ml/24 fl oz) chicken
    stock
2 cups (500 ml/16 fl oz) red wine
1 tablespoon redcurrant jelly
3 teaspoons cornflour
sprigs of thyme, to garnish

1 Preheat the oven to warm 160°C (315°F/Gas 2–3). Pat the lamb dry with paper towels. Heat the oil in a flameproof casserole or baking dish large enough to fit the shanks in a single layer, then brown the shanks over high heat for 3 minutes, turning frequently. Remove and set aside.
2 Peel three 5 cm (2 inch) strips of rind from the orange, avoiding the bitter white pith. Set aside.
3 Add the onion and garlic cloves to the dish and cook over medium heat for 2 minutes, stirring. Add the carrot, parsnip and celery and place the shanks snugly on top. Add the rind strips and bay leaves, then pour in the stock and red wine. Cover and bake for 2 hours, or until the meat is very tender and comes away from the bone.
4 Using tongs, carefully remove the shanks from the dish; cover with foil to keep warm. Remove the rind and bay leaves and strain the juices into a pan. Set the vegetables aside.
5 Add the redcurrant jelly to the dish and stir to dissolve. Boil rapidly for 20 minutes, or until the sauce is reduced to 1½ cups (375 ml/12 fl oz). Combine the cornflour with a little water and whisk into the sauce, stirring until thickened and glossy.
6 To serve, place the lamb shanks on serving plates, arrange the vegetables on top, drizzle with the sauce and garnish with thyme.

COOK'S FILE

Note: This recipe can be made 2 days ahead, or frozen for up to 2 months.

Heat the oil in a baking dish and brown the shanks over high heat.

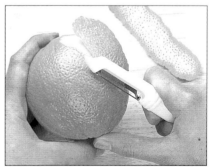

Peel strips of rind from the orange, avoiding the bitter white pith.

VEAL WITH ALMONDS AND MUSHROOMS

Preparation time: 20 minutes
Total cooking time: 1 hour 50 minutes
Serves 4–6

75 g (2½ oz) blanched
    almonds
olive oil, for cooking
2 onions, chopped
1 kg (2 lb) diced veal
plain flour, seasoned with salt
    and black pepper
½ cup (125 ml/4 fl oz) red wine
500 g (1 lb) very ripe tomatoes,
    chopped
2 tablespoons chopped oregano
50 g (1¾ oz) butter
400 g (13 oz) mushrooms (such
    as tiny buttons, shiitake or
    porcini)

1 Preheat the oven to slow 150°C (300°F/Gas 2). Scatter the almonds on a baking tray and bake for 10 minutes, or until golden. Cool and roughly chop.
2 Heat 2 tablespoons of oil in a deep, heavy-based pan. Cook the onion over low heat for 15 minutes, stirring often. Remove and set aside, leaving as much oil as possible in the pan.
3 Toss the veal in the flour, shaking off any excess. Reheat the pan and brown the veal over medium heat in batches, adding more oil if necessary.
4 Return all the veal to the pan with any juices; add the onion and wine. Bring to the boil and stir well. Reduce the heat to very low, cover with foil and a tightly fitting lid, then simmer very gently for 1 hour.
5 Stir well, then mix in the tomatoes and oregano. Cover and simmer for another 20 minutes. Season to taste.

6 Melt the butter until foamy in a frying pan over medium heat. Cut any large mushrooms and cook until just wilted, tossing well.
7 To serve, dish the stew onto serving plates, top with the mushrooms, drizzle over any juices and sprinkle with the chopped toasted almonds.

Gently cook the onion for 15 minutes, or until golden. Remove and set aside.

Return the browned veal to the pan with any juices. Add the onions and red wine.

When the butter is foaming, add all the mushrooms and cook until just wilted.

OXTAIL RAGOUT

Preparation time: 20 minutes +
  3 hours soaking
Total cooking time: 4 hours
Serves 4

1 kg (2 lb) oxtail, cut into short
    pieces (ask your butcher to
    do this)
1/4 cup (30 g/1 oz) plain flour
1 tablespoon ghee or oil
2 rashers bacon, chopped
1 small onion, peeled and
    studded with 6 whole cloves
2 cloves garlic, peeled
2 carrots, quartered lenghways
1½ cups (375 ml/12 fl oz) beef
    or chicken stock
425 g (14 oz) can tomato purée
1 parsnip, peeled and
    quartered lengthways
1 leek, thickly sliced

1 Trim any fat from the oxtail and discard. Put the oxtail in a large bowl, cover with water and set aside for 3 hours. Drain and transfer the meat to a large heavy-based pan, cover with fresh water and bring to the boil. Reduce the heat and simmer for 10 minutes, skimming any froth from the surface with a spoon or absorbent paper towel. Drain the meat, allow to cool and pat dry with paper towels.

2 Preheat the oven to slow 150°C (300°F/Gas 2). Put the seasoned flour, in a large plastic bag then add the oxtail and shake until it is evenly coated in flour. Heat the ghee or oil in a large frying pan, add the bacon and cook over medium heat for 3 minutes, stirring frequently. Remove from the pan.

3 Add the oxtail and cook, stirring continuously over medium-high heat for 2–3 minutes, or until browned. Transfer to a casserole dish.

4 Add the bacon, onion, garlic and half the carrot. Stir in the stock and tomato purée. Cover and bake for 3 hours. Add the parsnip, leek and remaing carrot and cook for 40 minutes, or until the vegetables are tender.

COOK'S FILE:

Storage time: Best made a day in advance and refrigerated.

Press the cloves firmly into the onion so they don't fall out during cooking.

Put the oxtail in a plastic bag with the flour and shake to coat evenly.

Cook the oxtail over medium-high heat until browned.

Add the remaining carrot with the parsnip and leek.

Use a couple of wooden spoons to toss the lamb cubes in the marinade.

Remove the cardamom pods and cinnamon stick and discard.

Add the marinade and apricot nectar to the meat in the pan.

Add the apricots and prunes and stir through gently.

LAMB AND APRICOT STEW

Preparation time: 30 minutes + marinating
Total cooking time: 1 hour 30 minutes
Serves 4–6

2 kg (4 lb) leg lamb, boned
　(ask your butcher to do this)
1 onion, thickly sliced
$1/2$ cup (125 ml/4 fl oz) white
　wine
1 tablespoon grated lemon rind
$1/4$ cup (60 ml/2 fl oz) lemon
　juice
1 tablespoon ground coriander
4 cardamom pods
1 cinnamon stick
2 tablespoons oil
170 ml ($5^{1}/2$ fl oz) can apricot
　nectar
$1/2$ cup (95 g/3 oz) dried apricots
$1/2$ cup (110 g/$3^{1}/2$ oz) pitted
　prunes
1 tablespoon cornflour
$1/2$ cup (80 g/$2^{3}/4$ oz) roasted
　unsalted cashew nuts
$1/4$ cup (7 g/$1/4$ oz) finely
　chopped fresh parsley

1 Trim away the skin and excess fat and cut the meat into 3 cm ($1^{1}/4$ inch) cubes. In a large non-metallic bowl, combine the onion, wine, lemon rind, juice, coriander, cardamom pods and cinnamon stick. Season with salt and freshly ground pepper. Toss the lamb cubes in the marinade, cover and refrigerate for a minimum of 8 hours or overnight. Stir 2 or 3 times.
2 Drain the meat and onion mixture, reserving the marinade, and dry on paper towels. Discard the cardamom pods and cinnamon stick. Heat the oil in a large heavy-based frying pan and brown the meat and onion, in batches, over high heat for 2–3 minutes.
3 Return all the meat and onion to the pan; add the marinade and apricot nectar. Bring to the boil, cover with a tight-fitting lid, reduce the heat to low and simmer for 30 minutes, stirring once. Add the apricots and prunes, stir gently through, cover and simmer for a further 30 minutes.
4 Mix 1 tablespoon water with the cornflour until smooth. Add to the pan and stir until thickened; simmer for a further 15 minutes, or until the lamb is tender. Scatter with the roasted cashews and parsley. Serve with steamed rice.

CHICKEN CURRY

Preparation time: 25 minutes
Total cooking time: 1 hour 45 minutes
Serves 4

2 tablespoons ghee
1 kg (2 lb) chicken drumsticks
   and thighs
1 tablespoon hot curry powder
1 tablespoon curry paste
1/2 teaspoon black mustard
   seeds
1/2 teaspoon ground coriander
1 teaspoon paprika
1/4 teaspoon cinnamon
1/2 teaspoon cumin
1/2 teaspoon turmeric
1 tablespoon finely chopped
   coriander root
2 cloves garlic, crushed
2 cm (3/4 inch) piece fresh
   ginger, grated
1 onion, chopped
1 kg (2 lb) potatoes, quartered
1 1/2 cups (375 ml/12 fl oz)
   chicken stock
1 tablespoon lemon juice
2 x 425 g (14 oz) cans peeled
   whole tomatoes
250 g (8 oz) packet frozen
   spinach, defrosted
1/4 cup (60 ml/2 fl oz) coconut
   cream
shredded fresh coriander leaves,
   to garnish

1 Melt 1 tablespoon of ghee in a heavy-based pan, and cook the chicken in batches for 2–3 minutes, or until browned all over. Remove. Melt the remaining ghee in the pan, add the curry powder, paste and remaining dry spices, and cook over low heat for 1–2 minutes, or until fragrant. Increase the heat, add the coriander root, garlic, ginger and onion, and cook for 3–5 minutes, or until the onion is soft.
2 Return the chicken pieces to the pan, add the potato and gently toss in the spices to coat. Season generously with salt and freshly ground black pepper. Pour in the chicken stock, and stir to ensure that any spices on the bottom of the pan are incorporated. Add the lemon juice and tomatoes, bring the mixture to the boil, then reduce the heat and simmer for 1–1 1/2 hours, or until the potato is tender and the chicken meat is falling off the bones.
3 Carefully remove the chicken from the pan, let it cool slightly and pull the meat off the bones. Return the meat to the pan. Stir in the spinach and coconut cream and cook for 3–5 minutes, or until heated through. Garnish with the coriander leaves and serve with jasmine rice.

Melt the ghee, then cook the chicken in batches until browned all over.

Cook the curry powder, curry paste and dry spices until fragrant.

Gently toss the chicken and potatoes in the spices to coat.

LAMB WITH BORLOTTI BEANS

Preparation time: 20 minutes +
   overnight soaking
Total cooking time: 2 hours
Serves 6

1 cup (200 g /6¹/2 oz) dried
   borlotti beans
1 tablespoon olive oil
12 lamb loin chops
1 onion, finely chopped
1 stick celery, chopped
1 carrot, chopped
3 cloves garlic, finely chopped
¹/2 teaspoon dried chilli flakes
1 teaspoon cumin seeds
2 cups (500 ml/16 fl oz) lamb or
   chicken stock
2 bay leaves
3 tablespoons lemon juice
¹/3 cup (20 g/³/4 oz) chopped
   parsley
1 tablespoon shredded mint

1 Soak the beans overnight in cold water. Drain, rinse well and set aside.
2 Preheat the oven to moderate 180°C (350°F/Gas 4). Heat the oil in a large heavy-based pan. Brown the lamb over high heat in batches and transfer to a casserole dish.

3 Add the onion, celery and carrot to the pan and cook over low heat for about 10 minutes, or until soft and golden. Add the garlic, chilli and cumin seeds and cook for 1 minute, then transfer to the casserole dish.
4 Add the stock, beans and bay leaves. Cover tightly; bake for 1¹/2–1³/4 hours, or until the lamb is very tender and the beans are cooked. Season with salt and freshly ground black pepper. Stir in the lemon juice, parsley and mint just before serving.

When the oil is hot, brown the lamb over high heat in batches.

Add the onion, celery and carrot to the pan and cook until soft and golden.

Add the stock, drained borlotti beans and bay leaves to the casserole.

RED WINE AND PORK STEW

Preparation time: 30 minutes +
  overnight marinating
Total cooking time: 1 hour 30 minutes
Serves 4–6

750 g (1½ lb) pork, cut into
  3 cm (1¼ inch) cubes
¼ cup (60 ml/2 fl oz) oil
plain flour, seasoned with salt
  and black pepper
12 bulb spring onions, trimmed
3 rashers bacon, cut into
  thin strips
2 carrots, chopped
200 g (6½ oz) button mushrooms
2 sticks celery, sliced

1½ cups (375 ml/12 fl oz)
  chicken stock
1 teaspoon thyme leaves
1 tablespoon chopped parsley

Marinade
1 cup (250 ml/8 fl oz) red wine
1 tablespoon olive oil
4 cloves garlic, crushed
1 tablespoon thyme leaves
2 teaspoons rosemary leaves
2 tablespoons chopped parsley

1 Combine the marinade ingredients
in a large bowl. Add the pork and mix
well. Cover and refrigerate overnight.
2 Reserving the marinade, drain the
pork. Heat 2 tablespoons of the oil in a
large, deep saucepan. Coat the pork in

the seasoned flour and brown in
batches over high heat. Remove and
set aside.
3 Heat the remaining oil. Cook the
onions and bacon over medium-high
heat for 5 minutes. Add the carrots,
mushrooms and celery and cook for
5 minutes, stirring constantly.
4 Add the pork, chicken stock and
reserved marinade. Bring to the boil,
then reduce the heat and simmer for
1¼–1½ hours, or until the pork is
very tender, stirring often to prevent
sticking. Season well with salt and
freshly ground black pepper. Stir in
the herbs and serve.

*Combine the marinade ingredients and
the pork in a large bowl.*

*Lightly coat the drained pork in the
seasoned flour.*

*Add the reserved marinade to the meat
and vegetables.*

ROSEMARY-INFUSED LAMB AND LENTIL CASSEROLE

Preparation time: 20 minutes
Total cooking time: 2 hours 30 minutes
Serves 6

25 g (³/4 oz) butter
2 tablespoons olive oil
1 onion, finely sliced
2 cloves garlic, crushed
1 small carrot, finely chopped
2 teaspoons cumin seeds
¹/4 teaspoon chilli flakes
2 teaspoons finely chopped
   fresh ginger
1 kg (2 lb) boned leg of lamb,
   cut into 4 cm (1¹/2 inch)
   cubes
2 teaspoons rosemary leaves
3 cups (750 ml/24 fl oz) lamb
   or chicken stock
1 cup (185 g/6 oz) green or
   brown lentils
3 teaspoons soft brown sugar
2 teaspoons balsamic vinegar
sprigs of rosemary, to garnish

1 Preheat the oven to moderate 180°C (350°F/Gas 4). Heat the butter and half the oil in a large, heavy-based pan. Add the onion, garlic and carrot and cook over medium heat for about 5 minutes, or until soft and golden. Add the cumin seeds, chilli flakes and ginger, cook for 1 minute, then transfer to a large casserole dish.
2 Heat the remaining oil in the pan and brown the lamb in batches over high heat. Transfer to the casserole dish.
3 Add the rosemary to the pan and stir in 2¹/2 cups (625 ml/20 fl oz) of the stock, scraping up all the brown bits from the base and side of the pan. Heat until the stock is bubbling, then

pour into the casserole dish. Cover and bake for 1 hour.
4 Add the lentils, sugar and vinegar and cook for 1 hour more, or until the lentils are cooked. If the mixture is too thick, stir in the remaining stock. Season with salt and freshly ground

black pepper and garnish with rosemary sprigs to serve.

When the oil is hot, add the onion, garlic and carrot and cook until soft and golden.

After browning the lamb, add the rosemary and stock, scraping up the brown bits.

Bake the casserole for 1 hour, then add the lentils, sugar and vinegar.

OSSO BUCO WITH GREMOLATA AND MILANESE RISOTTO

Preparation time: 40 minutes
Total cooking time: 2 hours 20 minutes
Serves 4

Gremolata
1 tablespoon finely shredded or
   zested lemon rind
1–2 cloves garlic, finely chopped
1/4 cup (7 g/1/4 oz) finely chopped
   parsley

Osso Buco
4 veal shank pieces, each
   5 cm (2 inches) thick
plain flour, seasoned with salt
   and black pepper
2 tablespoons olive oil
2 large onions, sliced
6 egg tomatoes, finely chopped
2 tablespoons tomato paste
1 1/2 cups (375 ml/12 fl oz) white
   wine
1 tablespoon cornflour
2–3 cloves garlic, crushed
1 cup (30 g/1 oz) finely chopped
   parsley

Milanese Risotto
1 litre (4 litres) chicken stock
50 g (1 3/4 oz) butter
2 tablespoons olive oil
1 onion, finely chopped
1–2 cloves garlic, crushed
1/4 teaspoon saffron threads
1 1/4 cups (250 g/8 oz) arborio rice
1/2 cup (50 g/1 2/3 oz) freshly
   grated Parmesan

1 To make the gremolata, combine the lemon rind, garlic and parsley and set aside.

2 Coat the veal with seasoned flour, shaking off any excess. Heat half the oil in a heavy-based pan large enough to fit the shanks in a single layer. When the oil is hot, brown the veal well on all sides. Remove and set aside.

3 Heat the remaining oil in the pan and cook the onion for 2–3 minutes, or until soft but not brown. Add the meat in a single layer, sitting snugly in the pan. Season to taste.

4 Mix together the chopped tomatoes, tomato paste and wine and pour over the meat. Bring to the boil, reduce the heat, cover and simmer for 1 1/2 hours.

5 Remove 1 cup (250 ml/8 fl oz) of the cooking liquid and allow to cool a little. Place the cornflour in a small bowl and whisk in the liquid, then stir in the garlic and chopped parsley and add the mixture to the dish. Simmer, uncovered, for about 30 minutes, or until the meat is very tender and the sauce has thickened. Sprinkle with the gremolata just before serving.

6 While the sauce is simmering, make the risotto. Heat the stock in a pan and keep it at a simmer. In another heavy-based pan, heat the butter and oil. Add the onion, garlic and saffron and cook, stirring, for 2–3 minutes without browning. Add the rice and stir for 1–2 minutes, or until well coated.

7 Add the stock, 1/2 cup (125 ml/ 4 fl oz) at a time, stirring constantly over low heat until all the liquid is absorbed before adding more stock. Repeat until all the stock is absorbed and the rice is tender—this will take 25–30 minutes, and requires constant stirring. Stir in the Parmesan, season and serve at once with the veal.

To make the gremolata, combine the lemon rind, garlic and parsley.

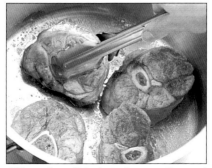

When the oil is hot, brown the veal shanks well all over.

Pour the chopped tomatoes, tomato paste and wine over the meat and onions.

In a bowl, blend some of the cornflour with a cup of the cooled liquid.

Add the rice to the fried onion, garlic and saffron mixture; stir until coated.

Add the stock a little at a time, stirring until absorbed before adding more stock.

CHICKEN MARSALA

Preparation time: 20 minutes
Total cooking time: 1 hour 10 minutes
Serves 4

¼ cup (60 ml/2 fl oz) olive oil
3 leeks, finely sliced
1 teaspoon finely chopped
    rosemary
3 bay leaves, torn
1 kg (2 lb) chicken pieces
plain flour, seasoned with salt
    and black pepper
1 large eggplant, cut into cubes
2 zucchini, roughly chopped
½ cup (125 ml/4 fl oz) Marsala
300 ml (10 fl oz) chicken stock

2 cups (500 ml/16 fl oz) tomato
    purée
200 g (6½ oz) button mushrooms,
    halved

1 Heat the oil in a large, heavy-based pan. Fry the leek, rosemary and bay leaves over low heat for 5 minutes, or until soft, stirring occasionally. Remove with a slotted spoon, leaving as much oil in the pan as possible.
2 Toss the chicken pieces in the seasoned flour. Add the chicken to the pan and brown well in batches over medium heat. Return all the chicken to the pan with the leek mixture.
3 Add the eggplant and zucchini and cook, stirring, for 2–3 minutes, or until softened, turning the chicken pieces

over. Add the Marsala and stock and cook for about 15 minutes over medium-high heat.
4 Add the tomato purée and season well with salt and freshly black ground pepper. Bring to the boil, turning the chicken pieces in the sauce. Reduce the heat to a very gentle simmer, then cover and cook for 35 minutes. Add the mushrooms and cook, uncovered, for 5 minutes.

COOK'S FILE

Note: Marsala is a famous Italian fortified wine. It has a smoky, rich flavour and ranges from dry to sweet.

Remove the softened leeks and herbs from the pan with a slotted spoon.

Add the chopped eggplant and zucchini to the chicken and leek mixture.

Stir in the tomato purée and season well with salt and pepper.

CHICKEN CALVADOS WITH GLAZED APPLES

Preparation time: 15 minutes
Total cooking time: 1 hour 10 minutes
Serves 4

1.25 kg (2 lb 8 oz) chicken pieces
plain flour, seasoned with salt
    and black pepper
2 tablespoons light olive oil
30 g (1 oz) butter
1 large onion, roughly chopped
1 tablespoon chopped marjoram
1 chicken stock cube, crumbled
3/4 cup (185 ml/6 fl oz) apple juice
1/3 cup (80 ml/2 3/4 fl oz) Calvados
3/4 cup (185 ml/6 fl oz) cream

Glazed Apples
2 red apples
40 g (1 1/4 oz) butter
2 teaspoons sugar

1 Preheat the oven to moderate 180°C (350°F/Gas 4). Trim the chicken of excess fat and sinew, then toss in the flour to coat, shaking off any excess. In a large, heavy-based pan, heat the oil and butter and brown the chicken all over, in batches if necessary. Transfer to a large casserole dish.
2 Add the onion to the pan and cook over low heat until soft but not brown. Add the marjoram, stock cube, apple juice and Calvados and bring to the boil, stirring. Season well and simmer for 5 minutes.

3 Pour the sauce over the chicken and bake, covered, for 45 minutes, or until the chicken is tender. Stir in the cream and bake for 5 minutes—the sauce will be thin but delicious.
4 Meanwhile, core (but do not peel) the apples, then cut into wedges. Melt the butter in a pan, add the apples and sugar and cook over very low heat, turning occasionally, until tender and glazed. Serve with the casserole.

COOK'S FILE

Note: Calvados is a French apple brandy. Cognac may be used instead.

Toss the trimmed chicken lightly in the flour to coat, shaking off any excess.

Add the marjoram, stock cube, apple juice and Calvados to the fried onions.

Glaze the apple wedges in the sugar and butter and cook on both sides until tender.

BEEF OLIVES

Preparation time: 20 minutes
Total cooking time: 1 hour 30 minutes
Serves 4

1 kg (2 lb) skirt steak, cut into
    thin slices lengthways
1/4 cup (30 g/1 oz) plain flour
1 tablespoon olive oil
1 carrot, finely chopped
1 cup (250 ml/8 fl oz) red
    wine
425 g (14 oz) can crushed
    tomatoes
2 bay leaves

Traditional sage filling
1 tablespoon olive oil
1 small onion, chopped
2 cloves garlic, chopped
2 large tomatoes, diced
1/2 cup (40 g/1 1/4 oz) fresh
    breadcrumbs
2 tablespoons chopped sage

Sun-dried tomato filling
1 tablespoon olive oil
4 spring onions, chopped
2 cloves garlic, crushed
100 g (3 1/2 oz) mushrooms,
    chopped
8 sun-dried tomatoes, chopped
60 g (2 oz) black olives, chopped
1/2 cup (40 g/1 1/4 oz) fresh
    breadcrumbs
2 tablespoons finely chopped
    basil

1 Put the steak between sheets of
plastic wrap and pound with a meat
mallet until very thin, taking care not
to tear the meat. Set aside.
2 To make the sage filling, heat
the oil in a deep heavy-based pan and
cook the onion and garlic, stirring,
for 3 minutes. Transfer the mixture
to a bowl and add the tomatoes,
breadcrumbs, sage and salt and pepper to taste. Mix well and set aside.
To make the sun-dried tomato filling,
heat the oil in a heavy-based pan,
add the spring onion, garlic and
mushrooms and cook for 3 minutes,
stirring continuously, over medium
heat. Transfer to a bowl, add the
tomatoes, olives, breadcrumbs, basil
and salt and pepper, to taste. Mix
well and set aside.
3 Lay a slice of meat on a board and
place about 1/3 cup of filling neatly
along the short edge. Roll up firmly,
folding in a little of the sides as you
roll, and tie with string to secure.
4 Repeat with the remaining meat
and filling. Roll the beef olives lightly
in flour, shaking off any excess.
5 Wipe out the pan with paper towels
and add the oil. Brown the carrots and
beef olives in batches over medium
heat, turning regularly, and then
return them all to the pan.
6 Add the wine, undrained tomatoes
and bay leaves to the pan and turn the
olives to coat them. Cover and
simmer very gently over low heat
for 1 hour, or until tender. Remove
from the sauce, trim away the string
and slice the olives. Remove the bay
leaves and purée the sauce in a food
processor or blender until smooth.
Serve poured over the beef olives.

COOK'S FILE

Storage time: Beef olives may be
prepared to the end of step 4 and
refrigerated for up to 1 day.
Note: Beef olives can be filled with
the traditional sage filling or the sun-
dried tomato filling. Each filling will
serve 4 people.

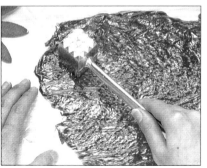

*Pound the steak with a meat mallet
between two sheets of plastic wrap.*

*For the sage filling add the breadcrumbs
with the other ingredients and mix well.*

*Roll the olives firmly, folding in a little
from the sides as you roll.*

Once they are rolled up, secure the olives with string.

Brown the olives in batches and then return them all to the pan.

Use a pair of tongs to lift the beef olives from the sauce.

PORK AND EGGPLANT POT

Preparation time: 20 minutes
Total cooking time: 1 hour 40 minutes
Serves 4

1/4 cup (60 ml/2 fl oz) olive oil
375 g (12 oz) slender eggplant,
    cut into 3 cm (1 1/4 inch) slices
8 bulb spring onions
400 g (13 oz) can chopped
    tomatoes
2 cloves garlic, crushed
2 teaspoons ground cumin
500 g (1 lb) pork fillet, sliced
    3 cm (1 1/4 inches) thick
plain flour, seasoned with salt
    and black pepper
2/3 cup (170 ml/5 1/2 fl oz) cider
1 sprig of rosemary
2 tablespoons finely chopped
    toasted almonds

1 Heat the olive oil in a large, heavy-based pan. Brown the eggplant in batches over high heat, adding oil as needed. Remove and set aside.
2 Quarter the spring onions along their length. Add some oil to the pan and fry over medium heat for 5 minutes. Add the tomatoes, garlic and cumin; cook for 2 minutes. Remove and set aside.
3 Coat the pork in the flour, shaking off any excess. Brown in batches over medium-high heat until golden, adding oil as needed. Remove and set aside.
4 Add the cider to the pan and stir well, scraping down the side and base. Allow to boil for 1–2 minutes, then add 1/2 cup (125 ml/4 fl oz) water. Reduce the heat and stir in the spring onions and tomatoes. Add the pork, season to taste and poke the rosemary sprig into the stew. Partially cover and simmer gently for 20 minutes.
5 Layer the eggplant on top, partially cover and cook for 25 minutes, or until the pork is tender. Just before serving, gently toss the almonds through.

Fry the eggplant in batches over high heat until browned on both sides.

Add the cider to the frying pan, scraping the brown bits from the side and base.

Layer the eggplant over the top of the pork and tomato mixture.

BEEF SAUSAGE AND MUSHROOM STEW

Preparation time: 20 minutes +
    30 minutes standing
Cooking time: 1 hour
Serves 4–6

15 g (1/2 oz) packet dried
    porcini mushrooms
12 thick beef sausages
300 g (10 oz) piece speck or bacon
2 teaspoons oil
2 onions, cut into eighths
8 cloves garlic
1 sprig of thyme
3 bay leaves
1 1/2 cups (375 ml/12 fl oz)
    red wine
1 cup (250 ml/8 fl oz) beef stock
1 teaspoon Dijon mustard
1 bunch baby carrots
100 g (3 1/2 oz) Swiss brown
    mushrooms, halved
100 g (3 1/2 oz) button
    mushrooms, halved
1 tablespoon cornflour
chopped parsley, for serving

1 Soak the mushrooms for 30 minutes in enough boiling water to cover.
2 Brown the sausages well all over in a lightly oiled pan over medium heat. Drain on paper towels and place in a large, flameproof casserole dish.
3 Remove the rind from the speck or bacon; cut the meat into small strips. Heat the oil in a pan and add the speck, onions and garlic. Cook, stirring, until the onions are golden, then place in the casserole dish with the thyme, bay leaves, wine, stock and mustard. Cover, bring to the boil, then reduce the heat and simmer for 20 minutes.
4 Drain the mushrooms, reserving 3 tablespoons of the soaking liquid. Add the carrots and all mushrooms to the stew. Cover and simmer for 20 minutes. Mix the cornflour into the reserved liquid; stir into the stew until it boils and thickens. Sprinkle with parsley to serve.

COOK'S FILE

Note: Speck is a type of smoked bacon sold in delicatessens.

Cover the porcini mushrooms with boiling water and soak for 30 minutes.

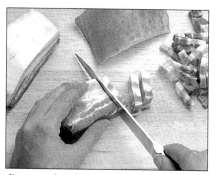

Remove the rind from the speck and cut the meat into small strips.

Add the carrots and all the mushrooms to the sausages. Simmer for 20 minutes.

43

CHICKEN CHASSEUR

Preparation time: 20 minutes
Total cooking time: 1 hour 30 minutes
Serves 4

1 kg (2 lb) chicken thigh fillets
2 tablespoons oil
1 clove garlic, crushed
1 large onion, sliced
100 g (3¼ oz) button mushrooms, sliced
1 teaspoon thyme leaves
400 g (13 oz) can chopped tomatoes
¼ cup (60 ml/2 fl oz) chicken stock
¼ cup (60 ml/2 fl oz) white wine
1 tablespoon tomato paste

1 Preheat the oven to moderate 180°C (350°F/Gas 4). Trim the chicken of excess fat and sinew. Heat the oil in a heavy-based frying pan and brown the chicken in batches over medium heat. Drain on paper towels, then transfer to a casserole dish.

2 Add the garlic, onion and mushrooms to the pan and cook over medium heat for 5 minutes, or until soft. Add to the chicken with the thyme and tomatoes.

3 Combine the stock, wine and tomato paste and pour over the chicken. Cover and bake for 1¼ hours, or until the chicken is tender.

COOK'S FILE

Storage time: This dish may be cooked a day ahead. Refrigerate in an airtight container overnight.

Note: Don't be tempted to use poor quality wine for cooking, as the taste will affect the flavour of the dish.

Brown the chicken in the hot oil over medium heat and drain on paper towels.

Add the garlic, onion and mushrooms to the pan and cook until soft.

Pour the combined stock, wine and tomato paste over the chicken mixture.

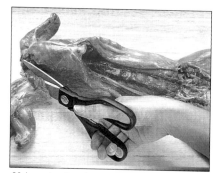

Using sharp scissors, cut the forelegs off the rabbit through the connective tissue.

Cutting where the hind legs join the body, remove the legs and cut in half to separate.

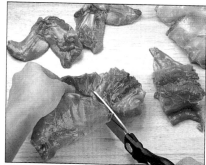

Cut the ribcage and body of the rabbit into 4 even pieces.

COUNTRY RABBIT IN RED WINE

Preparation time: 15 minutes
Total cooking time: 1 hour 30 minutes
Serves 4

1.25 kg (2 lb 8 oz) rabbit
½ cup (125 ml/4 fl oz) olive oil
2 cloves garlic, crushed
1 sprig of rosemary, finely
    chopped
1 cup (250 ml/8 fl oz) red wine
½ cup (125 ml/4 fl oz) chicken
    stock
4 tomatoes, peeled and chopped

1 Cut the forelegs from the rabbit by cutting through the connective tissue joining the body. Cut across the back of the rabbit just above the legs, then cut the legs in half. Cut the body (saddle) of the rabbit into 2 pieces, then cut the ribcage and backbone into 4 pieces, to form 8 portions.
2 Heat the oil in a heavy-based pan. Add the rabbit, garlic and rosemary and brown the rabbit over medium heat on all sides.
3 Add the wine and stock; season with salt and freshly ground black pepper. Cover and simmer gently for 30 minutes. Add the tomatoes and cook, covered, for another 45 minutes over low heat, or until the rabbit is tender. Serve with crusty Italian bread to mop up the juices.

COOK'S FILE

Note: To save time, ask your butcher or poulterer to cut the rabbit for you.

Add the peeled and chopped tomatoes to the pan and simmer for 45 minutes.

LEMON GRASS, CORIANDER AND FISH STEW

Preparation time: 15 minutes
Total cooking time: 40 minutes
Serves 4

4 fish cutlets (200 g/6¹/₂ oz each)
plain flour, seasoned with salt
    and black pepper
2–3 tablespoons peanut oil
2 stems lemon grass
4 Kaffir lime leaves
2 onions, sliced
1 teaspoon ground cumin
1 teaspoon ground coriander
1 teaspoon finely chopped red
    chilli
³/₄ cup (180 ml/6 fl oz) chicken
    stock
1¹/₂ cups (375 ml/12 fl oz)
    coconut milk
¹/₄ cup (15 g/¹/₂ oz) chopped
    coriander
2 teaspoons fish sauce

1 Preheat the oven to moderate 180°C (350°F/Gas 4). Toss the fish lightly in the flour. Heat half the oil in a large heavy-based frying pan and cook the fish over medium heat until lightly browned on both sides. Transfer to a shallow ovenproof dish.

2 Finely chop the white part of the lemon grass stems, and finely shred the lime leaves.

3 Heat the remaining oil in the pan. Add the onion and lemon grass and cook, stirring, for 5 minutes, or until the onion softens. Add the lime leaves and ground spices with the chilli and stir for about 2 minutes, or until fragrant.

4 Add the stock and coconut milk and bring to the boil. Pour over the fish,

then cover and bake for 30 minutes, or until the fish is tender.

5 Transfer the fish to a serving plate. Stir the chopped coriander and the fish sauce into the remaining sauce, and season to taste with salt and freshly ground pepper. Pour the sauce over the fish to serve.

COOK'S FILE

Note: Kaffir lime leaves are glossy and dark green, with double leaves and a floral citrus smell. They can be frozen.

Heat half the peanut oil and brown the lightly floured fish over medium heat.

Finely chop the white part of the lemon grass stems; shred the lime leaves.

Add the lime leaves, ground spices and chilli to the fried onions.

SEAFOOD STEW WITH FETA AND OLIVES

Preparation time: 20 minutes
Total cooking time: 35 minutes
Serves 4

500 g (1 lb) fresh mussels
12 raw king prawns
750 g (1½ lb) firm white fish
    fillets
2 tablespoons olive oil
1 large onion, sliced
2 x 400 g (13 oz) cans tomatoes,
    chopped
2 strips lemon rind
1 tablespoon chopped lemon
    thyme

⅓ cup (80 ml/2¾ fl oz) dry
    vermouth or white wine
1 teaspoon sugar
12 black olives
125 g (4 oz) feta cheese, cubed

1 Discard any open mussels; scrub the rest and remove the beards. Place the mussels in a pan of simmering water: as soon as the shells open, place the mussels in a bowl of cold water, discarding any unopened ones. Open them up and leave on their half shells, discarding the other half.

2 Peel and devein the prawns, leaving the tails intact. Cut the fish into bite-sized pieces, removing any bones. Cover and refrigerate. Preheat the oven to moderate 180°C (350°F/Gas 4).

3 Heat the oil in a large, heavy-based pan and cook the onion over low heat for 5 minutes, or until soft but not brown. Add the tomatoes, lemon rind, lemon thyme, vermouth and sugar. Bring to the boil and season to taste. Reduce the heat, cover and simmer for 10 minutes.

4 Place the seafood in a shallow, ovenproof dish and cover with the hot sauce. Bake, covered, for 10 minutes. Add the remaining ingredients, covering the seafood with the sauce. Bake for 10 minutes, or until heated through. Serve immediately.

Scrub the mussels, remove the beards, then place in a pan of simmering water.

Peel and devein the prawns and cut the fish into bite-sized pieces.

Add the tomatoes, lemon rind, thyme, vermouth and sugar to the softened onion.

HEARTY PORK AND RED LENTILS

Preparation time: 35 minutes
Total cooking time: 2 hours
Serves 4–6

1 kg (2 lb) lean pork neck,
    sliced 2 cm (3/4 inch) thick
plain flour, seasoned with salt
    and black pepper
50 g (1 3/4 oz) butter
1 tablespoon olive oil
1 large onion, finely chopped
3 cloves garlic, finely chopped
2 tablespoons chopped sage
1 1/4 cups (310 ml/10 fl oz)
    vegetable stock
1 1/4 cups (310 ml/10 fl oz) red
    wine
1 cup (250 g/8 oz) red lentils,
    rinsed
2 carrots, chopped
2 potatoes, chopped
3 sticks celery, chopped
1 bay leaf, torn in three
2 teaspoons finely grated lemon
    rind
2 tablespoons chopped parsley

1 Coat the pork in the flour, shaking off any excess. In a large, deep, heavy-based pan, heat the butter and oil over medium heat until foamy. Brown the pork well, in batches if necessary.
2 Return all the pork to the pan. Add the onion, garlic, sage, stock and wine; season well. Bring to the boil, turning the pork to coat in the liquid. Reduce the heat, cover and simmer for 1 hour, turning the pork during cooking. If the sauce becomes too thick, add about 1 cup (250 ml/8 fl oz) water.
3 Add the lentils, carrots, potatoes, celery and bay leaf to the stew with 2 cups (500 ml/16 fl oz) water, and plenty of salt and freshly ground black pepper. Bring to the boil, then reduce the heat to low. Simmer, covered, for 40 minutes.
4 Add the rind. Cook, uncovered, for 30 minutes, or until the sauce is thick and mash-like. If the pork is falling apart, remove and keep warm. To serve, pile the sauce onto the plates, rest some pork on top and sprinkle with parsley. Serve with mashed potato and steamed green beans.

Brown the pork well in the foamy butter and oil mixture.

When the wine mixture boils, turn the pork over to coat in the cooking liquid.

Add the lemon rind to the stew and cook, covered, for 30 minutes.

VEAL WITH SWEET VEGETABLES

Preparation time: 30 minutes
Total cooking time: 2 hours 30 minutes
Serves 4

olive oil, for cooking
8 veal shank pieces, each 2 cm
   (3/4 inch) thick
2 cloves garlic, finely chopped
2 onions, chopped
2 carrots, chopped
1 stick celery, chopped
2 bay leaves, torn
3 cups (750 ml/24 fl oz)
   beef stock
50 g (1³/4 oz) butter

200 g (6¹/2 oz) white sweet potato
200 g (6¹/2 oz) parsnips
150 g (5 oz) baby turnips
150 g (5 oz) new potatoes
2 teaspoons soft brown sugar
2 tablespoons balsamic vinegar

1 Preheat the oven to warm 160°C (315°F/Gas 2–3). Heat 3 tablespoons oil in a roasting pan over medium heat and brown the veal all over. Remove and set aside. Add the garlic, onion, carrot and celery and brown lightly for 10 minutes. Add the veal, bay leaves and stock and stir well. Bring to the boil, cover tightly with foil, then bake for 1¹/2 hours.
2 Towards the end of baking, cut the sweet potato and parsnips into large

chunks; trim the turnips and cut in half. Heat the butter and a little oil in a deep frying pan until foamy. Toss all the root vegetables over medium heat for 5–6 minutes, or until the edges are golden. Sprinkle with sugar and vinegar and toss well. Cook gently for 10 minutes, or until the vegetables soften and the juices caramelise.
3 Turn the veal in the stock, add the vegetables and toss well. If the meat is drying out, stir in 1 cup (250 ml/ 8 fl oz) water. Season well, then cover and cook for 20 minutes. This dish is delicious served with steamed rice or creamy polenta.

Heat the oil in a roasting pan, add the veal shanks and brown all over.

Add the root vegetables to the foaming butter. Cook until the edges are golden.

Add the caramelised vegetables to the veal mixture and toss well.

CHILLI CON CARNE

Preparation time: 10 minutes
Total cooking time: 50 minutes
Serves 4

1 tablespoon olive oil
1 medium onion, chopped
3 cloves garlic, crushed
1 stick celery, sliced
500 g (1 lb) lean minced beef
2 teaspoons chilli powder
pinch cayenne pepper
1 teaspoon dried oregano
440 g (14 oz) can crushed
    tomatoes
2 tablespoons tomato paste
1 teaspoon soft brown sugar
1 tablespoon cider or
    red wine vinegar
420 g (14 oz) can red kidney
    beans

1 Heat the oil in a large heavy-based pan and then add the onion, garlic and celery. Stir over medium heat for 5 minutes, or until softened. Add the beef to the pan and stir over high heat for 5 minutes, or until well browned.

2 Add the chilli powder, cayenne and oregano to the pan. Stir well and cook over medium heat for a further 5 minutes. Add the crushed tomatoes, tomato paste and 1/2 cup (125 ml/4 fl oz) water and stir well.

3 Simmer, uncovered, for 30 minutes, stirring occasionally. Add the sugar, cider or vinegar, drained beans and season with salt and freshly ground black pepper. Heat for 5 minutes. Serve hot with white or brown rice.

COOK'S FILE

Storage time: Keep covered and refrigerated for up to 3 days.

Hint: For a more spicy dish, add some chopped fresh red chillies when you are cooking the onions.

Use a fork to break up any lumps of meat as it browns.

Add the tomatoes, water and tomato paste and stir well.

Add the sugar, cider or vinegar, seasoning and kidney beans and heat through.

MEDITERRANEAN VEGETABLE POT

Preparation time: 20 minutes
Total cooking time: 40 minutes
Serves 4

1/4 cup (60 ml/2 fl oz) olive oil
1 onion, chopped
2 cloves garlic, crushed
1 green capsicum, chopped
1 red capsicum, chopped
3 zucchini, sliced
3 slender eggplant, sliced

2 cups (400 g/13 oz) long-grain rice
100 g (3½ oz) button
  mushrooms, sliced
3 cups (750 ml/24 fl oz) chicken
  stock
1 cup (250 ml/8 fl oz) white wine
400 g (13 oz) can crushed
  tomatoes
2 tablespoons tomato paste
150 g (5 oz) feta cheese

1 Heat the oil in a large heavy-based pan and cook the onion over medium heat for about 10 minutes until very soft but not browned. Add the garlic and cook for a further minute.

2 Add the capsicums and cook, stirring, for 3 minutes. Add the zucchini and eggplant and stir-fry for a further 5 minutes. Add the rice and stir-fry for 2 minutes.

3 Add the mushrooms, stock, wine, undrained crushed tomatoes and tomato paste. Stir to combine. Bring to the boil, reduce the heat, cover and simmer for 20 minutes. The rice should be tender and have absorbed most of the liquid. Serve immediately, topped with crumbled feta cheese.

Cook the onion until it is very soft but not browned.

Add the zucchini and eggplant to the pan and stir-fry a little longer.

Add the mushrooms, stock, wine, crushed tomatoes and tomato paste.

PORK AND APPLE BRAISE

Preparation time: 20 minutes
Total cooking time: 40 minutes
Serves 4

2 tablespoons oil
1 large onion, thinly sliced
1 clove garlic, chopped
2 teaspoons soft brown sugar
2 green apples, cut into wedges
4 pork loin steaks or medallions
2 tablespoons brandy
2 tablespoons seeded mustard

1 cup (250 ml/8 fl oz) rich
   chicken stock
1/2 cup (110 g/3 1/2 oz) pitted
   prunes
3/4 cup (185 ml/6 fl oz) cream

1 Heat the oil in a large heavy-based pan. Cook the onion and garlic for 10 minutes over low heat, stirring often, until softened and golden brown. Add the sugar and apple and cook, stirring regularly, until the apple begins to brown. Remove from the pan.
2 Reheat the pan and lightly brown the pork steaks, two at a time; return to the pan. Add the brandy and stir until it has nearly all evaporated. Add the mustard and stock. Simmer over low heat, covered, for 15 minutes.
3 Return the apple to the pan with the prunes and cream and simmer for 10 minutes, or until the pork is tender. Season to taste before serving.

COOK'S FILE

Hint: Take care not to overcook pork or it can become tough and dry.

Stir the apple regularly over the heat until it begins to brown.

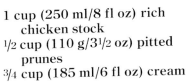

Brown the pork steaks two at a time and then return them all to the pan.

Put the browned apple back in the pan with the prunes and cream.

VEGETABLE STEW WITH COUSCOUS

Preparation time: 30 minutes
Total cooking time: 40 minutes
Serves 4

2 tablespoons olive oil
1 onion, sliced
2 teaspoons mustard seeds
2 teaspoons ground cumin
1 teaspoon paprika
1 clove garlic, crushed
2 teaspoons grated ginger

2 sticks celery, thickly sliced
2 small carrots, thickly sliced
2 small parsnips, peeled, cubed
300 g (10 oz) pumpkin, diced
2 zucchini, thickly sliced
1½ cups (375 ml/12 fl oz)
   vegetable stock
1 cup (185 g/6 oz) instant
   couscous
30 g (1 oz) butter

1 Heat the oil in a large heavy-based pan. Add the onion and cook over medium heat for 10 minutes, until very soft and lightly golden, stirring occasionally. Add the mustard seeds, cumin, paprika, garlic and ginger and stir for 1 minute. Add the vegetables and stir to coat with spices.

2 Add the stock and bring to the boil. Reduce the heat and simmer, partially covered, for 30 minutes, until tender.

3 Put the couscous in a heatproof bowl. Add ¾ cup (185 ml/6 fl oz) boiling water and leave to stand for 2 minutes. Add the butter and stir until melted, then fluff up the grains with a fork. Serve with the vegetables.

Add the mustard seeds, cumin, paprika, garlic and ginger.

Simmer until the vegetables are tender but not breaking up.

Separate the grains of couscous and fluff them up with a fork.

SMOKED SAUSAGE AND KIDNEY BEAN STEW

Preparation time: 20 minutes
Total cooking time: 2 hours 30 minutes
Serves 4–6

1 small red capsicum, halved
2 tablespoons olive oil
2–3 cloves garlic, crushed
1 large onion, thinly sliced
1 carrot, cut into cubes
420 g (14 oz) can kidney beans, rinsed and drained
2 cups (500 ml/16 fl oz) beef stock
1 tablespoon treacle
600 g (1¼ lb) piece speck or bacon
425 g (14 oz) can chopped tomatoes, juice reserved
2 tablespoons tomato paste
150 g (5 oz) smoked sausages

1 Grill the capsicum halves, skin-side-up, under a hot grill until the skin is black and blistered. Cool, then peel off the skin and dice the flesh.

2 Heat the oil in a large, heavy-based pan. Add the garlic, onion and carrot and cook, stirring, over low heat for 4–5 minutes without browning.

3 Add the beans, stock, treacle and freshly ground black pepper to taste. Slowly bring to the boil, then add the speck or bacon. Reduce the heat; cover and simmer for 1 hour. Stir through the undrained tomatoes and tomato paste and simmer for 30 minutes.

4 Place the sausages in a pan of cold water. Slowly bring to the boil, then drain and add to the stew. Simmer, uncovered, for 45 minutes, or until the sauce is thick and rich.

5 Remove the speck or bacon and sausages, using tongs. Slice them, removing any fat and skin, and return to the stew for serving. Serve hot.

COOK'S FILE

Note: Speck is a kind of smoked bacon, often sold in delicatessens.

Serving suggestion: This stew is lovely with a pumpkin and white bean purée. For the recipe, see page 192.

Add the beans, stock, treacle and pepper to the onion mixture.

Simmer the stew until rich and thick, then remove the speck and sausages.

Remove the skin and excess fat from the speck. Slice the sausages and speck.

LAMB STEW WITH ROSEMARY DUMPLINGS

Preparation time: 25 minutes
Total cooking time: 2 hours
Serves 4

8 lamb neck chops
plain flour, seasoned with salt
    and black pepper
2 tablespoons oil
2 rashers bacon, finely chopped
1 large onion, sliced
2 cups (500 ml/16 fl oz) beef
    stock
1 tablespoon chopped thyme
2 carrots, thickly sliced
2 potatoes, chopped

Rosemary dumplings
1 cup (125 g/4 oz) self-raising
    flour
20 g (3/4 oz) butter, chopped
1 tablespoon chopped rosemary
1/3 cup (80 ml/2 3/4 fl oz) milk

1 Trim the lamb of fat and sinew and toss lightly in the flour, shaking off any excess. Heat the oil in a large, heavy-based pan, then brown the lamb in batches over medium-high heat. Remove and set aside.
2 Add the bacon to the pan and cook over medium heat for 2 minutes, or until brown. Add the onion and cook for about 5 minutes, or until soft.
3 Return the browned lamb to the pan. Add the stock, thyme and 1/2 cup (125 ml/4 fl oz) water, then simmer, covered, over low heat for 30 minutes. Add the carrot and potato and simmer for a further 1 hour.
4 To make the rosemary dumplings, sift the flour into a bowl, then rub in the butter with your fingertips until

the mixture is fine and crumbly. Mix in the rosemary. Add most of the milk and mix to a soft dough with a knife, adding more milk if needed. Turn out onto a lightly floured surface and gently knead until smooth. Divide the dough into 12 portions and form into rough balls. Place the dumplings on top of the stew, then cover and cook for 15 minutes. Serve immediately.

Lightly toss the trimmed lamb in the seasoned flour, shaking off any excess.

Sift the flour into a bowl. Rub in the butter with your fingertips until fine.

Divide the dough into 12 portions, then form into rough balls.

CHICKEN WITH SHERRY, RAISINS AND PINE NUTS

Preparation time: 30 minutes
Total cooking time: 50 minutes
Serves 4

1.5 kg (3 lb) chicken pieces
   (about 8 portions)
plain flour, seasoned with salt
   and black pepper
¼ cup (60 ml/2 fl oz) olive oil
2 onions, thinly sliced
2 red capsicums, sliced
4 cloves garlic, finely sliced

1 cup (250 ml/8 fl oz) chicken stock
½ cup (125 ml/4 fl oz) dry sherry
½ cup (125 ml/4 fl oz) orange
   juice
125 g (4 oz) raisins
125 g (4 oz) pine nuts, toasted

1 Toss the chicken in the seasoned flour to coat. Heat the oil in a large, heavy-based pan. Brown the chicken in batches over medium heat until crisp and golden all over. Remove from the pan and set aside.
2 Drain the pan of any oil and add the onion, capsicum and garlic. Cover and cook for about 3 minutes.

3 Add the chicken, chicken stock, sherry, orange juice and raisins and season to taste with salt and freshly ground pepper. Cover and simmer for about 35 minutes, turning the chicken now and then in the sauce.
4 Remove the chicken, keep warm and simmer the sauce for 5 minutes to thicken. Pour the sauce over the chicken and scatter with pine nuts to serve.

Toss the chicken in the seasoned flour to coat evenly all over.

Add the onion, capsicum and garlic to the pan. Cover and cook for 3 minutes.

Add the chicken, stock, sherry, orange juice and raisins to the capsicum mixture.

CHICKEN CACCIATORE

Preparation time: 20 minutes
Total cooking time: 1 hour 15 minutes
Serves 4

1.25 kg (2 lb 8 oz) chicken pieces
2 tablespoons plain flour
1 tablespoon olive oil
1 large onion, finely chopped
2 cloves garlic, chopped
2 x 425 g (14 oz) cans tomatoes,
   roughly chopped

2 cups (500 ml/16 fl oz) chicken
   stock
½ cup (125 ml/4 fl oz) white wine
2 tablespoons tomato paste
1 teaspoon caster sugar
2 tablespoons chopped basil
2 tablespoons chopped parsley
½ cup (90 g/3 oz) black olives

1 Toss the chicken in the flour to coat. Heat the oil in a large, heavy-based pan and brown the chicken in batches over medium heat. Remove from the pan and drain on paper towels.

2 Cook the onion and garlic in the pan for 10 minutes over low heat, stirring. Add the tomatoes, stock and wine. Bring to the boil, reduce the heat and simmer for 15 minutes. Add the tomato paste, sugar and chicken; mix well.
3 Cover and simmer for 30 minutes, then add the herbs and olives and season to taste. Simmer for another 15 minutes, stirring occasionally.

Brown the chicken in batches in the hot oil and drain on paper towels.

Add the tomatoes, stock and wine to the softened onion and garlic mixture.

Stir in the herbs, olives and salt and pepper to taste.

BEEF AND GLOBE ARTICHOKE STEW

Preparation time: 30 minutes
Total cooking time: 2 hours 15 minutes
Serves 4–6

2 tablespoons olive oil
1 kg (2 lb) stewing beef, cut into
    large cubes
2 red onions, sliced
4 cloves garlic, crushed
1 teaspoon cumin seeds
2 teaspoons ground cumin
1 teaspoon ground coriander
2 teaspoons sweet paprika
1 tablespoon plain flour
2 cups (500 ml/16 fl oz) beef
    stock
1 teaspoon grated lemon rind
1 tablespoon soft brown sugar
1 tablespoon tomato paste
1/4 cup (60 ml/2 fl oz) lemon juice
4 fresh globe artichokes
3 tablespoons small black olives

1 Preheat the oven to moderate 180°C (350°F/Gas 4). Heat half the oil in a large heavy-based pan. Brown the meat in batches over medium-high heat and transfer to a large casserole dish.
2 Add the remaining oil to the pan and cook the onion over medium heat for 5 minutes, or until soft. Add the garlic, cumin seeds, cumin, coriander and paprika and cook for 1 minute.
3 Add the flour, cook for 30 seconds and remove from the heat. Add the stock, return to the heat and stir until the mixture bubbles. Add to the meat with the rind, sugar and tomato paste. Cover tightly and bake for 1½ hours.
4 Meanwhile, add the lemon juice to a bowl of water. Cut the top third from each artichoke, trim the stem to 5 cm

(2 inches) and cut away the dark outer leaves. Cut the artichokes lengthways in half. Remove the prickly lavender-topped leaves in the centre and scoop out the hairy choke. Drop into the lemon-water until ready to use.
5 Drain the artichokes and add to the casserole, covering them in the liquid. Cover and cook for 30 minutes, or until tender. For a thicker gravy, cook

uncovered for 15 minutes more. Season and stir in the olives to serve.

COOK'S FILE

Note: Tiny black olives have a great flavour and are sold in delicatessens.

Add the garlic and spices to the fried onion and cook for 1 minute.

Cut the trimmed artichokes lengthways in half and place them in the lemon-water.

Drain the artichokes and add them to the casserole, covering them with the liquid.

CHILLI BEANS

Preparation time: 45 minutes +
  overnight soaking
Total cooking time: 1 hour 35 minutes
Serves 4–6

1/2 cup (110 g/31/2 oz) dried
  black beans
1/2 cup (110 g/31/2 oz) dried
  pinto beans
1/2 cup (110 g/31/2 oz) dried
  chickpeas
2 small red chillies
1 small green chilli
1 tablespoon olive oil
1 onion, sliced
4 cloves garlic, finely chopped

4 cm (11/2 inch) piece fresh
  ginger, finely chopped
1/4 teaspoon chilli powder
2 teaspoons ground cumin
2 teaspoons ground coriander
4 cups (1 litre) vegetable stock
440 g (14 oz) can chopped
  tomatoes
1 small red capsicum, diced
1 small yellow capsicum, diced
1/4 cup (7 g/1/4 oz) chopped
  coriander leaves
1/4 cup (60 ml/2 fl oz) lime juice

1 Cover the beans and chickpeas in boiling water and soak overnight. Drain and rinse well.
2 Discard the seeds and membranes from the chillies. Chop finely; set aside.

3 Heat the oil in a large pan. Cook the onion over low heat for 5 minutes, or until soft and transparent. Add the garlic, ginger, chillies, ground spices, stock, beans and chickpeas. Bring to the boil, reduce the heat, cover and simmer for 1 hour. (There should be just enough liquid to coat the beans.)
4 Add the tomatoes and the red and yellow capsicums and simmer gently for 30 minutes, or until the capsicum and beans are tender. Stir in the coriander leaves and lime juice. Season to taste with salt and freshly ground black pepper and serve.

Cover the dried beans and chickpeas with boiling water and leave to soak overnight.

Remove the seeds and membranes from the red and green chillies.

Add the drained beans and chickpeas to the spiced stock mixture.

TOMATO AND POTATO STEW

Preparation time: 30 minutes
Total cooking time: 1 hour 15 minutes
Serves 6

1/4 cup (60 ml/2 fl oz) olive oil
2 red capsicums, chopped
2 green capsicums, chopped
3 onions, thinly sliced
4 cloves garlic, crushed
2 x 400 g (13 oz) cans chopped
    tomatoes
3–4 sprigs of thyme, and extra
    to garnish
2 bay leaves
2 teaspoons caster sugar
1.2 kg (2 lb 7 oz) potatoes, cut
    into chunks
1 cup (125 g/4 oz) black olives,
    pitted
small block of Parmesan cheese,
    for shaving

1 Heat the oil in a large, heavy-based pan. When the oil is hot, cook the capsicum, onion and garlic over medium heat for 10 minutes, or until softened. Add the chopped tomatoes, 1/2 cup (125 ml/4 fl oz) water, thyme sprigs, bay leaves and sugar. Season to taste and leave to simmer gently for 15 minutes.
2 Add the potato chunks, cover and cook very gently for 50–60 minutes, or until tender. Stir in the olives.
3 Using a vegetable peeler, carefully shave thin slivers from the Parmesan block, arrange over the stew and garnish with a sprig of thyme.

When the oil in the pan is hot, fry the capsicum, onion and garlic until soft.

Add the potato chunks to the tomato sauce mixture.

Using a vegetable peeler, carefully shave thin slivers from the Parmesan block.

LENTIL BHUJIA STEW

Preparation time: 30 minutes +
  overnight soaking + 30 minutes
  refrigeration
Total cooking time: 1 hour 10 minutes
Serves 4–6

2 cups (370 g/12 oz) green
  or brown lentils
1 large onion, grated
1 large potato, grated
1 teaspoon ground cumin
1 teaspoon ground coriander
1 teaspoon ground turmeric
3/4 cup (90 g/3 oz) plain flour
oil, for shallow-frying
2 cloves garlic, crushed
1 tablespoon grated fresh
  ginger
1 cup (250 ml/8 fl oz) tomato
  purée
2 cups (500 ml/16 fl oz)
  vegetable stock
1 cup (250 ml/8 fl oz) cream
200 g (6½ oz) green beans,
  topped, tailed and cut in half
2 carrots, sliced
2 hard-boiled eggs, chopped
sprig of rosemary, to garnish

1 Soak the lentils overnight in cold water. Drain well. Squeeze the excess moisture from the lentils, onion and potato using a tea towel. Place them in a bowl with the ground spices and flour; mix well and leave for 10 minutes. With floured hands, shape the mixture into walnut-sized balls and place on a foil-lined tray. Cover and refrigerate for 30 minutes.
2 Heat 2 cm (3/4 inch) of oil in a heavy-based pan. Cook the balls in batches over high heat until golden brown. Drain on paper towels.

3 Heat 2 tablespoons of oil in a pan; gently fry the garlic and ginger for 2 minutes. Stir in the purée, stock and cream. Bring to the boil, reduce the heat and simmer for 10 minutes. Add the beans, lentil balls and carrots. Cook, covered, for 30 minutes, stirring twice. Add the egg; cook for 10 minutes. Garnish with rosemary to serve.

COOK'S FILE

Variation: Split peas can be used in this recipe in place of the lentils. Soak them in cold water overnight, then drain well before using.

Shape the lentil mixture into walnut-sized balls. Place on a foil-lined tray.

Fry the lentil balls in oil in batches over high heat, until golden brown.

Add the beans, lentil balls and carrots to the simmering sauce.

BOMBAY LAMB CURRY

Preparation time: 25 minutes
Total cooking time: 1 hour 25 minutes
Serves 4–6

1.5 kg (3 lb) leg lamb, boned
   (ask your butcher to do this)
2 tablespoons ghee or oil
2 onions, finely chopped
2 cloves garlic, crushed
2 small green chillies,
   finely chopped
5 cm (2 inch) piece fresh
   ginger, grated
1¹/2 teaspoons turmeric
2 teaspoons ground cumin
3 teaspoons ground coriander
¹/2–1 teaspoon chilli powder
1–1¹/2 teaspoons salt
425 g (14 oz) can crushed
   tomatoes
2 tablespoons coconut cream

1 Cut the meat into cubes, removing any skin and fat. You will have about 1 kg meat remaining. Heat the ghee or oil in a large heavy-based frying pan (with a lid). Add the onion and cook, stirring frequently, over medium high heat for 10 minutes until golden brown. Add the garlic, chillies and ginger and stir for a further 2 minutes, taking care not to burn them.

2 Mix together the turmeric, cumin, coriander and chilli powder in a small bowl. Stir to a smooth paste with 2 tablespoons water and add to the frying pan. Stir constantly for 2 minutes, taking care not to burn them.

3 Add the meat a handful at a time, stirring well to coat with spices. It is important to make sure all the meat is well-coated and browned.

4 Add the salt to taste and stir in the undrained tomatoes. Bring to the boil, cover and reduce the heat to low. Simmer for 45–60 minutes, or until the lamb is tender. Stir in the coconut cream 30 minutes before the end of the cooking time.

COOK'S FILE

Variation: Use 1 kg (2 lb) beef, such as topside or round, if preferred. If you do so, increase the cooking time to 1 hour 15–30 minutes.

Cut the meat into bite-sized chunks, about 3 cm (1¹/4 inch) square.

Once the onion is golden brown, stir in the garlic, chilli and ginger.

Blend the ground spices to a smooth paste with a little water.

Add the meat a handful at a time to make sure it is thoroughly coated.

PERSIAN CHICKEN

Preparation time: 20 minutes
Total cooking time: 1 hour
Serves 6

1.5 kg (3 lb) chicken thighs
1/2 cup (60 g/2 oz) plain flour
2 tablespoons olive oil
1 large onion, chopped
2 cloves garlic, chopped
1/2 teaspoon ground cinnamon
4 ripe tomatoes, chopped
6 fresh dates, stones removed,
   halved
2 tablespoons currants

2 cups (500 ml/16 fl oz) rich
   chicken stock
2 teaspoons finely grated
   lemon rind
1/2 cup (80 g/2³/4 oz) almonds,
   toasted and roughly chopped
2 tablespoons chopped
   fresh parsley

1 Coat the chicken with flour and shake off any excess. Heat the oil in a large heavy-based pan over moderate heat. Brown the chicken on all sides, turning regularly, and then remove from the pan. Drain any excess oil.
2 Add the onion, garlic and ground cinnamon to the pan and cook for

5 minutes, stirring regularly, until the onion is soft.
3 Add the tomatoes, dates, currants and stock. Bring to the boil, return the chicken to the pan, cover with sauce, lower the heat and simmer uncovered for 30 minutes. Add the lemon rind and season to taste with salt and freshly ground black pepper. Bring back to the boil and boil for 5 minutes, or until thickened. Garnish with almonds and parsley and serve with buttered rice.

An easy way to coat the chicken with flour is to toss them both in a bag.

Brown the chicken on all sides, turning it regularly to prevent sticking.

Add the tomatoes, dates, currants and stock to the softened onion.

HUNGARIAN VEAL GOULASH

Preparation time: 20 minutes
Total cooking time: 2 hours
Serves 4

2 tablespoons olive oil
2 medium onions, chopped
500 g (1 lb) stewing veal,
    cubed
1 tablespoon Hungarian paprika
1/4 teaspoon caraway seeds
425 g (14 oz) can chopped
    tomatoes

2 cups (500 ml/16 fl oz)
    beef stock
1 large potato, peeled and diced
1 large carrot, sliced
1 green capsicum, chopped
1/2 cup (125 g/4 oz) sour cream

1 Heat the oil in a large heavy-based pan. Fry the onion for 10 minutes, stirring often, until soft and golden brown. Remove the onion, increase the heat and brown the veal in batches. Return the veal and onion to the pan.
2 Add the paprika, caraway seeds, tomatoes and stock. Bring to the boil,

reduce the heat, cover and simmer for 11/4 hours.
3 Add the diced potato, carrot and capsicum and cook, uncovered, for 20 minutes, or until the vegetables are tender. Season to taste and stir in the sour cream. Serve with rice or pasta.

COOK'S FILE

Hint: Hungarian paprika has a brighter colour and is not as sweet as ordinary paprika. It is available from good supermarkets and delicatessens.

Brown the meat in small batches so that it browns but doesn't stew in the liquid.

Stir in the paprika, caraway seeds, undrained tomatoes and stock.

Add the potato, carrot and capsicum for the last 20 minutes of cooking.

Use the prawn shells and trimmings to make a good base stock.

Use a slotted spoon to lift the sausage from the oil in the pan.

Add the canned tomatoes and their juice to the pan with the herbs.

After 25 minutes the rice should have absorbed most of the liquid.

SEAFOOD JAMBALAYA

Preparation time: 20 minutes
Total cooking time: 1 hour 10 minutes
Serves 6

1 kg (2 lb) raw king prawns
1 small onion, chopped
1 stick celery, chopped
1 cup (250 ml/8 fl oz) dry white
 wine
1/4 cup (60 ml/2 fl oz) vegetable oil
200 g (6 1/2 oz) spicy sausage,
 chopped
1 medium onion, chopped
1 medium red capsicum,
 chopped
1 stick celery, chopped
425 g (14 oz) can crushed
 tomatoes
1/2 teaspoon cayenne pepper
1/2 teaspoon cracked
 black pepper
1/4 teaspoon dried thyme

1/4 teaspoon dried oregano
2 cups (400 g/13 oz) long-grain
 rice

1 Shell the prawns, devein and set the prawns aside. Put the trimmings in a pan with the small onion, celery, wine and 4 cups (1 litre) water. Bring to the boil, then reduce the heat and simmer for 20 minutes. Strain, reserving the stock.
2 Heat the oil in a large heavy-based pan and cook the sausage for 5 minutes, until browned. Remove from the pan and set aside.
3 Add the onion, capsicum and celery to the pan and cook, stirring often, for 5 minutes. Add the tomatoes, pepper and herbs, bring to the boil and then reduce the heat to simmer, covered, for 10 minutes.
4 Return the sausage to the pan and add the rice and prawn stock. Bring back to the boil, reduce the heat and simmer, covered, for 25 minutes, until almost all the liquid has been absorbed and the rice is tender. Add the prawns, cover and cook for 5 minutes. Serve immediately.

CASSEROLE OF AUTUMN VEGETABLES

Preparation time: 25 minutes
Total cooking time: 30 minutes
Serves 4–6

185 g (6 oz) frozen broad
   beans, thawed
150 g (5 oz) pickling onions
50 g (1³/₄ oz) butter
2 teaspoons olive oil
400 g (13 oz) small parsnips
150 g (5 oz) Jerusalem
   artichokes
2 tablespoons plain flour
2¹/₃ cups (600 ml/20 fl oz)
   chicken stock
300 ml (10 fl oz) cream
2 teaspoons grated lemon rind
1 teaspoon grated orange rind
400 g (13 oz) baby carrots,
   trimmed
500 g (1 lb) baby turnips,
   trimmed

1 Peel and discard the tough outer skin of the broad beans. Carefully peel the onions, leaving the flat root end attached, then cut a cross through the root end of each onion.

2 Heat the butter and oil in a large, heavy-based pan until foamy. Add the onions and cook for 7 minutes over low-medium heat, turning often to colour evenly.

3 While the onions are browning, peel the parsnips and artichokes and cut into bite-sized pieces. Add to the pan and toss well. Scatter with the flour, toss to coat and cook for 2 minutes.

4 Stir in the stock, cream and rinds. Bring to the boil, stirring, then reduce the heat and simmer for 7 minutes, or until the vegetables are half-cooked.

5 Add the carrots and turnips; toss well. Cover and cook for 4–5 minutes, or until the vegetables are just tender. Season well with salt and freshly ground pepper, stir in the broad beans to heat through, and serve.

COOK'S FILE

Notes: Baby vegetables have a sweet, delicate flavour. If unavailable, choose the smallest vegetables and cook them for a few minutes longer.

• Fresh broad beans can be used. Add them with the carrots and turnips.

Skin the broad beans and cut a cross through the root end of the peeled onions.

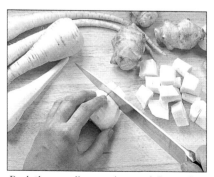

Peel the small parsnips and Jerusalem artichokes and cut into bite-sized pieces.

COQ AU VIN

Preparation time: 20 minutes
Total cooking time: 1 hour
Serves 6

2 kg (4 lb) chicken pieces
plain flour, seasoned with salt and
    black pepper
3 tablespoons oil
4 thick bacon rashers, sliced
12 small pickling onions
2 cloves garlic, crushed
2 tablespoons brandy
1½ cups (375 ml/12 fl oz) good
    red wine
1½ cups (375 ml/12 fl oz)
    chicken stock
2 bay leaves
1 fresh bouquet garni
¼ cup (60 g/2 oz) tomato paste
250 g (8 oz) small button
    mushrooms

1 Coat the chicken in the seasoned flour and shake off any excess. Heat 2 tablespoons of the oil in a heavy-based pan and brown the chicken in small batches; drain on paper towels.
2 Heat the remaining oil in the cleaned pan. Add the bacon, onions and garlic and cook, stirring, until the onions are browned. Add the chicken, brandy, wine, stock, bay leaves, bouquet garni and tomato paste. Bring to the boil, reduce the heat and simmer, covered, for 30 minutes.
3 Add the mushrooms, stirring to combine, and simmer, uncovered, for a further 10 minutes, or until the chicken is tender and the sauce has thickened a little. Delicious served sprinkled with chopped fresh herbs and French bread.

Wrap some fresh herbs in muslin to make a bouquet garni.

Brown the chicken well and drain on paper towels.

Add the chicken, brandy, wine, stock, bouquet garni and tomato paste.

STUFFED PORK CHOPS WITH WILD RICE

Preparation time: 15 minutes
Total cooking time: 2 hours 30 minutes
Serves 6

Stuffing
90 g (3 oz) butter
1/2 cup (40 g/11/4 oz) fresh
    breadcrumbs
1 small onion, finely chopped
5 button mushrooms, finely
    chopped
2 tablespoons pine nuts
1/2 teaspoon chopped thyme
2 tablespoons chopped parsley

6 pork loin chops, trimmed
plain flour, seasoned with salt and
    black pepper
2 tablespoons olive oil
60 g (2 oz) butter
1 large tomato, sliced into rounds
1 onion, sliced into rounds
1 cup (190 g/61/2 oz) wild rice
1/2 cup (125 ml/4 fl oz) cider
1 cup (250 ml/8 fl oz) chicken
    stock
1 clove garlic, crushed
1/4 teaspoon paprika

1 Preheat the oven to warm 170°C (325°F/Gas 3). To make the stuffing, heat a third of the butter in a pan. Add the breadcrumbs and stir over medium heat until golden; remove and set aside. Heat the remaining butter and fry the onion for 5 minutes, or until soft. Add the remaining stuffing ingredients and fry for 3 minutes. Remove from the heat, add the breadcrumbs and season well.
2 Cut a pocket in the meaty part of each pork chop, then fill with the stuffing. Secure with a toothpick and coat in the seasoned flour.
3 Heat the oil and half the butter in the pan. Brown the chops over high heat; transfer to an oiled ovenproof dish wide enough to fit them in a single layer. Place a slice of tomato and onion on each; secure with a toothpick. Scatter the rice around and pour on the cider.
4 Add the stock, garlic and paprika to the same pan the pork was browned in. Cook over high heat for 1 minute, scraping the base and side of the pan. Pour the sauce over the chops, adding

water if needed to cover the rice. Dot with the remaining butter; cover tightly and bake for 11/2 hours. Check the liquid: you may need to add more water to cover the rice. Cover tightly and bake for 30 minutes more, or until the pork is very tender. Remove the toothpicks before serving.

COOK'S FILE

Serving suggestion: This dish is lovely served with pea purée with chives and sour cream. See page 191.

Fill each pork chop with the prepared stuffing and secure with a toothpick.

Scatter the rice around the pork and pour the cider over the top.

ITALIAN SAUSAGE CASSEROLE

Preparation time: 15 minutes
Total cooking time: 45 minutes
Serves 4

2 large red capsicums
1 tablespoon olive oil
2 large red onions, sliced into
    thick wedges
2 cloves garlic, finely chopped
600 g (1¼ lb) Italian-style thin
    pork sausages
300 g (10 oz) can chickpeas,
    drained
150 g (5 oz) flat mushrooms,
    thickly sliced
½ cup (125 ml/4 fl oz) dry
    white wine

2 bay leaves
2 teaspoons chopped fresh
    rosemary
400 g (13 oz) can diced
    tomatoes

1 Cut the capsicums into large pieces, removing the seeds and membrane. Place skin-side-up, under a hot grill until the skin blackens and blisters. Allow to cool in a plastic bag. Peel away the skin, and slice diagonally into thick strips.

2 Meanwhile, heat the oil in a large non-stick frying pan. Add the onion and garlic, and stir over medium heat for 6 minutes, or until the onion is soft and browned. Remove the onion from the pan and set aside. Add the sausages to the same pan. Cook over medium heat, turning occasionally, for 8 minutes, or until the sausages are browned. Remove the sausages and slice diagonally into 3 cm (1¼ inch) pieces.

3 Combine the capsicum, onion, sausage, chickpeas and mushrooms in the pan and cook over medium-high heat.

4 Add the wine, bay leaves and rosemary. Bring to the boil, then reduce the heat to low and simmer for 3 minutes. Stir in the tomatoes and simmer for 20 minutes, or until the sauce has thickened slightly. Remove the bay leaves and season to taste with sugar, salt and ground black pepper. Delicious served with fettucine, noodles, grilled ciabatta bread, mashed potato, soft polenta, or Parmesan cheese shavings.

Grill the capsicums under a hot grill until the skin blackens and blisters.

Remove the skin from the cooled capsicums and slice them into thin strips.

Use a pair of tongs to hold the sausages as you slice them into pieces.

SAUSAGE CARBONADE

Preparation time: 15 minutes
Total cooking time: 45 minutes
Serves 4–6

750 g (1½ lb) good quality
  beef sausages
1 tablespoon olive oil
1 large onion, chopped
2 cloves garlic, chopped
2 teaspoons soft brown sugar

2 tablespoons plain flour
1½ cups (375 ml/12 fl oz) beer
2 cups (500 ml/16 fl oz) beef
  stock
2 bay leaves
2 tablespoons chopped parsley

1 Put the sausages in a pan and cover with cold water. Bring to the boil, reduce the heat and simmer for 5 minutes. Drain and cool.
2 Heat the oil in a large heavy-based pan and cook the onion and garlic for

5 minutes, stirring regularly. Add the sugar and flour and cook, stirring, for 5–8 minutes over low heat, until the flour is golden brown.
3 Gradually stir in the beer and stock. Add the sausages and bay leaves, bring to the boil, then reduce the heat, cover the pan and simmer for 20 minutes. Remove the bay leaves, stir in the parsley and season.

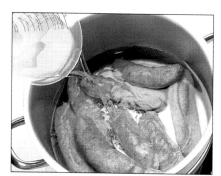

Put the sausages in a pan with enough cold water to cover them.

Cook the onion and garlic for 5 minutes, stirring regularly.

Lift the bay leaves out of the pan just before serving.

HAM, BEAN AND SWEDE CASSEROLE

Preparation time: 35 minutes
Total cooking time: 1 hour 45 minutes
Serves 4

1 cup (200 g/6½ oz) black-eyed
    beans, soaked in cold water
    overnight
1 smoked ham hock
18 small pickling onions
30 g (1 oz) butter
2 tablespoons oil
2 cloves garlic, crushed

2 tablespoons golden syrup
3 teaspoons ground cumin
1 tablespoon German or
    French mustard
1 swede or turnip, peeled, diced
2 tablespoons tomato paste

1 Drain the beans and put them in a large heavy-based pan. Add the ham hock and 8 cups (2 litres) water, cover and bring to the boil. Reduce the heat to low and simmer for a further 25–30 minutes. Drain, reserving 2 cups (500 ml) of the stock. Remove the skin from the hock and chop the meat into bite-sized pieces.

2 Peel the onions, leaving the bases intact. Heat the butter, oil, garlic and syrup in the cleaned pan. Add the onions and cook for 5–10 minutes, or until just starting to turn golden.
3 Stir in the ham, cumin, mustard and swede or turnip and cook for 2 minutes until golden. Season to taste and return the beans to the pan. Add the reserved stock and tomato paste, bring to the boil, reduce the heat and simmer, covered, for 1 hour. Uncover and simmer for 5–10 minutes longer, or until reduced and thickened.

Remove the skin and chop the cooked ham hock into bite-sized pieces.

Peel the onions, leaving the bases intact so that they hold their shape.

Stir in the ham, cumin, mustard and swede or turnip.

PEPPERED VEGETABLE HOTPOT

Preparation time: 30 minutes
Total cooking time: 1 hour 5 minutes
Serves 8–10

2 tablespoons olive oil
2 onions, chopped
2 leeks, washed and chopped
2 cloves garlic, crushed
6 cups (1.5 litres) chicken stock
2 tablespoons chopped fresh
   rosemary
1–2 teaspoon green peppercorns

4 large potatoes, peeled and
   cubed
2 large turnips, cubed
200 g (6½ oz) broccoli, cut into
   small florets
200 g (6½ oz) cauliflower, cut
   into small florets
1 cup (155 g/5 oz) fresh peas

1 Heat the oil in a large heavy-based pan and cook the onion and leek over medium heat for 10 minutes, or until they are tender.
2 Add the garlic and cook for 1 minute further, then add the stock, rosemary, peppercorns and potato to the pan. Bring to the boil and then reduce the heat, cover and leave to simmer for 30 minutes. Add the pieces of turnip and allow to simmer for a further 15 minutes.
3 Add the broccoli, cauliflower and peas and simmer, uncovered, for a further 5 minutes. Season to taste.

COOK'S FILE

Hint: Serve as a main course with pesto and crusty bread.

Wash the turnips well and roughly chop into large cubes.

Add the stock, rosemary, peppercorns and potato to the pan.

Add the broccoli, cauliflower and peas for the last 5 minutes of cooking.

MINTY LAMB SHANKS

Preparation time: 20 minutes
Total cooking time: 2 hours 10 minutes
Serves 6

6 lamb shanks
1 tablespoon olive oil
1 red onion, finely chopped
2 cloves garlic, crushed
1 sprig fresh thyme
2 bay leaves
3/4 cup (35 g) chopped mint leaves

425 g (14 oz) can crushed
   tomatoes
2 cups (500 ml/16 fl oz)
   vegetable stock
1/4 cup (60 ml/2 fl oz) white wine

1 Preheat the oven to moderately hot 200°C (400°F/Gas 6). Put the shanks in a baking dish in a single layer, close together. Season and bake, uncovered, for 20 minutes. Turn the shanks over, reduce the oven to 180°C (350°F/Gas 4) and bake for a further 20 minutes.
2 Heat the oil in heavy-based frying pan. Add the onion and garlic and fry for 5–8 minutes, or until the onion is soft. Stir in the thyme, bay leaves and 1/2 cup (25 g) of the mint leaves. Scatter over the meat, return to the oven and cook, uncovered, for 15 minutes.
3 Combine the tomato, stock and wine and pour over the meat. Cover the dish tightly with foil or a lid and bake for 1 hour 15 minutes. Garnish with the remaining mint and serve with pasta. Best made a day or two in advance and refrigerated.

Put the shanks in one layer, close together and season with salt and pepper.

Once the onion is soft, stir in the thyme, bay leaves and mint.

Mix together the tomato, stock and wine and pour over the lamb shanks.

CHICKEN AND COCONUT CREAM CURRY

Preparation time: 20 minutes
Total cooking time: 50 minutes
Serves 4

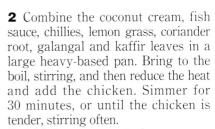

1.5 kg (3 lb) chicken thigh
   fillets
1 tablespoon vegetable oil
400 ml (13 fl oz) can coconut
   cream
2 tablespoons fish sauce
1–2 small chopped red chillies
1 lemon grass, chopped finely

4 coriander roots, chopped,
   leaves reserved
6 pieces dried galangal
6 dried kaffir lime leaves
1 tablespoon red curry paste
2 teaspoons soft brown sugar
1 tablespoon lemon juice
2 small zucchini, thickly
   sliced
1/2 cup (80 g/2 3/4 oz) green peas

1 Trim the skin and fat from the chicken, chop into bite-sized pieces and pat dry with paper towels. Heat the oil in a frying pan and brown the chicken in batches. Set aside.

2 Combine the coconut cream, fish sauce, chillies, lemon grass, coriander root, galangal and kaffir leaves in a large heavy-based pan. Bring to the boil, stirring, and then reduce the heat and add the chicken. Simmer for 30 minutes, or until the chicken is tender, stirring often.
3 Add the curry paste, brown sugar and lemon juice and stir well. Taste and add more, if you prefer. Stir in the zucchini and peas and simmer for a further 5 minutes, or until the vegetables are just tender. Remove the galangal and lime leaves to serve.

Lemon grass, like kaffir lime leaves and galangal, is available from Asian stores.

Reduce the heat and return the browned chicken to the pan.

Use a pair of tongs to lift out and discard the galangal and lime leaves.

CHICKPEA AND VEGETABLE CURRY

Preparation time: 30 minutes
Total cooking time: 35 minutes
Serves 4

1 tablespoon oil
1 onion, chopped
1 tablespoon grated fresh ginger
3 cloves garlic, crushed
1/2 teaspoon fennel seeds
2 teaspoons curry powder
1 teaspoon finely chopped
   chilli, optional
400 ml (13 fl oz) coconut milk

425 g (14 oz) chickpeas,
   drained
3 medium zucchini, chopped
200 g (6½ oz) sweet potato,
   chopped
150 g (5 oz) green beans,
   chopped
200 g (6½ oz) broccoli, cut into
   small florets
1/3 cup (30 g/1 oz) shredded
   coconut

1 Heat the oil in a large heavy-based pan and cook the onion over medium heat for about 10 minutes, until soft and golden. Add the ginger, garlic, fennel seeds, curry powder and chilli (if using). Cook, stirring, for 2 minutes, until fragrant.

2 Stir in the coconut milk, chickpeas, zucchini, sweet potato, beans and broccoli and bring to the boil. Reduce the heat, cover and leave to simmer for 20 minutes, or until the vegetables are tender.

3 Preheat the oven to moderate 180°C (350°F/Gas 4). Spread the coconut on a baking tray and toast in the oven for a few minutes until lightly golden. Serve over the curry as a garnish.

Add the ginger, garlic and spices and cook until fragrant.

Add the drained chickpeas to the pan with the other vegetables.

Spread the coconut on a baking tray and toast until lightly golden.

In a bowl, combine the leeks, shallots, garlic, parsley, mint and zucchini.

Brush the veal with browned butter, then overlap a layer of veal over the vegetables.

Cut the bacon in half crossways and arrange over the top layer of vegetables.

Evenly pour the cream in around the edge of the dish.

SPRING VEAL WITH BACON AND ZUCCHINI

Preparation time: 20 minutes
Total cooking time: 1 hour 50 minutes
Serves 4–6

3 medium leeks, thinly sliced
6 French shallots, chopped
2 cloves garlic, crushed
2 tablespoons chopped parsley
2 tablespoons chopped mint
200 g (6¹/2 oz) small young
    zucchini, thickly sliced
85 g (3 oz) butter
1 kg (2 lb) thin leg veal slices
4 rashers lean bacon
¹/3 cup (80 ml/2³/4 fl oz) cream
4 baby zucchini, with flowers

1 Combine the leeks, shallots, garlic, parsley, mint and sliced zucchini. Spread a thin layer in a deep, oiled ovenproof dish; season well. Preheat the oven to warm 170°C (325°F/Gas 3).

2 Gently melt the butter in a pan until golden brown with a nutty aroma. Remove from the heat.

3 Cut the veal into 9 cm (3¹/2 inch) pieces, brush with the browned butter and season well. Overlap a veal layer over the vegetables. Repeat the layers, finishing with a layer of vegetables.

4 Remove the rind from the bacon. Cut the bacon in half crossways and arrange over the vegetables. Cover and bake for 40 minutes. Pour the cream in around the edge, then bake, partially covered, for 40 minutes more.

5 Arrange the baby zucchini over the bacon rashers. Cover and bake for 15–20 minutes: the vegetables and veal will shrink in from the sides of the dish to form a mould. If the sauce is thin, simmer in a pan until thick. Cut the mould into portions and drizzle with the sauce to serve.

POLENTA WITH SPICY VEGETABLES

Preparation time: 30 minutes
Total cooking time: 1 hour 10 minutes
Serves 4

1 tablespoon olive oil
1 large onion, sliced
4 cloves garlic, finely chopped
1/4 teaspoon chilli powder
2 teaspoons ground cumin
2 teaspoons ground coriander
1/2 teaspoon ground turmeric
1/2 teaspoon ground cinnamon
2 potatoes, cubed
3 carrots, thickly sliced
1 1/2 cups (375 ml/12 fl oz)
    vegetable stock
300 g (10 oz) baby yellow
    squash, halved
3 zucchini, cut into chunks
300 g (10 oz) pumpkin, cut into
    chunks
2 tablespoons chopped
    parsley

Polenta
4 cups (1 litre) vegetable stock
    or water
1 2/3 cups (250 g/8 oz) fine
    polenta
100 g (3 1/2 oz) butter, chopped
1/3 cup (35 g/1 1/4 oz) finely
    grated fresh Parmesan
    cheese

1 Heat the oil in a large saucepan. Fry the onion over low heat for 5 minutes, or until soft and translucent. Add the garlic and spices and cook over medium heat for 3 minutes.
2 Add the potato, carrot and stock. Bring to the boil, reduce the heat, then cover and simmer for 10 minutes.

3 Add the squash and zucchini. Cover partially and simmer for 15 minutes. Add the pumpkin; cook for 10 minutes more, or until the vegetables are soft and the mixture is thick and gravy-like. Season well with salt and freshly ground black pepper. Remove from the heat, cover and keep warm.
4 To make the polenta, bring the stock to the boil. Add the polenta in a thin stream, stirring constantly with a wooden spoon. Simmer gently for 20 minutes, stirring constantly so it doesn't stick. When thick, add the butter and Parmesan and mix until melted. Season well and serve at once.
5 Stir the parsley into the vegetables. Spoon the polenta onto serving plates, swirling it into nests with a hole in the centre. Spoon in the spicy vegetables and serve immediately.

Add the pumpkin to the partially cooked vegetable mixture.

Simmer the polenta gently for 20 minutes, stirring constantly until thick.

When the polenta has thickened, add the butter and Parmesan. Stir until melted.

VIETNAMESE CHICKEN AND NOODLE CASSEROLE

Preparation time: 40 minutes
Total cooking time: 25 minutes
Serves 4

1 stem lemon grass
4 Kaffir lime leaves
4 cups (1 litre) chicken stock
400 ml (13 fl oz) coconut cream
1/4 cup (30 g/1 oz) coconut milk
    powder
2 tablespoons peanut oil
400 g (13 oz) chicken breast
    fillet, cut into strips
12 raw king prawns, peeled and
    deveined, tails intact
8 spring onions, sliced
2 teaspoons finely chopped
    fresh ginger
4 cloves garlic, finely chopped
2 small red chillies, seeded and
    finely chopped
500 g (1 lb) Hokkien noodles
1 teaspoon dried shrimp paste
2 tablespoons lime juice
1 cup (90 g/3 oz) bean sprouts
mint leaves, to garnish
coriander leaves, to garnish

1 Finely chop the white stem of the lemon grass. Remove the centre stem from the Kaffir lime leaves, then finely shred the leaves.
2 Place the lemon grass and lime leaves in a large, heavy-based pan with the stock, coconut cream and coconut milk powder. Bring to the boil, stirring constantly to dissolve the coconut milk powder. Reduce the heat and simmer, covered, for 15 minutes.
3 Heat a wok over high heat and add the peanut oil. Toss in the chicken, prawns, spring onion, ginger, garlic and chillies. Stir-fry for 5–10 minutes, or until the chicken and prawns are cooked through.
4 Place the noodles in the simmering coconut cream, then add the chicken and prawn mixture from the wok. Add the shrimp paste and lime juice. Allow the noodles to heat through.
5 Divide the sprouts among warmed deep bowls and place the noodles, chicken and prawns on top. Ladle the sauce over, scatter with mint and coriander and serve at once.

Using a sharp knife, finely chop the white stem of the lemon grass.

Stir-fry the chicken, prawns, spring onions, ginger, garlic and chilli.

Add the noodles to the simmering coconut cream mixture.

BEEF BOURGUIGNON

Preparation time: 10 minutes
Total cooking time: 2 hours
Serves 4–6

1 kg (2 lb) topside or round steak
plain flour, seasoned with salt and
    black pepper
3 rashers bacon, rind removed
oil, for cooking
12 pickling onions
1 cup (250 ml/8 fl oz) red wine
2 cups (500 ml/16 fl oz) beef
    stock

1 teaspoon dried thyme
200 g (6½ oz) button mushrooms
2 bay leaves

1 Trim the steak of fat and sinew and cut into 2 cm (¾ inch) cubes. Lightly toss in the seasoned flour to coat, shaking off the excess.
2 Cut the bacon into 2 cm (¾ inch) squares. Heat some oil in a large pan and quickly cook the bacon over medium heat. Remove the bacon from the pan, then add the meat and brown well in batches. Remove and set aside. Add the onions to the pan and cook until golden.

3 Return the bacon and meat to the pan with the remaining ingredients. Bring to the boil, reduce the heat and simmer, covered, for 1½ hours, or until the meat is very tender, stirring now and then. Remove the bay leaves to serve. Mashed potato and steamed green beans are a nice accompaniment.

COOK'S FILE

Storage time: Refrigerate in an airtight container for up to 3 days.

Trim the meat of fat and sinew and cut into cubes.

Fry the bacon in the hot oil over medium heat until lightly browned.

Return the bacon and meat to the pan and add the remaining ingredients.

PORK AND MUSTARD STEW

Preparation time: 15 minutes
Total cooking time: 1 hour 10 minutes
Serves 4–6

2 tablespoons oil
1 kg (2 lb) pork neck, cut into
    3 cm (1¼ inch) cubes
20 g (¾ oz) butter
1 large onion, sliced
1 clove garlic,
    crushed

250 g (8 oz) button mushrooms,
    halved
1 tablespoon plain flour
⅓ cup (80 ml/2¾ fl oz) lemon
    juice
1 cup (250 ml/8 fl oz) chicken
    stock
2 tablespoons wholegrain mustard
2 teaspoons honey
½ teaspoon ground cumin

1 Preheat the oven to moderate 180°C (350°F/Gas 4). Heat the oil in a large, heavy-based pan and brown the pork

in batches over high heat. Transfer to a large casserole dish.
2 Add the butter to the pan and cook the onion and garlic until soft but not brown. Add the mushrooms and cook for 1 minute. Stir in the flour, then the remaining ingredients. Stirring, bring to the boil. Season to taste and spoon the mixture over the pork. Cover and bake for 45 minutes, or until tender.

Using a sharp knife, cut the pork neck into large cubes.

In the same pan, melt the butter, add the onion and garlic and cook until soft.

Stir the flour into the onion and garlic mixture. Add the remaining ingredients.

CASSEROLE OF CURRIED VEGETABLES

Preparation time: 25 minutes
Total cooking time: 1 hour 25 minutes
Serves 4–6

1 tablespoon vegetable oil
1 leek, thickly sliced
2–3 cloves garlic, crushed
1 stick celery, thickly sliced
1 large carrot
1 large parsnip
1 large potato
1 medium swede or turnip
500 g (1 lb) sweet potato
500 g (1 lb) pumpkin
280 g (9 oz) can curried cooking
    sauce (see Notes)
400 ml (13 fl oz) coconut milk
1 cup (155 g/5 oz) shelled fresh
    green peas
1/2 cup (15 g/1/2 oz) chopped
    coriander leaves

1 Preheat the oven to moderate 180°C (350°F/Gas 4). Heat the oil in a large flameproof casserole dish. Cook the leek, garlic and celery over medium heat for 2–3 minutes, or until tender. Remove the pan from the heat.
2 Peel the root vegetables and cut into 5 cm (2 inch) pieces. Add them to the dish, place over medium heat and stir well to combine. Stir in the curry sauce and coconut milk and cook, stirring, for 2–3 minutes.
3 Cover and bake for about 1¼ hours, or until the vegetables are tender, stirring gently once or twice.
4 Meanwhile, cook the peas in boiling water until just tender. Drain, refresh under cold water and stir into the casserole with the coriander leaves. Serve immediately.

COOK'S FILE

Notes: Curried cooking sauces are not to be confused with concentrated curry pastes. They are available in many brands and flavours, ranging from mild to hot. Choose one to suit your taste.
● If fresh peas are not available, frozen peas can be substituted.

In a flameproof casserole dish, fry the leek, garlic and celery until tender.

Peel the root vegetables and cut them into 5 cm (2 inch) pieces.

BEEF CARBONNADE

Preparation time: 15 minutes
Total cooking time: 3 hours 25 minutes
Serves 4

1 leek, green part only
1 bay leaf
1 sprig fresh thyme
1 sprig celery leaves
4 sprigs fresh parsley
2 tablespoons butter
1 tablespoon oil
1 kg (2 lb) chuck or stewing
    steak, cubed
2 onions, sliced
2 cloves garlic, crushed
2 tablespoons plain flour
$1^1/_2$ cups (375 ml/12 fl oz)
    brown ale or stout
1 long bread stick
$^1/_2$ tablespoon French mustard
$^1/_2$ tablespoon butter, softened

1 To make a bouquet garni, wrap the green part of the leek loosely around the bay leaf, thyme sprig, celery leaves and parsley, then tie together with string. Leave a long tail to the string for easy removal.

2 Preheat the oven to moderate 180°C (350°F/Gas 4). Heat the butter and oil in a large pan and cook the beef in batches for 3–4 minutes, or until well browned. Remove from the pan. Lower the heat and cook the onion and garlic for 4 minutes, or until translucent. Sprinkle in the flour, stir well, then cook for 1 minute. Combine the beer with $1^1/_2$ cups (375 ml/12 fl oz) water and pour into the pan. Stir well, scraping the pan to incorporate ingredients that are stuck to the base of the pan. Bring to the boil and return the meat to the pan. Add the bouquet garni and return to the boil. Transfer to a 10 cup (2.5 litre) casserole dish,

cover well with foil and cook gently in the oven for $2^1/_2$ hours.

3 Cut the bread into 2 cm ($^1/_2$ inch) slices and spread with the combined mustard and butter. Remove the casserole from the oven, take out the bouquet garni and skim off any fat. Put the bread slices on the surface of the casserole, mustard-side-up, and press down gently to cover with juice. Return to the oven and cook, uncovered, for another 30–40 minutes, or until the bread becomes crusty. Serve with steamed green vegetables.

Leave a long tail of string on the bouquet garni for easy removal.

Cook the beef in batches until well browned all over.

LANCASHIRE HOTPOT

Preparation time: 20 minutes
Total cooking time: 2 hours
Serves 8

8 forequarter chops,
    cut 2.5 cm (1 inch) thick
4 lamb kidneys, cut in quarters,
    cores removed
50 g (1¾ oz) dripping or butter
¼ cup (30 g/1 oz) plain flour
4 medium potatoes, thinly sliced
2 large brown onions, sliced
2 sticks celery, chopped
1 large carrot, peeled and chopped
1¾ cups (440 ml/14 fl oz)
    chicken or beef stock
200 g (6½ oz) button
    mushrooms, sliced
2 teaspoons chopped fresh
    thyme
1 tablespoon Worcestershire
    sauce

1 Preheat the oven to warm 160°C (315°F/Gas 2–3). Brush a large casserole dish with melted butter or oil. Trim the meat of excess fat and sinew and toss the chops and kidneys in flour, shaking off the excess. Heat the dripping or butter in a large frying pan and brown the chops quickly on both sides. Remove the chops from the pan and brown the kidneys. Layer half the potato slices in the base of the dish and place the chops and kidneys on top of them.

2 Add the onions, celery and carrot to the pan and cook until the carrot begins to brown. Layer on top of the chops and kidneys. Sprinkle the remaining flour over the base of the pan and cook, stirring, until dark brown. Gradually pour in the stock and bring to the boil, stirring. Add the mushrooms, thyme and Worcestershire sauce then season with salt and freshly ground black pepper. Reduce the heat and simmer for 10 minutes. Pour into the casserole dish.

3 Cover the meat and vegetables with a layer of the remaining potato. Cover and cook in the oven for 1 hour 15 minutes. Remove the lid and cook for a further 30 minutes, or until the potatoes are brown.

Brown the kidneys in the hot dripping or butter, stirring regularly.

Add the mushrooms, herbs, Worcestershire sauce and seasonings.

Layer the remaining potato over the top of the casserole.

GAME CASSEROLE

Preparation time: 30 minutes
Total cooking time: 2 hours
Serves 6

1 kg (2 lb) venison shoulder
2 tablespoons oil
3 rashers bacon, chopped
3 medium onions, thickly sliced
2 tablespoons plain flour
1 cup (250 ml/8 fl oz) red wine
1/2 cup (125 ml/4 fl oz) chicken
   stock
2 tablespoons port
2 medium carrots, chopped

1 stick celery, chopped
1 clove garlic, crushed
1 bay leaf
1 cinnamon stick
2 cloves
1/2 teaspoon ground nutmeg
1/2 teaspoon dried thyme
1/2 teaspoon chopped chilli
150 g (5 oz) button mushrooms,
   halved

1 Preheat the oven to moderate 180°C (350°F/Gas 4). Trim the excess fat and sinew from the venison and cut into cubes. Heat half the oil in a large heavy-based pan, add the bacon and fry over medium heat until brown.

Remove with a slotted spoon. Add the onion and cook until soft and golden. Remove and set aside.

2 Add the remaining oil to the pan. Brown the venison in small batches, return it all to the pan, sprinkle with flour and cook, stirring, for 1 minute. Remove from the heat and add the wine, stock, port, bacon, onion, carrot, celery, garlic, bay leaf, cinnamon stick, cloves, nutmeg, thyme and chilli. Stir until well combined.

3 Pour into a casserole dish, cover and cook in the oven for 1 1/2 hours. Add the mushrooms and cook for a further 30 minutes.

Cook the onion slices until they are soft and golden.

Return all the browned venison to the pan and sprinkle with flour.

Add the mushrooms to the casserole and cook for a further 30 minutes.

CHICKEN AND ORANGE CASSEROLE

Preparation time: 50 minutes
Total cooking time: 1 hour 30 minutes
Serves 4–6

2 small chickens
1 tablespoon olive oil
2 thick rashers bacon, rind
    removed and thinly sliced
50 g (1¾ oz) butter
16 small pickling onions, peeled
    (ensure ends are intact)
2–3 cloves garlic, crushed
3 teaspoons grated fresh ginger
2 teaspoons grated orange rind
2 teaspoons ground cumin
2 teaspoons ground coriander
2 tablespoons honey
1 cup (250 ml/8 fl oz) fresh
    orange juice
1 cup (250 ml/8 fl oz) white
    wine
½ cup (125 ml/4 fl oz) chicken
    or vegetable stock
1 bunch baby carrots
1 large parsnip, peeled
fresh coriander and orange zest,
    to serve

1 Using a sharp knife or a pair of kitchen scissors, cut each chicken into 8 pieces discarding the backbone. Remove any excess fat and discard (remove the skin as well, if preferred).
2 Heat about a teaspoon of the oil in a large, deep heavy-based pan. Add the bacon and cook over medium heat for 2–3 minutes, or until just crisp. Remove from the pan and set aside to drain on paper towels. Add the remaining oil and half the butter to the pan. Cook the onions over medium heat until dark golden brown. Shake the pan occasionally to ensure even cooking and browning. Remove from the pan and set aside.
3 Add the chicken pieces to the pan and brown in small batches over medium heat. Remove from the pan and drain on paper towels.
4 Add the remaining butter to the pan. Stir in the garlic, ginger, orange rind, cumin, coriander and honey and cook, stirring, for 1 minute. Add the orange juice, wine and stock to the pan. Bring to the boil and then reduce the heat and simmer for 1 minute. Return the chicken pieces to the pan, cover and leave to simmer over low heat for 40 minutes.
5 Return the onions and bacon to the pan and simmer, covered, for a further 15 minutes. Remove the lid and leave to simmer for a further 15 minutes.
6 Trim the carrots, leaving a little green stalk, and wash well or peel if necessary. Cut the parsnip into small batons. Add the carrots and parsnip to the pan. Cover and cook for 5–10 minutes, or until the carrots and parsnip are just tender. Do not over-cook the carrots or they will lose their bright colouring. When you are ready to serve, arrange 2–3 chicken pieces on each plate. Put a couple of carrots and a few parsnip batons on top and spoon over a little juice. Garnish with coriander leaves and orange zest.

COOK'S FILE

Storage time: Can be refrigerated for up to 1 day at the end of stage 5. Reheat the casserole gently over low heat and add the carrots and parsnip just prior to serving.

Cut each chicken into 8 even-sized pieces using a knife or pair of scissors.

Cook the pickling onions until they are dark golden brown.

Brown the chicken pieces in batches and drain on paper towels.

Add the orange juice, wine and stock to the pan.

Return the browned pickling onions and cooked bacon to the pan.

Cut the parsnip into batons and leave the stalks on the carrots to provide colour.

87

CAJUN SPICED FISH BRAISE

Preparation time: 15 minutes
Total cooking time: 25 minutes
Serves 4

750 g (1 1/2 lb) ling fillets or
 other firm meaty white-
 fleshed fish
2 tablespoons plain flour
2 tablespoons Cajun spice mix
2 tablespoons olive oil
30 g (1 oz) butter
1 large onion, thickly sliced
1 red capsicum, sliced

1/2 cup (125 ml/4 fl oz) white
 wine
2 cups (500 g/1 lb) good-quality
 bottled tomato pasta sauce
1 wide strip lemon rind
8 fresh raw prawns, peeled
 and deveined

1 Cut the fish into bite-sized, thick pieces. Mix together the flour and Cajun spice mix and use to lightly coat the fish. Heat the oil and butter in a heavy-based pan over medium heat. Cook the fish, turning occasionally, until browned on all sides. Remove from the pan.

2 Add the onion and capsicum to the pan and cook, stirring regularly, for 5 minutes. Add the wine and bring to the boil, stirring continuously. Add the tomato sauce and lemon rind. Bring to the boil, then reduce the heat and simmer for 10 minutes.

3 Add the fish and prawns; cook over low heat for about 3 minutes, or until the prawns are red and the fish tender and easily flaked with a fork. Season to taste, remove the lemon rind and serve immediately.

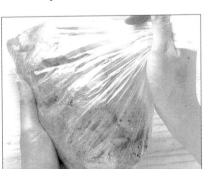

Coat the fish in flour and Cajun spice mix by putting in a bag and shaking.

Cook the fish in the oil and butter until browned on all sides.

When the fish is tender it should be easy to flake with a fork.

VEAL AND FENNEL CASSEROLE

Preparation time: 20 minutes
Total cooking time: 2 hours 15 minutes
Serves 4–6

1 tablespoon oil
30 g (1 oz) butter
4 veal shanks, cut into 4 cm
    (1¹/2 inch) pieces
1 large onion, sliced
1 clove garlic, crushed
2 sticks celery, thickly sliced
3 carrots, thickly sliced
2 small fennel bulbs, quartered
¹/4 cup (30 g/1 oz) plain flour

425 g (14 oz) can tomatoes
¹/3 cup (80 ml/2³/4 fl oz) white
    wine
1 cup (250 ml/8 fl oz) chicken
    stock
1 tablespoon chopped thyme
12 black olives

1 Preheat the oven to moderate 180°C (350°F/Gas 4). Heat the oil and butter in a large heavy-based pan and brown the meat quickly in batches on both sides over high heat. Transfer to a large, shallow casserole dish.
2 Add the onion and garlic to the pan and cook over medium heat until soft. Add the celery, carrot and fennel and cook for a further 2 minutes. Add the

flour, stir until golden, then add the tomatoes, wine, stock and thyme. Bring to the boil, reduce the heat and simmer for 5 minutes, or until thickened. Season with salt and freshly ground black pepper.
3 Add the sauce to the veal; cover and bake for 1¹/2–2 hours, or until tender. Scatter with olives to serve.

COOK'S FILE

Note: Many butchers sell veal shanks already cut into pieces. You will need 12 medium pieces for this recipe.

Trim the leaves and base from the celery stalks and thickly cut the stalks.

Heat the oil and butter, then brown the meat in batches over high heat.

Add the celery, carrots and fennel to the onion and garlic and cook for 2 minutes.

VEGETABLE TAGINE

Preparation time: 20 minutes
Total cooking time: 40 minutes
Serves 4

1 large potato
1 large carrot
1 turnip or swede, peeled
150 g (5 oz) sweet potato
400 g (13 oz) can tomatoes
1½ cups (375 ml/12 fl oz)
    chicken or vegetable stock
2 tablespoons olive oil
2 red onions, chopped
8 large cloves garlic,
    chopped
1 large red chilli, seeded
    and chopped
1 tablespoon ground cumin
1 cinnamon stick
1 zucchini
2 baby eggplants
100 g (3½ oz) blanched
    almonds
125 g (4 oz) dried apricots

1 Cut the potato, carrot, turnip or swede and sweet potato into large pieces. Place them in a large heavy-based pan and add the tomatoes and enough of the chicken or vegetable stock to just cover. Bring slowly to the boil then cover and simmer for 15 minutes, or until the vegetables are just tender.

2 Meanwhile, heat the oil in a frying pan. Cook the onion, garlic and chilli, stirring, for 5 minutes or until tender. Add the cumin and cinnamon stick and cook over low heat for a further 3 minutes.

3 Add the onion mixture to the pan with the vegetables. Cut the zucchini and eggplants into large pieces and add to the vegetables with the almonds and apricots. Stir to combine and bring slowly to the boil. Reduce the heat and simmer, covered, for 10 minutes. If still liquid, simmer, uncovered, for a further 5 minutes—the vegetables should be tender and the liquid thickened. Season to taste with salt and freshly ground black pepper. Serve with harrissa and couscous.

Wearing protective gloves, remove the seeds and chop the chilli.

Use a sharp knife to cut the vegetables into large pieces.

Heat the oil in a frying pan and cook the onion, garlic and chilli.

Cut the zucchini and eggplants into large pieces and add them to the pan.

RABBIT, CHORIZO AND OLIVE CASSEROLE

Preparation time: 35 minutes
Total cooking time: 2 hours 30 minutes
Serves 4–6

150 g (5 oz) French shallots
2 tablespoons olive oil
2 kg (4 lb) rabbit pieces
2 chorizo sausages, sliced
12 pickling onions
2 cloves garlic, crushed
1 teaspoon dried thyme
1 teaspoon paprika
1 tablespoon plain flour
1/2 cup (125 ml/4 fl oz) white wine
11/2 cups (375 ml/12 fl oz)
    chicken stock

1 tablespoon tomato paste
1/2 teaspoon grated orange rind
1/3 cup (80 ml/2³/4 fl oz) orange
    juice
12 Kalamata olives
2 tablespoons chopped parsley
2 tablespoons chopped chives

1 Soak the shallots in boiling water for 30 seconds; drain and peel. Preheat the oven to moderate 180°C (350°F/Gas 4).
2 In a large, heavy-based pan, heat half the oil and brown the rabbit in batches over high heat, then transfer to a large casserole dish. Heat the remaining oil; fry the chorizo, shallots and onions over medium heat until soft and golden.
3 Add the garlic, thyme and paprika and cook for 1 minute. Add the flour and cook for 30 seconds.

4 Remove from the heat, pour in the wine and stir well, scraping up any bits in the pan. Return to the heat, add the stock and stir until bubbling. Add the tomato paste, rind and orange juice, then add to the rabbit and mix well. Cover and cook for 2–2¹/4 hours, or until the rabbit is tender. Season to taste, stir in the olives and parsley and scatter with chives to serve.

COOK'S FILE

Note: Chorizo is a spicy Spanish pork sausage flavoured with cayenne.
Serving suggestion: Lovely with creamy parsnip mash, page 192.

Place the shallots in a bowl and cover with boiling water, then drain and peel.

Heat half the oil in a large pan. Brown the rabbit in batches over high heat.

Heat the remaining oil in the pan and add the chorizo, shallots and onions.

MOROCCAN SEAFOOD WITH CORIANDER PUREE

Preparation time: 50 minutes
Total cooking time: 50 minutes
Serves 6

2 tablespoons olive oil
2 red onions, roughly chopped
1 red capsicum, chopped
4 cloves garlic, crushed
2 teaspoons ground cumin
1 teaspoon ground coriander
2 teaspoons sweet paprika
1/2 teaspoon dried chilli flakes
1 cup (250 ml/8 fl oz) chicken
    or fish stock
425 g (14 oz) can chopped
    tomatoes
4 tablespoons orange juice
1 tablespoon sugar
1/4 cup (30 g/1 oz) seedless
    raisins
375 g (12 oz) baby new potatoes
12 raw king prawns
500 g (1 lb) baby octopus, cleaned
1 kg (2 lb) thick white fish
    fillets, cut into chunks

Coriander Purée
1 cup (30 g/1 oz) fresh
    coriander leaves
2 tablespoons ground almonds
1/3 cup (80 ml/2³/4 fl oz) extra
    virgin olive oil
1/2 teaspoon ground cumin
1 teaspoon honey

1 Heat the olive oil in a large pan and cook the onion over medium heat for about 5 minutes, or until soft. Add the capsicum and garlic and cook for another minute. Add the ground cumin, ground coriander, paprika and chilli flakes and cook until fragrant.

2 Pour in the stock, tomatoes, orange juice, sugar and raisins and bring to the boil. Add the potatoes, reduce the heat to low and gently simmer for 20–30 minutes, or until the potatoes are just tender. Season to taste.
3 Peel and devein the prawns, leaving the tails intact. Use a small sharp knife to remove the octopus heads; slit the heads open and remove the gut. Grasp the body firmly and push the beak out with your index finger; remove and discard. Add the prawns, octopus and fish to the pan and cook, covered, for 10 minutes, or until the fish flakes when tested with a fork.
4 To make the coriander purée, place the coriander leaves and ground almonds in a food processor. With the motor running, drizzle in the oil and process until smooth, then add the cumin, honey and salt to taste. Process until well combined.
5 To serve, dish the stew onto serving plates and drizzle a spoonful of purée on top. Serve with couscous and a green leaf salad.

Peel and devein the prawns and cut the cleaned octopus into bite-sized pieces.

Process the coriander leaves and ground almonds, gradually drizzling in the oil.

LAMB CASSEROLE WITH BEANS

Preparation time: 25 minutes +
   overnight soaking
Total cooking time: 2 hours 15 minutes
Serves 6

1½ cups (300 g/10 oz) borlotti
   beans or red kidney beans
1 kg (2 lb) boned leg lamb
1½ tablespoons olive oil
2 rashers bacon, rind removed,
   chopped
1 large onion, chopped
2 cloves garlic, crushed
1 large carrot, chopped
2 cups (500 ml/16 fl oz) red wine
1 tablespoon tomato paste
1½ cups (375 ml/12 fl oz) beef
   stock
2 large sprigs fresh rosemary
2 sprigs fresh thyme

1 Put the beans in a bowl and cover with plenty of water. Leave to soak overnight, then drain well.
2 Preheat the oven to warm 160°C (315°F/Gas 2–3). Trim any excess fat from the lamb and cut into 3 cm (1¼ inch) pieces.
3 Heat 1 tablespoon oil in a large flameproof casserole. Add half the meat and toss over medium–high heat for 2 minutes, or until browned. Remove from the pan and repeat with remaining lamb. Remove from the pan.

4 Heat the remaining olive oil in the casserole and add the bacon and onion. Cook over medium heat for 3 minutes, or until the onion is translucent. Add the garlic and carrot, and cook for 1 minute, or until aromatic.
5 Return the meat and any juices to the pan, increase the heat to high and add the wine. Bring to the boil and cook for 2 minutes. Add the beans, tomato paste, stock, rosemary and thyme, bring to the boil, then cover and cook in the oven for 2 hours, or until the meat is tender. Stir occasionally during cooking. Skim off any excess fat, remove the sprigs of herbs and season. Serve with bread.

Remove any excess fat from the lamb then cut it into pieces.

Heat the oil then add the lamb and toss until browned all over.

Return the meat and juices to the pan, add the wine, and bring to the boil.

KIDNEYS IN CREAMY MUSTARD SAUCE

Preparation time: 15 minutes
Total cooking time: 25 minutes
Serves 4

8 lamb kidneys
50 g (1¾ oz) butter
6 French shallots, finely sliced
1 cup (250 ml/8 fl oz) cream
2 teaspoons wholegrain mustard
2 teaspoons Dijon mustard
⅓ cup (20 g/¾ oz) chopped
   parsley

1 To prepare the kidneys, slice them in half lengthways. Using a pair of small sharp scissors, carefully snip out the core of each kidney and remove any membrane.
2 Melt half the butter in a small pan. Add the shallots and gently cook for 5 minutes, or until soft and golden. Add the cream and simmer for 10 minutes, or until reduced by one-quarter. Remove from the heat and stir in both mustards; mix well and set aside.
3 Melt the remaining butter in a frying pan over medium heat. When the butter foams, cook the kidney halves for 2 minutes on each side.

4 Pour the creamy mustard sauce over the kidneys and simmer, stirring, for 2 minutes. Stir in the chopped parsley and serve.

COOK'S FILE

Note: When buying kidneys, select those that are firm and have a rich, even colour.
Serving suggestion: This dish is delicious served with mashed potato and steamed green beans.

Cut the kidneys in half lengthways and remove the core and membrane.

Add the two mustards to the cream and stir until well combined.

Pour the cream and mustard sauce over the kidneys.

MEDITERRANEAN CHICKEN

Preparation time: 30 minutes
Total cooking time: 1 hour 10 minutes
Serves 4

8 chicken thigh cutlets
2 tablespoons olive oil
150 g (5 oz) French shallots
4 cloves garlic
½ cup (125 ml/4 fl oz) white wine
425 g (14 oz) can chopped
  tomatoes
12 Kalamata olives
1 tablespoon red wine vinegar
2 teaspoons tomato paste
1 tablespoon oregano leaves
1 tablespoon chopped basil
  leaves
1 teaspoon sugar
4 slices prosciutto
1 teaspoon grated lemon rind
½ cup (30 g/1 oz) chopped
  parsley
1 tablespoon capers, rinsed

1 Preheat the oven to moderate 180°C (350°C/Gas 4). Remove the skin and fat from the chicken thighs. Heat half the oil in a large pan and brown the chicken over high heat for 3–4 minutes on each side, then arrange in a large flameproof casserole dish.
2 Heat the remaining oil in the same pan. Add the shallots and garlic and cook over medium heat for 4 minutes, or until soft but not brown. Add the wine and bring to the boil.
3 Add the tomatoes, olives, vinegar, tomato paste, herbs and sugar. Season with salt and freshly ground black pepper. Boil, stirring, for 2 minutes, then pour over the chicken and cover with a lid. Bake for 45 minutes, or until the chicken is tender.

4 Meanwhile, place the prosciutto slices in a single layer in a frying pan, without any oil. Dry fry for 3 minutes, or until crispy, turning once. Break into large chunks and set aside.
5 Arrange the chicken on a serving dish; cover and keep warm. Transfer the casserole to the stove top and boil the pan juices for 5 minutes, or until thickened, stirring occasionally. Spoon the juices over the chicken, sprinkle with lemon rind, parsley and capers and top with the prosciutto to serve.

When the shallots and garlic are soft, add the wine.

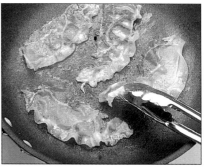

Place the prosciutto slices in a single layer in a dry frying pan and fry until crisp.

COUNTRY-STYLE CHICKEN WITH BABY VEGETABLES

Preparation time: 45 minutes
Total cooking time: 2 hours
Serves 4

1.5 kg (3 lb) chicken pieces
(about 8 portions)
60 g (2 oz) clarified butter
12 baby pickling onions
1 cup (250 ml/8 fl oz) dry white
wine
1 cup (250 ml/8 fl oz) chicken
stock
1 cup (250 ml/8 fl oz) cream
12 baby carrots
16 snowpeas
16 asparagus spears
12 button mushrooms
1 tablespoon chopped chives

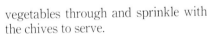

1 Season the chicken portions with a little salt and black pepper. Heat half the butter in a frying pan, then brown the chicken in batches for 2–3 minutes on each side to seal the flavours. Place in a casserole dish and add the onions. Preheat the oven to moderately hot 200°C (400°F/Gas 6).

2 Pour the wine into the frying pan and stir over medium heat, scraping down the side and base of the pan. Add the stock and whisk in the cream. Bring to the boil, then reduce the heat and simmer for 20 minutes. Pour the sauce over the chicken; cover and bake for 1 hour 10 minutes.

3 Meanwhile, bring a pan of salted water to the boil. In separate batches, boil or steam the carrots, snowpeas and asparagus until just cooked, but still slightly crunchy. Plunge in iced water, then drain and set aside.

4 Heat the remaining butter in a frying pan. Sauté the mushrooms for 2–3 minutes, stirring constantly.

5 Place the mushrooms on top of the stew with the blanched vegetables and cook for another 20 minutes, or until the chicken is tender. Skim off any fat, stir carefully to mix all the vegetables through and sprinkle with the chives to serve.

Lightly brown the seasoned chicken in half the melted butter.

Plunge the blanched vegetables into a bowl of iced water to stop them cooking.

Place the drained blanched vegetables on top of the stew and cook for 20 minutes.

GINGERED DUCK CURRY

Preparation time: 30 minutes +
  30 minutes refrigeration + soaking
Total cooking time: 1 hour 30 minutes
Serves 4

1.8 kg (3 lb 10 oz) duck
1 clove garlic, crushed
1 teaspoon grated fresh ginger
1 tablespoon dark soy sauce
1/2 teaspoon sesame oil
8 dried Chinese mushrooms
5 cm (2 inch) piece fresh ginger,
  peeled and thinly sliced
2 tablespoons yellow curry paste
2 tablespoons chopped lemon
  grass, white part only

400 ml (13 fl oz) can coconut milk
4 Kaffir lime leaves, shredded
100 g (3½ oz) Thai pea eggplants
2 teaspoons soft brown sugar
2 teaspoons fish sauce
1 tablespoon lime juice

1 Cut the duck in half by cutting down both sides of the backbone, through the breastbone. Discard the backbone. Cut each duck half into 4 portions, removing any fat. Rub the duck with the combined garlic, ginger, soy sauce and oil. Refrigerate for 30 minutes.
2 Soak the mushrooms in boiling water for 20 minutes. Drain, remove the stalks and cut in half.
3 Heat a lightly oiled pan. Brown the duck over medium heat. Leaving only 1 tablespoon of fat in the pan, stir-fry the ginger, curry paste and lemon grass for 3 minutes. Stir in the coconut milk, lime leaves and 1/2 cup (125 ml/4 fl oz) water. Add the duck; cover and simmer gently for 45 minutes. Skim well.
4 Remove the eggplant stems; add the eggplants to the pan with the sugar, fish sauce and mushrooms. Simmer, partly covered, for 30 minutes, or until tender. Stir in lime juice to taste.

COOK'S FILE

Note: To reduce the fat in this dish, use light coconut milk and skin the duck.

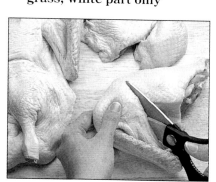

Cut the duck down the middle. Cut the legs and breasts in half to give 8 portions.

Stir the coconut milk, water and lime leaves into the stir-fried spice mixture.

Remove the stems from the pea eggplants and add the eggplants to the pan.

PORK WITH SOUR CHERRIES

Preparation time: 15 minutes
Total cooking time: 1 hour 35 minutes
Serves 4

1.5 kg (3 lb) pork neck (pork
  scotch fillet)
plain flour, seasoned with salt and
  black pepper
1/4 cup (60 ml/2 fl oz) olive oil
30 g (1 oz) butter
2 onions, sliced
1/2 cup (125 ml/4 fl oz) chicken
  stock
1/2 cup (125 ml/4 fl oz) red wine
2 tablespoons chopped tarragon
  leaves
700 g (1 lb 7 oz) jar pitted
  cherries, syrup reserved

1 Preheat the oven to warm 160°C
(315°F/Gas 2–3). Cut the pork into 4 cm
(1½ inch) cubes and toss lightly in the
seasoned flour, shaking off any excess.
Heat the oil in a large heavy-based
pan. In batches, quickly brown the
pork over medium heat and transfer
to a large, shallow casserole dish.
2 Melt the butter in the pan. Cook the
onion over low heat for 10 minutes, or
until soft but not brown.
3 Add the stock, wine, tarragon and
1 cup (250 ml/8 fl oz) of the reserved
cherry syrup. Stirring, bring to the
boil and season to taste. Pour the
mixture over the pork, then cover and
bake for 1 hour. Drain the cherries,
stir them through the mixture and
bake for 15 minutes to heat through.

*Add the pork to the hot oil and cook over
medium heat until well browned.*

*Add the onions to the melted butter and
cook until soft but not brown.*

*Add the stock, wine, tarragon and the
cherry syrup to the softened onions.*

SPICY VENISON AND VEGETABLE HOTPOT

Preparation time: 45 minutes
Total cooking time: 2 hours
Serves 6

1 tablespoon olive oil
25 g (³/4 oz) butter
100 g (3¹/2 oz) pancetta, chopped
1 kg (2 lb) trimmed shoulder
   of venison, cut into 4 cm
   (1¹/2 inch) cubes
2 onions, each cut into 8 wedges
2 cloves garlic, crushed
1 tablespoon chopped fresh ginger
1 teaspoon ground cinnamon

¹/2 teaspoon allspice
1 teaspoon dried thyme
1 bay leaf
500 g (1 lb) tomatoes, peeled,
   seeded and diced
1 cup (250 ml/8 fl oz) beef stock
¹/3 cup (80 ml/2³/4 fl oz) orange
   juice
¹/3 cup (80 ml/2³/4 fl oz) port
200 g (6¹/2 oz) turnip
200 g (6¹/2 oz) parsnip
200 g (6¹/2 oz) carrot
chopped chives, to garnish

1 Heat the oil and butter in a large, heavy-based pan. Cook the pancetta over medium heat until lightly golden. Remove and set aside.

2 Brown the venison in batches and set aside. Cook the onion until golden; add the garlic and ginger and cook for 1 minute. Add the pancetta and venison and all ingredients except the root vegetables. Bring to the boil, then reduce the heat, cover tightly and very gently simmer for 1 hour.
3 Peel the turnip, parsnip and carrot, cut into even-sized wedges and add to the pan. Cover and cook for 40 minutes, or until tender, then uncover to reduce the sauce. Season to taste, scatter with the chives and serve.

Brown the venison in batches in the hot oil and butter.

Add the pancetta and venison with all the ingredients except the root vegetables.

Peel and cut the turnip, parsnip and carrot into wedges about the same size.

TURKEY OSSO BUCO

Preparation time: 25 minutes +
  thawing
Total cooking time: 1 hour 30 minutes
Serves 4–6

3 red capsicums
2.1 kg (4 lb 3 oz) frozen turkey
  hindquarters (legs with
  thighs), chopped (see Note)
plain flour, seasoned with salt and
  black pepper
1/4 cup (60 ml/2 fl oz) olive oil
60 g (2 oz) butter
3/4 cup (185 ml/6 fl oz) chicken
  stock
1/4 teaspoon chilli flakes
4 fresh sage leaves, chopped, or
  1/2 teaspoon dried sage
2 cloves garlic, crushed
1 teaspoon finely grated lemon
  rind
150 g (5 oz) sliced pancetta, or
  thinly sliced bacon
1 sprig of rosemary
2 tablespoons chopped flat-leaf
  parsley

1 Preheat the grill to high. Cut the capsicums in half, then remove the seeds and membranes. Place the capsicum halves skin-side-up under the grill and cook for 5–8 minutes, or until the skin blackens and blisters. Transfer to a plastic bag, seal and allow to cool, then peel away the blackened skin. Cut the flesh into thick slices.
2 Thaw the turkey pieces in a single layer in the refrigerator. When they have thawed, pat the turkey pieces well with paper towels to remove all the excess moisture, then coat them well in the seasoned flour, dusting off any excess.

3 Heat the oil and butter in a large pan. Brown the turkey pieces in batches over medium-high heat, then drain the pan of excess oil.
4 Pour the chicken stock into the pan and stir well, scraping the base and side of the pan to mix in all the pan juices. Add the chilli flakes, sage, garlic and lemon rind and cook, stirring, for 1 minute.
5 Return all the turkey pieces to the pan. Cover with the grilled capsicum slices, then layer the pancetta over the top to completely cover. Add the rosemary sprig, cover the pan and cook over low heat for 1 hour, or until the turkey is succulent, yet not falling off the bone.
6 Discard the rosemary sprig and transfer the pancetta, capsicum slices and turkey pieces to a serving plate. Cover and keep warm. If the sauce is a little thin, place it over high heat and simmer for 3–4 minutes to thicken. Stir in the chopped parsley, adjust the seasoning if necessary, then spoon the sauce around the turkey to serve.

COOK'S FILE

Note: Ask your butcher or poulterer to saw the frozen turkey into 1 1/2–2 cm (5/8–3/4 inch) pieces for you.
● Pancetta is an Italian unsmoked bacon, rolled and cured with salt and spices, sold in many delicatessens. As an alternative, you could use prosciutto in this recipe.
Serving suggestion: This dish is delicious with a creamy mashed potato or polenta.

Place the grilled capsicum halves in a plastic bag, seal and allow to cool.

Coat the thawed turkey pieces lightly in the seasoned flour.

In batches, brown the turkey in the hot oil and butter over medium-high heat.

Pour the chicken stock into the pan and stir well to mix in all the pan juices.

Cover the turkey with the capsicum slices, then cover with the pancetta.

Stir the chopped flat-leaf parsley into the simmering pan juices.

CIOPPINO

Preparation time: 30 minutes +
    30 minutes soaking
Total cooking time: 1 hour
Serves 4

2 dried mushrooms
1 kg (2 lb) firm white fish fillets
375 g (12 oz) raw king prawns
1 raw lobster tail
12 mussels
¼ cup (60 ml/2 fl oz) olive oil
1 large onion, finely chopped
1 green capsicum, finely
    chopped
2–3 cloves garlic, crushed
425 g (14 oz) can crushed
    tomatoes
1 cup (250 ml/8 fl oz) white wine
1 cup (250 ml/8 fl oz) tomato
    juice
1 cup (250 ml/8 fl oz) fish stock
bay leaf
2 sprigs of parsley
6 basil leaves, chopped
1 tablespoon chopped parsley

1 Soak the mushrooms for 20 minutes. Cut the fish into bite-size pieces, removing any bones. Peel and devein the prawns, leaving the tails intact. Remove the meat from the lobster shell and cut into small pieces. Discard any open mussels; scrub the rest, remove the beards, then soak in cold water for 10 minutes. Drain the mushrooms, squeeze dry and chop finely.

2 Heat the oil in a heavy-based pan. Stirring, cook the onion, capsicum and garlic over medium heat for about 5 minutes, or until the onion is soft. Add the mushrooms, tomatoes, wine, tomato juice, stock, bay leaf, parsley sprigs and chopped basil. Bring to the boil, reduce the heat, then cover and simmer for 30 minutes.

3 Layer the fish and prawns in a large pan. Add the sauce mixture, then cover and leave on low heat for 10 minutes, or until the prawns are pink and the fish is cooked. Add the lobster and mussels and simmer for 2–3 minutes. Season to taste. Discard any unopened mussels, sprinkle with parsley, and serve with crusty bread.

Note: You can make your own fish stock for this recipe by simmering the trimmings from the fish, lobster and prawns in 1¼ cups (310 ml/10 fl oz) of water for about 20 minutes, then straining the liquid.

Remove the lobster meat from the shell and cut into small pieces.

When the onion is soft, add the chopped mushroom, tomatoes, liquids and herbs.

Add the lobster and mussels when the prawns are pink and the fish is cooked.

Trim the ends from the fennel and slice the bulb thinly.

Add the Pernod and wine to the softened fennel, leek and garlic mixture.

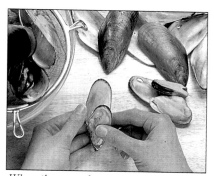

When the mussels are cool, remove them from their shells.

Cut off the octopus heads. Grasp the body firmly and push out the beak.

SEAFOOD, FENNEL AND POTATO STEW

Preparation time: 10 minutes
Total cooking time: 30 minutes
Serves 6

1 large fennel bulb
2 tablespoons olive oil
2 leeks, thinly sliced
2 cloves garlic, crushed
1/2 teaspoon paprika
2 tablespoons Pernod or Ricard
200 ml (6 1/2 fl oz) dry white wine
18 mussels, scrubbed and
    beards removed
1/4 teaspoon saffron threads
1/4 teaspoon thyme leaves
6 baby octopus
16 raw prawns, peeled and
    deveined
500 g (1 lb) swordfish steaks,
    cut into large chunks
400 g (13 oz) baby new potatoes
fennel greens, to garnish

1 Trim and thinly slice the fennel. Heat the oil in a large pan over medium heat. Add the fennel, leek and garlic. Stir in the paprika, season lightly and cook for 8 minutes, or until softened. Add the Pernod and wine and stir for 1 minute, or until reduced by a third.
2 Add the mussels, discarding any open ones. Cover and cook for 1 minute or until opened, discarding any which do not. Remove from the pan to cool; remove from the shells and set aside.
3 Add the saffron and thyme to the pan and cook for 1–2 minutes, stirring. Adjust the seasoning and transfer to a large, flameproof casserole dish.
4 Use a small sharp knife to remove the octopus heads. Grasp the bodies and push the beaks out with your index finger; remove and discard. Slit the heads and remove the gut. Mix the octopus, prawns, fish and potatoes into the stew. Cover and cook gently for 10 minutes, or until tender. Add the mussels, cover and heat through. Garnish with fennel greens and serve.

BEEF AND PEPPERCORN STEW

Preparation time: 15 minutes
Total cooking time: 2 hours
Serves 4

1 kg (2 lb) chuck steak, cut into
    3 cm (1¼ inch) cubes
2 teaspoons cracked black
    peppercorns
40 g (1¼ oz) butter
2 tablespoons oil
1 large onion, thinly sliced
2 cloves garlic, sliced
1½ tablespoons plain flour
2 tablespoons brandy

3 cups (750 ml/24 fl oz) beef
    stock
1 tablespoon Worcestershire
    sauce
2 teaspoons Dijon mustard
500 g (1 lb) baby new potatoes
¼ cup (60 ml/2 fl oz) cream
2 tablespoons chopped parsley

1 Toss the steak in the peppercorns. Heat half the butter and half the oil in a large heavy-based pan. Brown half the steak over high heat; remove and set aside. Heat the remaining butter and oil and brown the remaining steak. Remove and set aside.

2 Add the onion and garlic to the pan and cook, stirring, until the onion is golden. Add the flour and stir until browned. Remove from the heat.

3 Combine the brandy, beef stock, Worcestershire sauce and mustard, and gradually stir into the onion mixture. Return to the heat, add the steak and any juices, then simmer, covered, for 1¼ hours.

4 Add the potatoes and simmer, uncovered, for a further 30 minutes, or until the meat and potatoes are tender. Stir in the cream and parsley and season to taste with salt and freshly ground black pepper.

Cut the steak into 3 cm (1¼ inch) cubes, using a sharp knife.

Add the brandy, stock, Worcestershire sauce and mustard to the onion mixture.

Add the potatoes and simmer, uncovered, for a further 30 minutes, or until tender.

Peel two strips of orange rind. Remove the pith and slice the orange into rounds.

Combine the chicken stock and wine and add to the softened onion mixture.

Grill the capsicum, skin-side-up, until the skin is blistered and black.

Stir the capsicum strips, orange slices, olives and parsley into the sauce.

MAJORCAN CHICKEN

Preparation time: 30 minutes
Total cooking time: 1 hour 30 minutes
Serves 4

2 tablespoons olive oil
30 g (1 oz) butter
1.5 kg (3 lb) chicken pieces
1 orange
1 red onion, thinly sliced
2 cloves garlic, chopped
3/4 cup (185 ml/6 fl oz) chicken
   stock
1/2 cup (125 ml/4 fl oz) white
   wine
1 tablespoon plain flour
1 red capsicum, quartered
12 stuffed green olives
3 tablespoons chopped parsley

1 Preheat the oven to moderate 180°C (350°F/Gas 4). Heat the oil and butter in a large pan. Brown the chicken in batches over high heat and transfer to a flameproof casserole dish.

2 Cut two large strips of rind from the orange and set aside. Remove the pith from the orange, then slice the orange into thin rounds. Set aside.
3 Cook the onion and garlic in the pan for 3 minutes over medium heat, or until softened. Combine the stock and wine. Stir the flour into the pan, then slowly add the stock and wine and stir until the mixture comes to the boil. Add the orange rind strips, then pour over the chicken. Cover and bake for 1 hour.
4 Meanwhile, grill the capsicum, skin-side-up, for 8 minutes, or until black and blistered. Place in a plastic bag, seal and allow to cool. Peel away the skin and cut the flesh into strips.
5 Remove the chicken from the dish; cover and keep warm. Bring the sauce to the boil on the stove top, skimming off the fat. Boil for 5 minutes to thicken slightly. Add the capsicum strips, orange slices, olives and parsley. To serve, remove the orange rind, season to taste and spoon the sauce over the chicken.

ZARZUELA

Preparation time: 40 minutes
Total cooking time: 1 hour 10 minutes
Serves 4

Sofrito Sauce
1 tablespoon olive oil
2 onions, finely chopped
2 large tomatoes, peeled, seeded
    and chopped
1 tablespoon tomato paste

Picada Sauce
3 slices white bread, crusts
    removed
10 blanched almonds, toasted
3 cloves garlic
1 tablespoon olive oil

1 raw lobster tail
750 g (1¹/2 lb) white boneless
    fish, cut into bite-size pieces
plain flour, seasoned with salt
    and black pepper
1 tablespoon olive oil
125 g (4 oz) calamari rings
12 raw king prawns
¹/2 cup (125 ml/4 fl oz) white wine
12 mussels, scrubbed and
    beards removed
¹/2 cup (125 ml/4 fl oz) brandy
¹/4 cup (15 g/¹/2 oz) chopped
    parsley

1 To make the sofrito sauce, heat the oil in a pan over medium heat. Add the onion and cook, stirring, for 5 minutes without browning. Add the tomato, tomato paste and ¹/2 cup (125 ml/4 fl oz) water and cook, stirring, over medium heat for a further 10 minutes. Stir in another ¹/2 cup (125 ml/4 fl oz) water, season with salt and freshly ground black pepper and set aside.

2 To make the picada sauce, finely chop the bread, almonds and garlic in a food processor. With the motor running, gradually add the oil to form a paste, adding another ¹/2 tablespoon of oil if necessary.

3 Preheat the oven to moderate 180°C (350°F/Gas 4). Cut the lobster tail into rounds through the membrane that separates the shell segments. Set the rounds aside.

4 Lightly coat the fish in the flour. Heat the oil in a large pan and fry the fish over medium heat for 2–3 minutes, or until cooked and golden all over. Transfer to a large casserole dish.

5 Add the calamari to the pan and cook, stirring, for 1–2 minutes, then remove and add to the fish. Cook the lobster rounds and unshelled prawns for 2–3 minutes, or until just pink, then add to the casserole.

6 Add the wine to the pan and, when hot, add the mussels, discarding any which are already open. Cover and steam the mussels for 2–3 minutes. Discard any that do not open and add the rest to the casserole.

7 Ensuring nothing flammable is nearby, pour the brandy into one side of the pan and, when it has warmed, carefully ignite the brandy. Gently shake the pan until the flames have died down. Pour this mixture over the seafood in the casserole.

8 Pour over the sofrito sauce. Cover the casserole and bake for 20 minutes. Stir in the picada sauce and cook for a further 10 minutes, or until warmed through—do not overcook, or the seafood will toughen. Sprinkle with parsley to serve.

Add the tomatoes, tomato paste and water to the softened onions.

Finely chop the bread, almonds and garlic in a food processor. Gradually add the oil.

Cut the lobster tail into rounds through the membrane, separating the shell segments.

Transfer the lightly fried seafood to the casserole dish.

Add the mussels to the hot wine. Cover and steam for 2–3 minutes.

Remove the mussels and carefully pour the brandy into one side of the pan.

MOROCCAN LAMB SHANKS

Preparation time: 25 minutes
Total cooking time: 3 hours 15 minutes
Serves 4

Spicy Paste
30 g (1 oz) bunch coriander,
    roots intact
1 teaspoon ground turmeric
2 teaspoons ground cumin
1 teaspoon paprika
1 teaspoon ground coriander
1/2 teaspoon ground cinnamon
1 dried red chilli
2 cloves garlic, crushed
2 tablespoons honey
1/4 cup (60 ml/2 fl oz) olive oil

light olive oil, for cooking
8 lamb shanks
3 onions, sliced into thick rings
sugar, for sprinkling
1 cup (250 ml/8 fl oz) white wine
2 cups (500 ml/16 fl oz) chicken
    stock
4 lime quarters, to garnish
coriander leaves, to garnish

1 In a food processor, blend the spicy paste ingredients (including coriander roots) to a smooth paste. Set aside.
2 Heat 3 tablespoons of oil in a large, heavy-based pan. Brown the shanks in batches over high heat and transfer to a large, ovenproof dish. Preheat the oven to moderate 180°C (350°F/Gas 4).
3 Heat a tablespoon of oil in the pan. Add the onion rings, sprinkle with sugar and sauté over medium heat for 10–15 minutes, or until golden.
4 Add the spicy paste and sauté for 2 minutes. Season well, add the wine and stock and simmer for 15 minutes.
5 Pour the wine sauce over the lamb shanks. Cover and bake for 1 hour, then turn the shanks over and bake for another 1 1/2 hours, or until the meat is tender. Spoon any fat from the surface, transfer to plates and garnish with lime quarters and coriander leaves. Serve with couscous.

COOK'S FILE
Serving suggestion: Serve with preserved lemon couscous, page 190.

Blend all the spicy paste ingredients in a food processor until smooth.

Heat the oil in a large pan. Brown the shanks over high heat.

Add the spicy paste to the fried onion and sauté for 2 minutes.

BEEF IN BEER WITH CAPERS AND ANCHOVIES

Preparation time: 25 minutes
Total cooking time: 3 hours 20 minutes
Serves 4–6

1 kg (2 lb) gravy beef
plain flour, seasoned with salt and black pepper
olive oil, for cooking
4 cloves garlic, finely chopped
2 cups (500 ml/16 fl oz) beef stock
1¹/₂ cups (375 ml/12 fl oz) beer
2 onions, chopped
3 bay leaves

¹/₃ cup (55 g/2 oz) stuffed or pitted green olives, sliced
6 anchovies
2 tablespoons capers, drained

1 Cut the beef into 4 cm (1¹/₂ inch) chunks, following the sinew and separation of the meat. Lightly coat in the flour. Heat 3 tablespoons of oil in a deep heavy-based pan, add the garlic, then brown the beef over high heat.
2 Add the stock, beer, onions and bay leaves, season well and bring to the boil. Reduce the heat; cover and gently simmer for 2¹/₂ hours, stirring about three times during cooking. Remove the lid and simmer for 30 minutes more. Stir, then mix in the olives.

3 Heat 2 teaspoons of oil in a small pan. Add the anchovies and capers, gently breaking up the anchovies. Cook over medium heat for 4 minutes, or until brown and crisp. To serve, place the meat on serving plates, drizzle with the sauce, sprinkle with anchovies and capers, and season with salt and freshly ground black pepper.

COOK'S FILE

Note: The capers should be squeezed very dry before being added to the pan, or they will spit in the hot oil.

Cut the beef into large chunks, following the sinew and separation of the meat.

Add the stock, beer, onions and bay leaves to the browned beef.

Fry the anchovies and capers in a little hot oil until brown and crisp.

PIES

CHICKEN AND LEEK PIE

Preparation time: 20 minutes
Total cooking time: 40 minutes
Serves 4

50 g (1³/4 oz) butter
2 large leeks, washed and
    finely sliced
4 spring onions, sliced
1 clove garlic, crushed
¼ cup (30 g/1 oz) plain flour
1¹/2 cups (375 ml/12 fl oz)
    chicken stock
¹/2 cup (125 ml/4 fl oz) cream
1 medium barbecued chicken,
    chopped
2 sheets puff pastry, thawed
¼ cup (60 ml/2 fl oz) milk

1 Preheat the oven to moderately hot 200°C (400°F/Gas 6). In a pan, melt the butter and add the leek, spring onion and garlic. Cook over low heat for 6 minutes, or until the leek is soft but not browned. Sprinkle in the flour and mix well. Pour in the stock gradually and cook, stirring well, until the mixture is thick and smooth.
2 Stir in the cream and add the chicken pieces. Put the mixture in a shallow 20 cm (8 inch) pie dish and set aside to cool.
3 Cut a circle out of one of the sheets of pastry to cover the top of the pie. Paint around the rim of the pie dish with a little milk. Put the pastry on top and seal around the edge firmly. Trim off any overhanging pastry and decorate the edge with the back of a fork. Cut the other sheet into 1 cm (¹/2 inch) strips and roll each strip up loosely like a snail. Arrange the spirals on top of the pie, starting from the middle and leaving a gap between each one. The spirals may not cover the whole surface of the pie. Make a few small holes between the spirals to let out any steam, and brush the top of the pie lightly with milk. Cook in a hot 210°C (415°F/Gas 6–7) oven for 25–30 minutes, or until the top is brown and crispy. Make sure the spirals look well cooked and are not raw in the middle.

COOK'S FILE

Note: Make small pies by placing the mixture into 4 greased 1¹/4 cup (315 ml/10 fl oz) round ovenproof dishes. Cut the pastry into 4 rounds to fit. Bake for 15 minutes, or until the pastry is crisp.

Seal the edge firmly and trim off any overhanging pastry with a sharp knife.

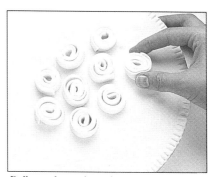

Roll up the strips of pastry like a snail and arrange them on top of the pie.

SHEPHERD'S PIE

Preparation time: 30 minutes + cooling
Cooking time: 1 hour 35 minutes
Serves 6

¼ cup (60 ml/2 fl oz) olive oil
1 large onion, finely chopped
2 cloves garlic, crushed
2 celery sticks, finely chopped
3 carrots, diced
2 bay leaves
1 tablespoon fresh thyme,
    chopped
1 kg (2 lb) good-quality lamb
    mince
1½ tablespoons plain flour
½ cup (125 ml/4 fl oz) dry red
    wine
2 tablespoons tomato paste
400 g (13 oz) can crushed
    tomatoes
1.5 kg (3 lb) floury potatoes
    (e.g. desiree), cut into
    even-sized pieces
¼ cup (60 ml/2 fl oz) milk
100 g (3½ oz) butter
½ teaspoon ground nutmeg

1 Heat 2 tablespoons oil over medium heat in a large, heavy-based saucepan and cook the onion for 3–4 minutes, or until softened. Add the garlic, celery, carrot, bay leaves and thyme and cook for 2–3 minutes. Transfer to a bowl and remove the bay leaves.
2 Add the remaining oil to the same pan, add the mince and cook over high heat for 5–6 minutes, or until it changes colour. Mix in the flour, cook for 1 minute, then pour in the red wine and cook for 2–3 minutes. Return the vegetables to the pan with the tomato paste and crushed tomato. Reduce the heat, cover and simmer for 45 minutes,

stirring occasionally. Season, to taste, then transfer to a shallow 3 litre (12 cups) ovenproof dish and leave to cool. Preheat the oven to moderate 180°C (350°F/Gas 4).
3 Meanwhile, boil the potatoes in salted water over medium heat for 20–25 minutes, or until tender. Drain, then mash with the milk and butter until smooth. Season with nutmeg and freshly ground black pepper. Spoon over the mince and fluff with a fork. Bake for 30 minutes, or until golden and crusty.

Return the softened vegetables to the pan with the mince mixture.

Spoon the mashed potato over the cooked mince in the ovenproof dish.

SPINACH PIE

Preparation time: 30 minutes
  + 30 minutes refrigeration
  + 10 minutes standing
Cooking time: 55 minutes
Serves 8–10

Pastry
2 cups (250 g/8 oz) plain flour
1/3 cup (80 ml/2³/4 fl oz) olive oil
1 egg, beaten
4–5 tablespoons iced water

1 kg (2 lb) spinach (silverbeet),
  stalks removed, roughly
  chopped
1 tablespoon olive oil
1 large leek, sliced
4 cloves garlic, crushed
2 cups (500 g/1 lb) ricotta
  cheese
1 cup (90 g/3 oz) grated
  pecorino cheese
300 g (10 oz) feta cheese,
  crumbled
3 eggs, lightly beaten
3 tablespoons chopped fresh dill
1/2 cup (15 g/1/2 oz) chopped
  fresh flat-leaf parsley

1 Sift the flour and 1/2 teaspoon salt into a large bowl and make a well in the centre. Mix the oil, egg and most of the water, add to the flour and mix with a flat-bladed knife until the mixture comes together in beads, adding a little more water if necessary. Gather the dough and press into a ball. Wrap in plastic wrap and refrigerate for about 30 minutes. (Pastry made with oil needs to be well chilled.)
2 Place the spinach in a large saucepan, sprinkle lightly with water, then cover and steam for 5 minutes, stirring occasionally, until wilted. Drain, squeeze out excess moisture, then finely chop.
3 Preheat the oven to moderately hot 200°C (400°F/Gas 6) and heat a baking tray. Grease a round, fluted tart tin with a removable base, 25 cm (10 inch) top, 23 cm (9 inch) base and 4 cm (1¹/2 inch) deep. Heat the oil in a frying pan, add the leek and garlic and cook over low–medium heat for 5 minutes, or until soft. Place in a large bowl with the ricotta, pecorino, feta, spinach, egg, dill and parsley. Season and mix.
4 Roll out two-thirds of the pastry between two sheets of baking paper until large enough to fit the tart tin. Line the tin, then fill with spinach mixture. Roll out the remaining pastry

between the baking paper and place over the mixture. Trim the edges with a knife and make two or three small slits in the pastry to allow the steam to escape.
5 Bake the pie on the hot tray for 15 minutes, then reduce the oven to moderate 180°C (350°F/Gas 4) and cook for another 30 minutes. Cover the top of the pie with foil if it is browning too much. Stand for 5–10 minutes before slicing.

Drain the wilted silverbeet well, then finely chop with a large, sharp knife.

CHICKEN, LEEK AND MUSHROOM PIES

Preparation time: 30 minutes
Cooking time: 1 hour
Makes 4

50 g (1³/₄ oz) butter
1 leek, thinly sliced
75 g (2¹/₂ oz) Swiss brown
    mushrooms, sliced
1 tablespoon peanut oil
500 g (1 lb) chicken breast
    fillet, cut into 2 cm (³/₄ inch)
    pieces
1 tablespoon plain flour
1 cup (250 ml/8 fl oz) chicken
    stock
150 g (5 oz) sliced ham, chopped
100 ml (3¹/₂ fl oz) crème fraîche
1 tablespoon chopped fresh
    flat-leaf parsley
4 sheets ready-rolled frozen puff
    pastry, thawed
2 egg yolks, lightly beaten

1 Preheat the oven to moderate 180°C (350°F/Gas 4). Grease two baking trays and lightly dust with flour. Melt half of the butter in a frying pan and cook the leek over medium heat for 4–5 minutes, or until soft but not browned. Add the mushrooms and cook for 1 minute. Remove from the heat and set aside.

2 Heat the remaining butter and oil in the same pan and cook the chicken over medium–high heat in two batches until golden. Stir in the flour, cook for 1 minute, then stir in the stock. Return the leek and mushrooms to the pan and simmer over low heat, stirring often, for 10–15 minutes. Add the ham and the crème fraîche and cook for 5 minutes. Season. Stir in the parsley and cool completely.

3 Cut each pastry sheet into an 18 cm (7 inch) square, reserving the offcuts. Spoon filling into the centre of each square. Brush the edges with the egg and bring them up over the filling, pinching them together. Cut out 16 large leaves from the offcuts and score veins on them. Carefully place a leaf over each seam. Brush with egg and bake for 20–25 minutes, or until golden.

Stir the chopped parsley into the creamy chicken mixture.

Bring the edges of the pastry squares up over the filling and pinch them together.

Place a pastry leaf over each seam on the top of each pie.

ASPARAGUS PIE

Preparation time: 40 minutes
  + 45 minutes refrigeration
Cooking time: 30 minutes
Serves 6

Pastry
350 g (11 oz) plain flour
**250 g (8 oz) butter, chilled
  and cubed**
²/3 cup (170 ml) iced water

**800 g (1 lb 10 oz) fresh
  asparagus**
20 g (³/4 oz) butter
**¹/2 teaspoon chopped fresh
  thyme**
1 French shallot, chopped
60 g (2 oz) sliced ham
¹/3 cup (80 ml/2³/4 fl oz) cream
**2 tablespoons grated Parmesan
  cheese**
1 egg
pinch of ground nutmeg
1 egg, extra, lightly beaten

1 To make the pastry, process the flour and a pinch of salt in a food processor for 3 seconds. Add the cubed butter and mix until it is cut finely, but not entirely blended into the flour—a few lumps are desirable. With the motor still running, gradually pour in the iced water until the dough just comes together. It should still have some small pebbles of butter.

2 Transfer to a lightly floured work surface and press into a rectangle about 30 x 12 cm (12 x 5 inch). Fold one end into the centre, then the opposite end over to cover the first. Roll into a rectangle again and repeat the folding three or four times. Wrap in plastic wrap and refrigerate for 45 minutes.

3 Trim the asparagus to 10 cm (2 inch). Slice thick spears in half lengthways. Heat the butter in a large frying pan over medium heat and add the asparagus, thyme and shallot. Add a tablespoon of water and season with salt and freshly ground black pepper. Cook, stirring, for 3 minutes, or until the asparagus is tender.

4 Preheat the oven to moderately hot 200°C (400°F/Gas 6) and grease a 21 cm (8¹/2 inch) fluted, loose-based flan tin. Roll the pastry out to a 2.5 mm (¹/8 inch) thick circle with a diameter of about 30 cm (12 inch). Line the flan tin and trim the pastry using kitchen scissors, leaving about 8 cm (3 inch) above the top of the tin. Place half the asparagus in one direction across the bottom of the dish. Layer the ham slices on top. Cover with the remaining asparagus, running in the opposite direction.

5 Combine the cream, Parmesan, egg and nutmeg and season. Pour over the asparagus. Fold the pastry over the filling, forming loose pleats. Brush with egg. Bake in the centre of the oven for 25 minutes, or until golden.

Fold the ends of the dough over and press into a rectangle.

Pour the combined cream, egg, Parmesan and nutmeg over the asparagus.

117

BEEF PIE

Preparation time: 35 minutes + chilling
Total cooking time: 2 hours 30 minutes
Serves 6

Filling
2 tablespoons oil
1 kg (2 lb) trimmed chuck
    steak, cubed
1 large onion, chopped
1 large carrot, finely chopped
2 cloves garlic, crushed
2 tablespoons plain flour
1 cup (250 ml/8 fl oz) beef
    stock
2 teaspoons fresh thyme leaves
1 tablespoon Worcestershire
    sauce

Pastry
2 cups (250 g/8 oz) plain flour
150 g (5 oz) cold butter,
    chopped
1 egg yolk
3–4 tablespoons iced water
1 egg yolk and 1 tablespoon
    milk, to glaze

1 Heat 1 tablespoon of the oil in a large pan and cook the meat in batches until browned all over. Remove from the pan and set aside. Heat the remaining oil, then add the onion, carrot and garlic and cook over medium heat until browned.

2 Return the meat to the pan and stir through the flour. Cook for 1 minute, then remove from the heat and slowly stir in the beef stock, mixing the flour in well. Add the thyme leaves and Worcestershire sauce, and bring to the boil. Season to taste with salt and freshly ground black pepper.

3 Reduce the heat to very low, cover and simmer for 1½–2 hours, or until the meat is tender. During the last 15 minutes of cooking remove the lid and allow the liquid to reduce so that the sauce is very thick and suitable for filling a pie. Allow to cool completely.

4 To make the pastry, sift the flour into a large bowl and add the butter. Using your fingertips, rub the butter into the flour until it resembles fine breadcrumbs. Add the egg yolk and 2 tablespoons of iced water, and mix with a knife using a cutting action until the mixture comes together in beads, adding a little more water if necessary. Turn out onto a lightly floured surface and gather together to form a smooth dough. Wrap in plastic wrap and refrigerate for 30 minutes.

5 Preheat the oven to moderately hot 200°C (400°F/Gas 6). Divide the pastry into two pieces and roll out one of the pieces on a sheet of baking paper until large enough to line a 23 cm (9 inch) pie dish. Line the pie dish with the pastry. Fill with the cold filling and roll out the remaining piece of pastry until large enough to fully cover the dish. Dampen the edges of the pastry with your fingers dipped in water. Lay the top piece of pastry over the pie and gently press the bottom and top pieces of pastry together. Trim the overhanging edges with a sharp knife, reroll the scrap pieces to make decorative shapes and press on the pie.

6 Cut a few slits in the top of the pastry to allow the steam to escape. Beat together the egg yolk and milk, and brush it over the top of the pie. Cook in the oven for 20–30 minutes, or until the pastry is golden and the filling is hot.

Add the butter and rub it into the flour with your fingertips.

Mix the egg yolk and water into the flour mixture with a flat-bladed knife.

Gather the mixture together to form a smooth dough.

The baking paper will help you lift the pastry into the pie dish.

Spoon in the filling then top with the second piece of pastry.

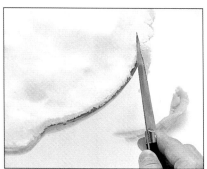

Press the pieces of pastry together and trim off the excess with a sharp knife.

CHARGRILLED VEGETABLE AND PARMESAN PIE

Preparation time: 45 minutes +
  1 hour standing
Cooking time: 1 hour 30 minutes
Serves 6

1 clove garlic, crushed
300 ml (9½ oz) olive oil
2 large eggplants
1 large orange sweet potato
3 large zucchini
3 red capsicums
3 yellow capsicums
2 tablespoons polenta
¾ cup (75 g/2½ oz) grated
  Parmesan cheese
1 egg, lightly beaten

Pastry
450 g (14 oz) plain flour
2 teaspoons cumin seeds
2 teaspoons paprika
100 g (3½ oz) butter, chopped

1 Place the garlic in a small bowl with the oil. Cut the eggplants and sweet potato into 5 mm (¼ inch) slices and the zucchini into 5 mm (¼ inch) lengths, then brush with the garlic oil. Quarter the capsicums, removing the seeds and membrane. Cook, skin-side-up, under a hot grill for 10 minutes, or until the skins blacken and blister. Cool in a plastic bag, then peel.

2 Chargrill the eggplant, orange sweet potato and zucchini in batches over high heat, turning occasionally, for 5–6 minutes, or until brown and tender. Set aside to cool.

3 Preheat the oven to moderate 180°C (350°F/Gas 4). Grease a deep 20 cm (8 inch) springform tin. Sift the flour into a bowl and add the cumin seeds, paprika and ½ teaspoon salt. Gently heat the butter in a saucepan with 220 ml (7 fl oz) water. Bring to the boil, pour into the flour and mix with a wooden spoon. When cool enough to handle, tip onto a floured surface and press gently together. Rest for 5 minutes.

4 Set aside one quarter of the dough and roll out the rest between two sheets of baking paper until large enough to cover the base and side of the tin. Line the tin, leaving some pastry overhanging. Sprinkle a layer of polenta over the base, then layer the red capsicum, zucchini, eggplant, sweet potato and yellow capsicum in the pie, brushing each layer with a little garlic oil, sprinkling with Parmesan and seasoning with salt and freshly ground black pepper as you go.

5 Roll out the remaining pastry between the baking paper to fit the top of the tin. Brush the edges of the bottom layer of pastry with egg. Cover with the pastry lid. Brush the edges with egg and trim with a sharp knife, crimping the edges to seal. Cut a small steam hole in the centre of the pie. Roll out the trimmings and use to decorate. Cook for 1 hour, or until crisp and golden (cover with foil if it browns too quickly). Cool for 1 hour. Serve at room temperature.

Layer the chargrilled vegetables and grated Parmesan in the pastry case.

LUXURY FISHERMAN'S PIE

Preparation time: 1 hour 10 minutes
Cooking time: 1 hour 10 minutes
Serves 6–8

1 kg (2 lb) raw medium prawns,
   peeled (heads and shells
   reserved)
1¹/₂ cups (375 ml/12 fl oz) fish
   stock
100 ml (3¹/₂ fl oz) dry white wine
6 black peppercorns
1 bay leaf
1.5 kg (3 lb) potatoes (e.g.
   desiree or pontiac), cut into
   3 cm (1¹/₄ inch) pieces
100 ml (3¹/₂ fl oz) milk
80 g (2³/₄ oz) butter
6 French shallots, chopped
¹/₃ cup (40 g/1¹/₄ oz) plain flour
300 ml (9¹/₂ fl oz) cream
2 egg yolks
2 tablespoons chopped fresh
   flat-leaf parsley
500 g (1 lb) salmon fillet,
   skinned and boned
500 g (1 lb) firm white-fleshed
   fish fillets (e.g. ling, blue eye)
pinch of cayenne pepper

1 Place the prawn heads and shells in a saucepan with the fish stock, wine, peppercorns and bay leaf and bring to the boil over medium–high heat. Reduce the heat and simmer for 25 minutes, or until you have about 1¹/₂ cups (375 ml/12 fl oz). Strain into a bowl, discarding the solids.

2 Meanwhile, put the potatoes in a saucepan of cold water, bring to the boil, then reduce the heat and simmer for 10–12 minutes, or until cooked. Drain, then mash with a potato masher. Heat the milk and 50 g (1³/₄ oz) of the butter in a small saucepan over low heat, then slowly beat into the potato with a wooden spoon until smooth. Stir in ¹/₂ teaspoon salt.

3 Preheat the oven to moderate 180°C (350°F/Gas 4). Lightly grease a 9 cup (4.25 litre) ovenproof dish. Melt the remaining butter in a frying pan over medium heat, add the shallots and cook for 5 minutes, or until soft but not brown. Add the flour and cook for another minute. Gradually stir in the reserved prawn stock and cook for 2–3 minutes, or until thickened, then add half the cream and cook for 5 minutes. Stir in the egg yolks and parsley and season.

4 Cut the fish into 2 cm (³/₄ inch) chunks and place in the base of the ovenproof dish, along with the prawns. Cover with the sauce, then spread the potato on top and rough up with a fork. Drizzle with the remaining cream, allowing it to soak through the topping. Sprinkle with cayenne pepper and bake for 30 minutes, or until golden.

Cover the combined fish pieces and prawns with the creamy sauce.

WHITE FISH AND BROAD BEAN PIE

Preparation time: 30 minutes
  + 20 minutes refrigeration
  + 15 minutes standing
Cooking time: 1 hour 10 minutes
Serves 6

60 g (2 oz) butter
700 g (1 lb 6½ oz) firm
    white-fleshed fish fillets such
    as ling, hake or gemfish
350 g (11 oz) shelled broad beans
1 baby fennel bulb, thick outer
    leaves removed, thinly sliced
1 leek, thinly sliced
¼ cup (30 g/1 oz) plain flour
1½ cups (375 ml/12 fl oz) milk
100 g (3½ oz) Cheddar cheese,
    grated
pinch of ground nutmeg
¼ teaspoon cayenne pepper
2 tablespoons chopped fresh
    flat-leaf parsley
375 g (12 oz) home-made or
    bought shortcrust pastry
1 egg, lightly beaten

1 Melt half the butter in a large frying pan over meduim heat and cook the fish for 3–4 minutes each side, or until opaque. Cool, then discard any bones and skin. Flake the flesh into chunks.
2 Cook the beans in a saucepan of boiling water for 2 minutes. Drain, cool slightly, then remove the skins.
3 Melt the remaining butter in the pan. Add the fennel and leek and cook for 3–4 minutes, or until soft. Stir in the flour for 1 minute, then gradually pour in the milk. Stir over medium heat until the sauce is thick and smooth. Add the cheese, nutmeg, cayenne and stir until the cheese melts. Season with salt and freshly ground black pepper then fold in the fish, beans and parsley. Refrigerate until required.
4 Grease a 6 cup (1.5 litre) oval ovenproof dish. Roll two-thirds of the pastry large enough for the pie lid. Roll the scraps and remaining pastry to the same size. Cover with a tea towel and refrigerate for 20 minutes. Preheat the oven to moderately hot 200°C (400°F/Gas 6) and heat a baking tray.
5 Spoon the filling into the dish and level the surface. Top with the pastry lid. Trim and crimp the edges with a fork. Brush with egg. Cut the other

sheet of pastry into a fish almost as long and wide as the pie. Lift onto the pie. Using scraps, make a mouth, eye and fins. Mark the tail with a knife and use the tip of a teaspoon to score scales. Brush with egg, then bake on the hot tray on the centre shelf for 45 minutes, covering with foil after 30 minutes. Cool in the dish for 15 minutes before serving.

Use a sharp knife to mark the tail of the pastry fish.

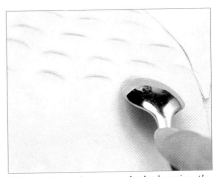

Make indentations over the body using the tip of a teaspoon.

ITALIAN ZUCCHINI PIE

Preparation time: 30 minutes
  + 30 minutes refrigeration
  + 30 minutes draining
Cooking time: 55 minutes
Serves 6

Pastry
2¹/₂ cups (310 g/10 oz) plain
    flour
¹/₃ cup (80 ml/2³/₄ oz) olive oil
1 egg, beaten
3–4 tablespoons iced water

600 g (1¹/₄ lb) zucchini
150 g (5 oz) provolone cheese,
    grated
120 g (4 oz) ricotta cheese
3 eggs
2 cloves garlic, crushed
2 teaspoons finely chopped fresh
    basil
pinch of ground nutmeg
1 egg, lightly beaten

1 To make the pastry, sift the flour and ¹/₂ teaspoon salt into a large bowl and make a well. Combine the oil, egg and almost all the water and add to the flour. Mix with a flat-bladed knife, using a cutting action, until the mixture comes together in beads, adding a little more water if necessary. Gather into a ball, wrap in plastic wrap and refrigerate for 30 minutes.

2 Preheat the oven to moderately hot 200°C (400°F/Gas 6) and heat a baking tray. Grease a 23 cm (9 inch) top, 18 cm (7 inch) base, 3 cm (1¹/₄ inch) deep pie dish. To make the filling, grate the zucchini and toss with ¹/₄ teaspoon salt. Place in a colander for 30 minutes to drain. Squeeze out any excess liquid with your hands. Place in a large bowl and add the provolone, ricotta, eggs, garlic, basil and nutmeg. Season well and mix thoroughly.

3 Roll out two-thirds of the pastry between two sheets of baking paper until large enough to line the base and side of the dish. Remove the top sheet and invert into the dish.

4 Spoon the filling into the pastry shell and level the surface. Brush the exposed rim of the dough with egg. Roll out two-thirds of the remaining dough between the baking paper to make a lid. Cover the filling with it, pressing the edges together firmly. Trim the edges and reserve the scraps. Crimp the rim. Prick the top all over with a skewer and brush with egg.

5 Roll the remaining dough into a strip about 30 x 10 cm (12 x 4 inch). Using a long sharp knife, cut this into nine lengths 1 cm (¹/₂ inch) wide. Press three ropes together at one end and press these onto the workbench to secure them. Plait the ropes. Make two more plaits with the remaining lengths. Trim the ends and space the plaits parallel across the centre of the pie. Brush with egg. Bake on the hot tray for 50 minutes, or until golden.

Spoon the filling into the pastry shell and level the surface.

ROAST VEGETABLE AND FETA PIES

Preparation time: 30 minutes + cooling
Cooking time: 45 minutes
Makes 6

3 zucchini, cut into 1.5 cm
    (5/8 inch) rounds
1/2 small butternut pumpkin
    (420 g/14 oz), cut into 2 cm
    (3/4 inch) cubes
1 red onion, cut into thin wedges
18 cap mushrooms, stalks
    removed
6 Roma tomatoes, quartered
    lengthways
3 cloves garlic, crushed

1 tablespoon roughly chopped
    fresh oregano
2 teaspoons roughly chopped
    fresh rosemary
2 tablespoons olive oil
6 sheets frozen ready-rolled
    shortcrust pastry, thawed
1 egg white, lightly beaten
200 g (6½ oz) feta cheese, cut
    into 1 cm (½ inch) cubes
1 tablespoon balsamic vinegar
200 g (6½ oz) ready-made
    tzatziki

1 Preheat the oven to 220°C (425°F/ Gas 7). Toss the zucchini, pumpkin, onion, garlic, mushrooms, tomatoes, herbs and oil together in a bowl, then bake in a large roasting dish for 20–30 minutes. Remove the vegetables from the oven and allow to cool.

2 Using a plate as a guide, cut out six 22 cm (8¾ inch) rounds from the pastry and lightly brush each one all over with egg white. Arrange the vegetables and feta over each pastry circle, leaving a 4 cm (1½ inch) border. Roughly tuck the pastry border in towards the filling. Brush the vegetables with balsamic vinegar.

3 Bake the pies for 10–15 minutes, or until the pastry is puffed and golden. Serve with tzatziki.

Bake the zucchini, pumpkin, onion, mushrooms, tomatoes, herbs and garlic.

Using a plate as a guide, cut out six rounds from the pastry.

Roughly tuck the pastry in towards the vegetable filling.

LAMB AND EGGPLANT PIE

Preparation time: 20 minutes
 + 30 minutes cooling
Cooking time: 1 hour 45 minutes
Serves 8–10

2 eggplants, cut into 2.5 cm
 (1 inch) cubes
1/4 cup (60 ml) olive oil
3 onions, finely chopped
3 cloves garlic, chopped
1 teaspoon paprika
1/2 teaspoon ground cinnamon
1/4 teaspoon ground nutmeg
650 g (1 lb 5 oz) lamb mince
1/4 cup (60 g/2 oz) tomato paste
1 cup (250 ml/8 fl oz) dry red
 wine
425 g (14 oz) can crushed
 tomatoes
1 cup (250 ml/8 fl oz) beef stock
200 g (6¹/2 oz) Greek-style
 natural yoghurt
2 eggs, lightly beaten
200 g (6¹/2 oz) feta cheese,
 crumbled
11 sheets filo pastry
olive oil spray

1 Preheat the oven to moderately hot 200°C (400°F/Gas 6) and grease a baking tray. Toss the eggplant with 2 tablespoons olive oil and place on the tray. Bake for 30 minutes, or until tender and brown. Remove, drain off any excess oil and set aside.

2 Meanwhile, heat the remaining oil in a large, deep frying pan over medium heat and cook the onion for 5 minutes, or until soft. Add the garlic and spices and cook for another minute.

3 Increase the heat to high, add the mince and cook for 5 minutes, or until brown. Add the tomato paste and cook for 2 minutes. Pour in the wine and cook for 3 minutes, stirring . Add the tomato and stock, bring to the boil, then reduce the heat and simmer for 30 minutes, or until the liquid has evaporated. Stir in the eggplant, then set aside for 30 minutes to cool.

4 Increase the oven to 220°C (425°F/Gas 7). Lightly grease a 8 cup (2 litre) pie dish. Combine the yoghurt, eggs and feta in a bowl.

5 Layer 6 sheets of filo in the base and sides of the pie dish, spraying each sheet with olive oil. Top with the

lamb, then pour in the yoghurt and feta mixture. Fold the overhanging pastry over the top, then top with another 5 filo sheets, spraying each sheet, to cover completely.

6 Bake on the lowest shelf for 30 minutes, then cook on the middle shelf for another 20–30 minutes, or until the pastry is crisp and golden.

Spoon the lamb and eggplant mixture into the pie dish.

Pour the yoghurt and feta mixture over the lamb and eggplant mixture.

INDIAN-STYLE SPICY LAMB AND APRICOT PIE

Preparation time: 40 minutes
+ 20 minutes refrigeration
+ cooling
Cooking time: 2 hours 45 minutes
Serves 8–10

Pastry
2¹/2 cups (310 g/10 oz) plain
    flour
160 g (5¹/2 oz) ghee, chilled and
    cut into small pieces
1 teaspoon cumin seeds
1 teaspoon sugar
¹/4–¹/2 cup (60–125 ml/2–4 fl oz)
    iced water

1.4 kg (1 lb 8 oz) boned lamb
    shoulder, cut into 1.5 cm
    (⁵/8 inch) cubes
1 cup (250 g/8 oz) natural
    yoghurt
2 teaspoons garam masala
1¹/2 tablespoons grated fresh
    ginger
1 teaspoon chilli powder
2 teaspoons ghee
2 onions, sliced
3 cloves garlic, crushed
1 long fresh green chilli, finely
    chopped
6 cardamom pods, crushed
1 teaspoon ground coriander
2 teaspoons ground cumin
2 x 425 g (14 oz) cans crushed
    tomatoes
100 g (3¹/2 oz) dried apricots,
    halved, soaked in 1 cup
    (250 ml/8 fl oz) warm water
¹/2 cup (125 g/4 oz) thick
    natural yoghurt (optional)

1 To make the pastry, sift the flour into a food processor and add the ghee, cumin seeds, sugar and 1 teaspoon salt. Process until the mixture resembles fine breadcrumbs, then gradually add the water until the pastry comes together in beads. Do not over-process. Gently gather the dough together into a ball, place on a lightly floured surface and press into a disc. Refrigerate for 20 minutes.

2 Combine the lamb, yoghurt, garam masala, ginger, chilli powder and ¹/2 teaspoon salt in a large bowl.

3 Heat the ghee in a large saucepan, add the onion and cook over medium heat for 10 minutes, or until soft and golden. Add the garlic and fresh chilli and cook for 1 minute, then add the remaining spices and cook for another minute.

4 Add the lamb and yoghurt mixture to the pan and cook, stirring occasionally, until combined. Add the tomato, bring to the boil, reduce the heat and simmer for 1¹/4 hours, then add the apricots and simmer for another 15 minutes, or until the lamb is tender. Set aside to cool.

5 Preheat the oven to 220°C (425°F/ Gas 7). Preheat a baking tray. Grease a deep 23 cm (9 inch) fluted tart tin or pie dish. Roll out two-thirds of the pastry between two sheets of baking paper to a size large enough to fit the tin. Remove the top sheet of paper and invert the pastry into the tin. Fill the pastry shell with the lamb curry. Brush the edges with a little water. Roll out the remaining pastry between the sheets of baking paper until large enough to cover the top of the pie dish. Position the lid on top of filling. Make two or three slits for the steam to escape, then trim the pastry edges.

6 Place the pie on the heated baking tray and bake on the lowest shelf for 30 minutes. Move to the centre shelf and bake for another 30 minutes, or until brown. Leave for 10 minutes before slicing. Serve with a dollop of yoghurt, if desired.

COOK'S FILE

Note: Because of the ghee content in the pastry for this pie, it is very difficult to make successfully by hand. It is better to use a food processor as described in the recipe. The filling mixture may seem a little runny when ready to go in the pie, but once it is cooked the sauce thickens. Ask your butcher to bone the lamb shoulder for you.

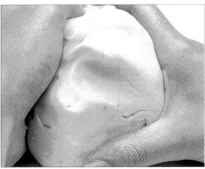

Gently gather the dough together into a ball and place on a lightly floured surface.

Add the spices to the onion mixture and cook for another minute.

Spoon the lamb curry mixture into the pastry shell.

Make steam holes on top of the pie and trim the pastry edges with a sharp knife.

PUMPKIN AND FETA PIE

Preparation time: 30 minutes
 + cooling + 20 minutes refrigeration
Cooking time: 1 hour 25 minutes
Serves 6

750 g (1¹/2 lb) butternut
 pumpkin, cut into 2 cm
 (³/4 inch) pieces
4 cloves garlic, unpeeled
5 tablespoons olive oil
2 small red onions, halved and
 sliced
1 tablespoon balsamic vinegar
1 tablespoon soft brown sugar
100 g (3¹/2 oz) good-quality
 feta cheese, broken into
 small pieces
1 tablespoon chopped fresh
 rosemary

Pastry
2 cups (250 g) plain flour
125 g butter, chilled and cubed
¹/2 cup (50 g) grated Parmesan
 cheese
3–4 tablespoons iced water

1 Preheat the oven to moderately hot
200°C (400°F/Gas 6). Place the garlic
and pumpkin on a baking tray, drizzle
with 2 tablespoons oil and bake for
25–30 minutes, or until the pumpkin is
tender. Transfer the pumpkin to a
large bowl and the garlic to a plate.
Leave the pumpkin to cool.
2 Meanwhile, heat 2 tablespoons oil
in a pan, add the onion and cook over
medium heat, stirring occasionally, for
10 minutes. Add the vinegar and
sugar and cook for 15 minutes, or until
the onion is caramelised. Remove from
the heat and add to the pumpkin.
Cool completely.
3 While the vegetables are cooling,
make the pastry. Sift the flour and
1 teaspoon salt into a large bowl and
rub in the butter with your fingertips
until the mixture resembles fine
breadcrumbs. Stir in the Parmesan.
Make a well, add almost all the water
and mix with a flat-bladed knife, using
a cutting action, until the mixture
comes together in beads. Add a little
more water if needed to bring the
dough together.
4 Gather the dough together and lift
onto a lightly floured work surface.
Press together into a ball and flatten
slightly into a disc. Cover in plastic
wrap and refrigerate for 20 minutes.
5 Add the feta and rosemary to the
pumpkin. Squeeze out the garlic flesh
and mix it through the vegetables.

Season with salt and freshly ground
black pepper.
6 Roll out the dough between two
sheets of baking paper to a 35 cm
(14 inch) circle. Remove the top sheet
of paper and place the bottom paper
with the pastry on a tray. Arrange the
pumpkin and feta mixture on top,
leaving a 6 cm (2¹/2 inch) border. Fold
over the edges, pleating as you fold,
and bake for 30 minutes, or until crisp
and golden.

*Fold the edges of the pastry over the
pumpkin and feta filling.*

RICH SNAPPER PIES

Preparation time: 20 minutes
Cooking time: 1 hour 20 minutes
Makes 4

2 tablespoons oil
4 onions, thinly sliced
¼ cup (30 g/1 oz) plain flour
2 cups (500 ml/16 fl oz) fish
   stock
½ cup (125 ml/4 fl oz) dry white
   wine
2 cups (500 ml) cream
1 tablespoon chopped fresh
   chives
1 kg (2 lb) skinless snapper
   fillets, cut into 2.5 cm
   (1 inch) pieces
2 teaspoons truffle-flavoured oil
   (optional)
1 sheet ready-rolled puff pastry,
   thawed
1 egg, lightly beaten

1 Preheat the oven to hot 210°C (415°F/Gas 6–7). Heat the oil in a large frying pan, add the onion and cook, stirring occasionally, over medium heat for 20 minutes, or until the onion is golden brown and slightly caramelised. Add the flour and cook, stirring, for 1 minute.

2 Gradually add the fish stock and wine to the pan, stir thoroughly, then bring to the boil and cook for 5 minutes, or until thickened. Stir in the cream and bring back to the boil. Reduce the heat and simmer for about 20 minutes, or until the liquid is reduced by half and has thickened. Stir in the chives, then the fish.

3 Divide the mixture among four 1¾ cup (440 ml) ramekins. Add ½ teaspoon truffle oil to each pie.

4 Cut the pastry sheets into rounds slightly larger than the tops of the ramekins and press onto the ramekins. Brush lightly with the beaten egg and make a cut in the tops for steam to escape. Bake for 30 minutes, or until crisp, golden and puffed. Serve with crusty bread.

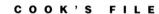

COOK'S FILE

Note: You can substitute bream, sea perch or a fleshy white fish for the snapper fillets.

Sprinkle the chives into the mixture, then stir through.

Place the pastry circle over the ramekin and press gently to seal.

BACON, TURKEY AND CIDER PIE

Preparation time: 45 minutes
+ 20 minutes refrigeration
Cooking time: 4 hours
Serves 6

Pastry

3¼ cups (405 g/13 oz) plain
    flour
1 teaspoon baking powder
200 g (6½ oz) lard, chilled and
    roughly chopped
3–4 tablespoons iced water

4 carrots
4 celery sticks (including leafy
    tops)
9 spring onions
3 onions
1.5 kg (3 lb) smoked bacon
    bones
2 teaspoons whole black
    peppercorns
1.5 litres (6 cups) apple cider
500 g (1 lb) turkey breast fillet,
    cut into 2 cm (¾ inch) cubes
plain flour, seasoned with salt
    and black pepper
60 g (2 oz) butter
1 egg, lightly beaten

1 Sift the flour and baking powder into a large bowl and add the lard and ½ teaspoon salt. Rub the lard into the flour with your fingertips until the mixture resembles fine breadcrumbs. Make a well in the centre, add almost all the water and mix with a flat-bladed knife, using a cutting action, until the mixture comes together in beads, adding more water, a teaspoon at a time, if necessary. Turn out onto a lightly floured surface and gather together into a smooth ball. Flatten slightly into a disc, wrap in plastic wrap and refrigerate for at least 20 minutes.

2 Roughly chop two of the carrots, three of the celery sticks (including the leafy tops), six of the spring onions and cut two of the onions into quarters and place them in a large saucepan with the bacon bones, peppercorns, cider and 2 litres (8 cups) cold water. Bring to the boil over high heat, then reduce the heat and simmer for 2 hours. Remove the bones with tongs, then strain the liquid into

a bowl. Return the liquid to the saucepan and gently simmer for another hour, or until reduced – you will need 2 cups (500 ml/16 fl oz). Meanwhile, pick the meat from the bacon bones, avoiding any gristle and small bones. You should have at least 200–250 g (6½–8 oz) meat.

3 Cut the remaining carrots and celery sticks into 1 cm (½ inch) roughly chop the onion and cut the remaining spring onions into 3 cm (1¼ inch) lengths. Melt half the butter in a large frying pan over medium heat. Add the carrot and onion and cook for 5 minutes, or until the onion is soft and golden. Stir in the celery and spring onion and cook for another 3 minutes, or until all the vegetables have softened. Transfer to a plate.

4 Toss the turkey cubes in the seasoned flour, shaking off any excess. Melt the remaining butter in the large frying pan over medium heat. Add the turkey and cook, turning constantly, for 8 minutes, or until browned all over. Return the vegetables and bacon meat to the pan and stir well, scraping the bottom of the pan to remove any flour. Slowly pour in the reserved stock. Stir for several minutes until the mixture has thickened, then remove from the heat and allow to cool.

5 Preheat the oven to moderate 180°C (350°F/Gas 4) and lightly grease a 25 cm (10 inch) ceramic pie dish. Divide the dough into two portions, one slightly larger than the other. Roll out the larger portion between two sheets of baking paper into a 35 cm (14 inch) circle, not too thin. Line the pie dish with the pastry. Spoon the filling into the shell. Roll out the remaining pastry between the baking paper to a 30 cm (12 inch) circle. Brush around the rim of the pastry base with egg, then place the top on. Trim off any excess pastry and pinch the edges together. If you wish, decorate the edges with pastry leaves. Brush the pie with egg, prick with a fork and bake for 45 minutes, or until golden.

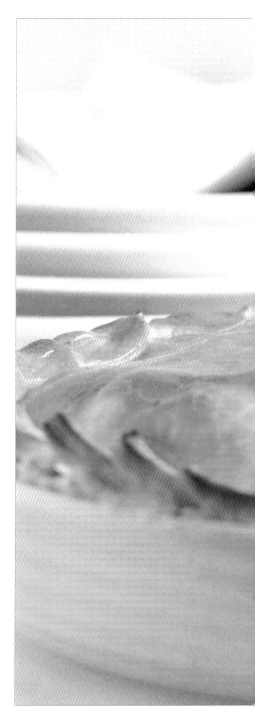

Gently gather the dough together into a smooth ball.

Using your fingers, remove the meat from the bacon bones.

Pour the reserved stock over the bacon and turkey mixture.

Brush the beaten egg over the rim of the filled pastry.

MINI SEAFOOD AND FENNEL PIES

Preparation time: 20 minutes
 + cooling time
Cooking time: 40 minutes
Makes 6

50 g (1¹/2 oz) butter
1 fennel bulb, chopped,
    1 teaspoon leaves reserved
    and chopped
1 clove garlic, crushed
3 tablespoons finely chopped
    French shallots
1¹/2 tablespoons plain flour
¹/2 cup (125 ml/4 fl oz) cream
1 teaspoon Pernod (optional)
pinch of cayenne pepper
350 g (11 oz) small raw prawns,
    peeled
170 g (5¹/2 oz) fresh scallops
600 g (1¹/4 lb) home-made or
    bought shortcrust pastry
1 egg, lightly beaten

1 Melt the butter in a large frying pan over medium heat. Add the fennel, garlic and shallots and gently cook, stirring, for 6–8 minutes, or until softened but not browned. Stir in the flour, cook for 20–30 seconds, then gradually add the cream and Pernod. Cook, stirring, until very thick. Add the cayenne pepper and season with salt and freshly ground black pepper. Stir the prawns, scallops and reserved fennel leaves into the mixture, then remove from the heat and set aside to cool.

2 Preheat the oven to moderate 180°C (350°F/Gas 4) and heat a baking tray. Grease six 11 cm (4¹/2 inch) top, 6 cm (2¹/2 inch) base, 2 cm (³/4 inch) deep pie tins. Divide the pastry into six and roll two-thirds of each portion out to a size large enough to fit the base and side of the tins. Line the tins with the pastry. Roll the remaining portions to a size large enough to form pie lids.

3 Divide the filling among the tins. Brush the pastry rims with egg. Top each with a lid, pressing the edges firmly. Trim with a sharp knife and seal with a fork. Brush with egg. Make a cross-hatch pattern over the tops using the fork—two lines in each direction—then make an incision in the middle. Place on the hot tray and bake for 25 minutes, or until the pastry is golden.

COOK'S FILE

Note: If small prawns aren't available, cut larger ones into 2.5 cm (1 inch) lengths. If you would prefer to discard the scallop coral, buy extra scallops to make up the weight.

Spoon the cooled seafood filling into the pastry-lined tins.

Make a cross-hatch pattern on the pastry, then make an incision in the middle.

BEEF, STOUT AND POTATO PIE

Preparation time: 30 minutes
Cooking time: 3 hours 10 minutes
Serves 6

2 tablespoons olive oil
1.25 kg (2 lb 4 oz) chuck steak,
    cut into 3 cm (1¹/₄ inch)
    cubes, excess fat trimmed
2 onions, sliced
2 rashers bacon, roughly
    chopped
4 cloves garlic, crushed
2 tablespoons plain flour
440 ml (14 oz) can stout
1¹/₂ cups (375 ml/12 fl oz) beef
    stock
1¹/₂ tablespoons chopped fresh
    thyme
2 large potatoes, thinly sliced
olive oil, for brushing

1 Heat 1 tablespoon of the oil over high heat in a large, heavy-based flameproof casserole dish, add the beef in batches and cook, turning occasionally, for 5 minutes, or until the meat is nicely coloured. Remove from the dish. Reduce the heat to low, add the remaining oil to the dish, then cook the onion and bacon for 10 minutes, stirring occasionally. Add the garlic and cook for another minute. Return the beef to the pan.

2 Sprinkle the flour over the beef, cook for a minute, stirring, and then gradually add the stout, stirring constantly. Add the stock, increase the heat to medium–high and bring to the boil. Stir in the thyme, season well, then reduce the heat and simmer for 2 hours, or until the beef is tender and the mixture has thickened.

3 Preheat the oven to moderately hot 200°C (400°F/Gas 6). Lightly grease a 5 cup (1.25 litre) ovenproof dish and pour in the beef mixture. Arrange potato slices in a single overlapping layer over the top to cover the meat. Brush with olive oil and sprinkle with salt. Bake for 30–40 minutes, or until the potato is golden.

Gradually add the stout to the beef mixture, stirring constantly.

Arrange the potato slices in a single overlapping layer to cover the meat.

RABBIT AND MUSHROOM PIE WITH POLENTA LID

Preparation time: 30 minutes
 + 15 minutes soaking
Cooking time: 1 hour 20 minutes
Serves 4–6

10 g (1/4 oz) dried porcini
  mushrooms
80 g (2³/4 oz) butter
1 kg (2 lb) trimmed rabbit meat,
  cut into 2 cm (³/4 inch) cubes
  (buy fillets or de-boned
  saddles)
200 g (6¹/2 oz) piece pancetta or
  bacon, diced
1 large onion, finely chopped
200 g (6¹/2 oz) button
  mushrooms, quartered
150 g (5 oz) shimeji mushrooms,
  trimmed
1 tablespoon plain flour
200 ml (6¹/2 fl oz) crème fraîche
150 ml (5 fl oz) cream
2 teaspoons chopped fresh
  thyme
2 tablespoons chopped fresh
  flat-leaf parsley

Topping
2 cups (500 ml/16 fl oz) milk
20 g (³/4 oz) butter
1/2 cup (75 g/2¹/2 oz) instant
  polenta
1/2 cup (50 g/1³/4 oz) shredded
  Parmesan cheese
pinch of ground nutmeg
1 egg, lightly beaten

1 Soak the porcini mushrooms in 1/2 cup (125 ml/4 fl oz) warm water for 15 minutes. Heat half the butter in a large, deep frying pan over medium heat and cook the rabbit in batches for 5 minutes each batch, or until brown all over. Remove from the pan. Add the pancetta to the pan and cook for 4–5 minutes, or until golden. Add the remaining butter and the onion, reduce the heat and cook for 5 minutes, or until softened.

2 Add the button and shimeji mushrooms to the pan and stir well. Squeeze dry the porcini mushrooms and chop. Add to the pan, along with the liquid. Simmer for 10 minutes, or until all the liquid evaporates. Add the flour and stir for 1 minute. Stir in the crème fraîche and cream and season with freshly ground black pepper. Return the rabbit to the pan

and simmer for 20 minutes, or until the sauce has reduced and thickened. Add the fresh herbs.

3 Preheat the oven to moderately hot 200°C (400°F/Gas 6). Grease a 5 cup (1.25 litre) ovenproof dish. Spoon in the rabbit and mushroom filling.

4 To make the topping, put the milk, butter and 1/2 teaspoon salt in a saucepan and heat until almost boiling. Add the polenta and stir constantly for 5 minutes, or until thick and smooth and the mixture pulls away from the sides. Remove from the heat and stir in the Parmesan. Add the nutmeg, beat in the egg and season. Spread over the rabbit mixture and bake for 20 minutes, or until golden.

Use a wooden spoon to spread the polenta topping over the rabbit mixture.

MINI THAI CHICKEN PIES

Preparation time: 15 minutes
  + 20 minutes refrigeration + cooling
Cooking time: 35 minutes
Makes 24

Pastry
4 cups (500 g/1 lb) plain flour
**250 g (8 oz) butter, chilled and
  cubed**
1 teaspoon chilli flakes, toasted
4–6 tablespoons iced water

1 tablespoon peanut oil
4 spring onions, finely chopped
2 cloves garlic, crushed
**1 stem lemon grass (white part
  only), finely chopped**
1 tablespoon green curry paste
**500 g (1 lb) chicken thigh fillets,
  trimmed and finely diced**
1 tablespoon plain flour
**1/3 cup (90 ml/3 fl oz) coconut
  cream**
**2 tablespoons finely chopped
  fresh coriander**
**1 teaspoon grated palm sugar or
  soft brown sugar**
2 teaspoons fish sauce
2 teaspoons lime juice
1 egg, lightly beaten

1 Sift the flour into a large bowl and rub in the butter with your fingertips until the mixture resembles fine breadcrumbs. Stir in the chilli flakes. Make a well in the centre, add almost all the water and mix with a flat-bladed knife, using a cutting action, until the mixture comes together in beads. Add more water if needed.

2 Gather the dough together and lift onto a lightly floured work surface. Press into a ball, cut in half, then flatten each portion into a disc and wrap in plastic wrap. Refrigerate for at least 20 minutes.

3 Preheat the oven to moderately hot 200°C (400°F/Gas 6). Place a baking tray in the oven to heat. Lightly grease two 12-hole shallow, round-based patty tins. Heat the oil in a large, deep frying pan over medium heat and cook the spring onion, garlic and lemon grass for 1 minute. Stir in the curry paste and cook for 1 minute, or until fragrant.

4 Increase the heat to high. Add the chicken and cook for 4–5 minutes, or until cooked. Reduce the heat to medium, stir in the flour and cook for 1 minute. Pour in the coconut cream and simmer for 2–3 minutes, or until thick. Add the coriander, sugar, fish sauce and lime juice, then set aside to cool.

5 Roll one portion of the dough out between two sheets of baking paper until 2 mm (1/8 inch) thick. Remove the top sheet of paper and, using a 7 cm (2³/4 inch) cutter, cut out 24 rounds. Gently place into the tins. Spoon the cooled filling into the rounds to come up to the top. Roll out the remaining pastry to 2 mm (1/8 inch) thick and, using a 7 cm (2³/4 inch) cutter, cut out 24 rounds. Brush the edges with egg, place the pastry lids over the filling and press the edges together with a fork. Lightly brush with beaten egg, prick with a fork, place on the hot tray and bake for 15–20 minutes, or until golden.

Carefully spoon the cooled filling into the pastry rounds.

STEWS, CASSEROLES, PIES & MASH

STEAK AND KIDNEY PIE

Preparation time: 40 minutes + cooling
Cooking time: 3 hours 10 minutes
Serves 6

1/2 cup (60 g/2 oz) plain flour,
   seasoned
1.5 kg (3 lb) chuck steak, cut
   into 2 cm (3/4 inch) cubes
1 ox kidney (500 g/1 lb), cut
   into 2 cm (3/4 inch) cubes
2 tablespoons olive oil
2 onions, chopped
125 g (4 oz) button mushrooms,
   quartered
40 g (11/4 oz) butter
1 cup (250 ml/8 fl oz) beef or
   veal stock
3/4 cup (185 ml/6 fl oz) stout
2 tablespoons Worcestershire
   sauce
1 tablespoon anchovy essence
1 tablespoon chopped fresh
   flat-leaf parsley
600 g (11/4 lb) quick flaky
   pastry
1 egg, lightly beaten

1 Place the flour in a bowl. Toss the steak and kidney pieces through the flour and shake off any excess.
2 Heat the oil in a large saucepan over medium heat, add the onion and cook for 5 minutes, or until soft and golden. Add the mushrooms and cook for another 5 minutes. Remove the onion and mushrooms from the pan.
3 Melt a third of the butter in the saucepan, add a third of the beef and kidney and cook over medium heat, turning occasionally, for 5 minutes, or until brown. Remove and repeat with the remaining butter, beef and kidney. Return all the meat to the saucepan, add the stock and stout, stir and bring slowly to boil. Reduce the heat and simmer for 2 hours, or until the meat is tender. Remove from the heat and allow the meat to cool.
4 Add the onion and mushrooms, Worcestershire sauce, anchovy essence and parsley to the meat.
5 Preheat the oven to moderate 180°C (350°F/Gas 4). Place the cooled filling into a 25 cm top, 20 cm base, 4 cm (11/2 inch) deep ceramic pie dish. Roll out the pastry between two sheets of

baking paper to a round to fit the top of the pie dish. Moisten the rim of the dish with milk and place the pastry over the filling. Press firmly into place and brush with egg. Roll any scraps to decorate the top, brush with egg and bake for 40–45 minutes, or until golden.

Cook the beef and kidney in three batches until browned.

EGG AND BACON PIE

Preparation time: 20 minutes
  + 30 minutes refrigeration + cooling
Cooking time: 50 minutes
Serves 4–6

Pastry
450 g (14 oz) plain flour
**125 g (4 oz) butter, chilled and
  cubed**
250 g (8 oz) mascarpone

1 tablespoon olive oil
300 g (10 oz) bacon, diced
**2 onions, halved and thinly
  sliced**
**1 tablespoon chopped fresh
  flat-leaf parsley**
6 eggs
1 egg yolk

1 Sift the flour into a large bowl and rub in the butter with your fingertips until the mixture resembles fine breadcrumbs. Add the mascarpone and mix with a flat-bladed knife, using a cutting action, until the mixture begins to form lumps which leave the side of the bowl.

2 Turn the dough out onto a lightly floured surface and gently gather into a smooth ball. Flatten slightly into a disc, then cover in plastic wrap and refrigerate for 30 minutes.

3 Preheat the oven to 170°C (325°F/ Gas 3). Lightly grease a 23 cm (9 inch) top, 18 cm (7 inch) base, 3 cm (1½ inch) deep metal pie dish. Place a baking tray in the oven to preheat. Heat the oil in a frying pan and cook the bacon and onion over medium heat, stirring occasionally, for 5–7 minutes, or until just browning. Stir in the parsley. Set aside to cool.

4 Divide the pastry into two portions, one slightly larger than the other. Roll out the larger portion between two sheets of baking paper until large enough to line the base and side of the pie dish. Line the pie dish. Place the onion and bacon in the pastry shell and make six well-spaced holes in the mixture with the back of a spoon. Crack an egg into each of the holes. Brush the rim of the pastry with water. Roll out the remaining pastry between the baking paper until large enough to cover the top of the pie. Lift it onto the pie. Trim the excess pastry

and seal the edges well. Re-roll the trimmings and make leaves to decorate the pie. Brush with egg yolk and bake on the hot tray for 40 minutes. Cover if it browns too quickly. Leave for 10 minutes before serving.

Add the mascarpone and mix with a flat-bladed knife until lumps start to form.

Crack an egg into each hole in the onion and bacon filling mixture.

FISH PIE

Preparation time: 10 minutes
Total cooking time: 45 minutes
Serves 4

2 large potatoes (500 g/1 lb),
    chopped
1/4 cup (60 ml/2 fl oz) milk or
    cream
1 egg
60 g (2 oz) butter
1/2 cup (60 g/2 oz) grated cheese
800 g white fish fillets, cut
    into large chunks
1 1/2 cups (375 ml/12 fl oz) milk
1 onion, finely chopped
1 clove garlic, crushed
2 tablespoons plain flour
2 tablespoons lemon juice
2 teaspoons lemon rind
1 tablespoon chopped
    fresh dill

1 Preheat the oven to moderate 180°C (350°F/Gas 4). Boil or steam the potatoes until tender. Drain and mash well with the milk or cream, egg and half the butter. Mix in half the cheese, then set aside and keep warm.
2 Put the fish in a shallow frying pan and cover with the milk. Bring to the boil, then reduce the heat and simmer for 2–3 minutes, or until the fish flakes when tested with a knife. Drain the fish well, reserving the milk, and set aside.

3 Melt the remaining butter over medium heat in a pan and cook the onion and garlic for 2 minutes. Stir in the flour and cook for 1 minute, or until pale and foaming. Remove from the heat and gradually stir in the reserved milk. Return to the heat and stir constantly until the sauce boils and thickens. Reduce the heat and simmer for 2 minutes. Add the lemon juice, lemon rind and dill, and season.
4 Put the fish into a 6 cup (1.5 litre) ovenproof dish and gently mix in the sauce. Spoon the potato over the fish and top with the remaining cheese. Bake in the oven for 35 minutes, or until the top is browned.

Use a potato masher to mash the potatoes with the milk or cream, egg and butter.

Put the pieces of fish in a frying pan and cover with the milk.

Put spoonfuls of the potato mixture on top of the fish.

TUNA MORNAY

Preparation time: 20 minutes
Total cooking time: 25 minutes
Serves 4

60 g (2 oz) butter
2 tablespoons plain flour
2 cups (500 ml/16 fl oz) milk
1/2 teaspoon dry mustard
3/4 cup (90 g/3 oz) grated cheese
425 g (14 oz) can tuna in brine,
    drained
180 g (6 oz) can tuna in brine,
    drained
2 tablespoons finely chopped
    fresh parsley
2 eggs, hard boiled and chopped
1/3 cup (25 g/3/4 oz) fresh
    breadcrumbs
paprika, to season

1 Preheat the oven to moderate 180°C (350°F/Gas 4). Melt the butter in a

small pan, then add the flour and stir over low heat for 1 minute. Remove the pan from the heat and add the milk gradually, stirring until smooth between each addition.
2 Return the pan to the heat and stir constantly until the sauce boils and thickens. Reduce the heat and simmer for 2 minutes. Remove from the heat, whisk in the mustard and 1/2 cup (60 g/2 oz) cheese until smooth.

3 Flake the tuna with a fork, and mix into the sauce, along with the parsley and egg. Season with salt and freshly ground black pepper. Spoon the mixture into four 1 cup (250 ml) ovenproof ramekins. Mix together the breadcrumbs and remaining cheese and sprinkle over the mornay. Dust very lightly with paprika. Bake for 15–20 minutes, or until the topping is golden brown.

Gradually add the milk, stirring until smooth between each addition.

Use a fork to flake the tuna, then stir it into the sauce.

BURGUNDY BEEF PIE

Preparation time: 30 minutes + cooling
Cooking time: 3 hours 10 minutes
Serves 6

2 tablespoons olive oil
40 g (1 1/4 oz) butter
185 g (6 oz) bacon, diced
1.25 kg (2 lb 6 oz) chuck steak,
    trimmed and cut into 2.5 cm
    (1 inch) cubes
2 onions, diced
3 cloves garlic, crushed
2 carrots, cut into 1.5 cm
    (5/8 inch) cubes
1/4 cup (30 g/1 oz) plain flour
1 1/4 cups (315 ml/10 fl oz)
    Burgundy
1 1/2 cups (375 ml/12 fl oz) beef
    stock
2 tablespoons tomato paste
1 teaspoon chopped fresh thyme
1 bay leaf
275 g (9 oz) small Swiss brown
    mushrooms, halved
pinch of ground nutmeg
3 tablespoons chopped fresh
    flat-leaf parsley
375 g (12 oz) home-made or
    bought puff pastry
1 egg, lightly beaten

1 Heat 1 tablespoon of oil and 20 g (3/4 oz) of butter in a large, heavy-based, flameproof casserole dish or saucepan over medium heat. Add the bacon and cook for 2–3 minutes. Transfer the bacon to a plate. Increase the heat to high, add the beef to the pan in batches and cook, turning, for 7–8 minutes, or until browned. Add to the bacon.
2 Heat the remaining oil in the pan over medium heat, add the onion and garlic and cook for 4–5 minutes. Add the carrot and cook, stirring once or twice, for 5 minutes. Stir in the flour, add the beef, bacon, wine, stock and tomato paste and stir for 5 minutes, or until the sauce has thickened slightly and is smooth. Add the thyme and bay leaf and season. Reduce the heat, cover and cook for 1 1/4 hours, or until the meat is tender, adding 1/4 cup (60 ml/ 2 fl oz) hot water, if necessary, to make a thick gravy.
3 Meanwhile, melt the remaining butter in a frying pan over low heat. Add the mushrooms and fry until

golden. Stir in the nutmeg and chopped parsley.
4 Preheat the oven to moderately hot 200°C (400°F/Gas 6) and grease a 2 litre (8 cups) oval ovenproof dish that has 5–6 cm (2–2 1/2 inch) sides. Roll out the pastry between two sheets of baking paper until about 6 mm (2 1/4 inch) thick and slightly larger than the dish. Roll out the scraps to a 35 x 10 cm (14 x 4 inch) strap, 5 mm (1/4 inch) thick. Cut into 1.5 cm (5/8 inch) wide strips.
5 Remove the bay leaf from the meat, then stir in the mushrooms. Spoon into

the dish. Cover the dish with the pastry lid, press the edges firmly down onto the lip of the dish, then trim off any excess. Brush the edges with egg. Make three 2.5 cm (1 inch) slits in the centre. Take a strip of pastry and twist a tight scroll. Repeat with the other strips. Run them around the rim, pressing joins together. Brush with egg and bake for 55–60 minutes, or until golden.

Cook the beef mixture until the sauce has thickened slightly and is smooth.

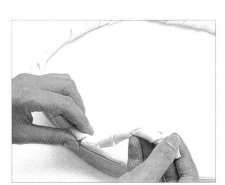

Twist the pastry strips to form long, tight scrolls and place them around the pie rim.

SWEET POTATO AND FENNEL PIE

Preparation time: 20 minutes
+ 30 minutes refrigeration
+ 10 minutes draining
Cooking time: 1 hour 10 minutes
Serves 6

2 fennel bulbs (540 g/1 lb
1¼ oz), thick outer leaves
removed, sliced
300 g (10 oz) sweet potato, cut
into 1 cm (½ inch) cubes
1 tablespoon dried juniper
berries, ground
¼ cup (60 ml/2 fl oz) olive oil
300 g (10 oz) ricotta cheese
1 cup (100 g/3½ oz) grated
Parmesan cheese

100 g (3½ oz) ground almonds
6 sheets ready-rolled shortcrust
pastry
milk, to glaze
3 sheets ready-rolled puff pastry

1 Preheat the oven to moderate 180°C (350°F/Gas 4). Grease six 11 cm (4½ inch) top, 9.5 cm (3¾ inch) base and 2.5 cm (1 inch) deep pie tins. Place the fennel, sweet potato and ground juniper berries in a deep roasting tin and toss with the oil. Season, cover with foil and cook for 35 minutes, or until the vegetables have softened. Drain any oil away, transfer the vegetables to a bowl and refrigerate for 30 minutes, or until cold.
2 Combine the ricotta, Parmesan and ground almonds in a large bowl. Transfer to a sieve and sit over a bowl

for 10 minutes to drain away any liquid from the ricotta.
3 Cut a 15 cm (6 inch) round from each sheet of shortcrust pastry and line the pie tins, leaving the excess overhanging. Brush the rims with the milk.
4 Divide the vegetables among the pastry shells, then top with ricotta mixture. Cut six 12 cm (5 inch) rounds from the puff pastry, place over the filled shells and trim. Seal the edges with a fork and prick a few holes in the tops. Brush with milk, then bake for 35 minutes, or until golden.

Roast the fennel and sweet potato until they have softened.

Cut a 15 cm (6 inch) round from each shortcrust sheet, using a saucer to help you.

Spoon the ricotta and Parmesan mixture into the vegetable-filled pie tins.

MOROCCAN LAMB PIE

Preparation time: 30 minutes + cooling
Cooking time: 2 hours 40 minutes
Serves 6–8

1/4 cup (60 ml/2 fl oz) olive oil
2 onions, finely chopped
4 cloves garlic, crushed
1 1/4 teaspoons ground cinnamon
1 1/4 teaspoons ground cumin
1 1/4 teaspoons ground coriander
1/2 teaspoon ground ginger
large pinch of cayenne pepper
1.2 kg (2 lb 6 1/2 oz) boned lamb
    leg, trimmed and cut into
    2 cm (3/4 inch) cubes
1 1/2 cups (375 ml/12 fl oz)
    chicken stock
2 teaspoons grated lemon rind
1 tablespoon lemon juice
2 carrots, cut into 1.5 cm
    (5/8 inch) cubes
1/3 cup (35 g/1 1/4 oz) ground
    almonds
1/2 cup (25 g/3/4 oz) chopped
    fresh coriander
500 g (1 lb) home-made or
    bought puff pastry
1 egg, lightly beaten

1 Heat the oil in a large saucepan. Add the onion, garlic, cinnamon, cumin, ground coriander, ginger and cayenne pepper and cook, stirring, over medium heat for 30–40 seconds. Add the lamb and stir until coated in the spices. Add the stock, lemon rind and lemon juice and cook, covered, over low heat for 45 minutes.

2 Add the carrot, cover and simmer for another 45 minutes, or until the lamb is tender. Stir in the almonds, increase the heat and boil, uncovered, for 30 minutes, or until the sauce becomes very thick. Stir in the fresh coriander, season to taste, and cool.

3 Preheat the oven to moderately hot 200°C (400°F/Gas 6) and heat a baking tray. Grease a 25 cm (10 inch) top, 20 cm (8 inch) base, 4 cm (1 1/2 inch) deep pie dish. Roll out the pastry to a 42 cm (16 3/4 inch) round and neaten the edge with a sharp knife. Line the dish with the pastry, with the excess hanging over.

4 Spoon the filling into the dish, levelling the surface. Fold the overhanging pastry up and over, forming pleats, to encase most of the filling, leaving an opening in the centre. Using kitchen scissors, cut out Vs of pastry where it falls into deep folds towards the middle. This reduces the thickness so that the pastry can bake evenly.

5 Brush with egg and bake on the hot tray in the centre of the oven for 20 minutes. Reduce the oven to moderate 180°C (350°F/Gas 4), cover the pie with foil and bake for another 20 minutes.

Boil the lamb mixture for 30 minutes, or until the sauce becomes very thick.

Fold the overhanging pastry up and over to encase most of the filling.

SALMON FILO PIE WITH DILL BUTTER

Preparation time: 25 minutes + cooling
Cooking time: 50 minutes
Serves 6

³/4 cup (150 g/5 oz) medium-grain white rice
80 g (2³/4 oz) butter, melted
8 sheets filo pastry
500 g (1 lb) fresh salmon fillet, skin and bones removed, cut into 1.5 cm (⁵/8 inch) chunks
2 French shallots, finely chopped
1¹/2 tablespoons baby capers
150 g (5 oz) Greek-style yoghurt
1 egg
1 tablespoon grated lemon rind
3 tablespoons chopped fresh dill
¹/4 cup (25 g/³/4 oz) dry breadcrumbs
1 tablespoon sesame seeds
2 teaspoons lemon juice

1 Put the rice in a large saucepan and add enough water to cover the rice by 2 cm (³/4 inch). Bring to the boil over medium heat, then reduce the heat to low, cover and cook for 20 minutes, or until all the water has been absorbed and tunnels appear on the surface of the rice. Set aside to cool.

2 Preheat the oven to moderate 180°C (350°F/Gas 4). Grease a 20 x 30 cm (8 x 12 inch) tin with melted butter. Cover the sheets of pastry with a damp tea towel. Put the salmon in a large bowl with the shallots, capers, rice, yoghurt and egg. Add the lemon rind, 1 tablespoon of the dill and season with salt and freshly ground black pepper.

3 Layer four sheets of pastry in the base of the tin, brushing each one with melted butter and leaving the sides of the pastry overlapping the side of the tin. Spoon the salmon mixture on top and pat down well. Fold in the excess pastry. Top with four more sheets of filo, brushing each one with melted butter and sprinkling all but the top layer with a tablespoon of

breadcrumbs. Sprinkle the top layer with sesame seeds.

4 Score the top of the pie into diamonds without cutting right through. Bake for 25–30 minutes on the lowest shelf until golden brown. Reheat the remaining butter, add the lemon juice and remaining dill and pour some over each portion of pie.

COOK'S FILE

Note: Some wastage occurs cutting into diamonds so you may want to cut into triangles which will resolve this problem.

Combine the salmon, shallots, capers, rice, yoghurt, egg, lemon rind and dill.

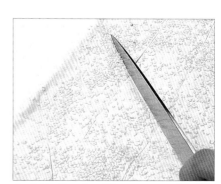

Sprinkle the pie with sesame seeds, then score the top into diamonds.

CREAMY MUSHROOM PIE

Preparation time: 45 minutes
  + 15 minutes soaking
  + 20 minutes refrigeration
  + cooling
Cooking time: 1 hour 5 minutes
Serves 4–6

Pastry
2 cups (250 g/8 oz) plain flour
¹/2 cup (75 g/2¹/2 oz) fine polenta
**125 g (4 oz) butter, chilled
    and cubed**
¹/4 cup (60 ml/2 fl oz) cream
2–3 tablespoons iced water

**10 g (¹/4 oz) dried porcini
    mushrooms**
150 g (5 oz) oyster mushrooms
1 large leek
150 g (5 oz) butter
2 large cloves garlic, crushed
**200 g (6¹/2 oz) shiitake
    mushrooms, thickly sliced**
**200 g (6¹/2 oz) Swiss brown
    mushrooms, thickly sliced**
**350 g (11 oz) field mushrooms,
    sliced**
**100 g (3¹/2 oz) enoki
    mushrooms**
2 tablespoons plain flour
**¹/2 cup (125 ml/4 fl oz) dry
    white wine**
**¹/2 cup (125 ml/4 fl oz)
    vegetable or chicken stock**
**¹/4 cup (60 ml/2 fl oz) thick
    cream**
**2 tablespoons chopped fresh
    thyme**
1 egg, lightly beaten

1 To make the pastry, sift the flour into a large bowl, then stir in the polenta and ¹/2 teaspoon of salt. Add the butter and rub into the dry ingredients with your fingertips until the mixture resembles fine breadcrumbs. Make a well in the centre, pour in the cream and mix with a flat-bladed knife, using a cutting action, until the mixture comes together in beads. Add a little water if the mixture is too dry.

2 Gently gather the dough together and lift out onto a lightly floured work surface. Press together into a ball and then flatten slightly into a disc. Wrap in plastic wrap and refrigerate for 20 minutes.

3 Soak the porcini mushrooms in ¹/4 cup (60 ml/2 fl oz) boiling water for about 15 minutes. Cut any large oyster mushrooms into halves. Thoroughly wash the leek and thinly slice it.

4 Preheat the oven to hot 210°C (415°F/Gas 6–7). Heat a baking tray in the oven. Lightly grease a 23 cm (9 inch) top, 18 cm (7 inch) base, 3 cm (1¹/4 inch) deep pie dish.

5 Drain the porcini mushrooms, reserving the soaking liquid, then coarsely chop them. Heat the butter in a large, deep frying pan over medium heat and cook the leek and garlic for 7–8 minutes, or until the leek is soft and golden. Add all the mushrooms to the pan and cook, stirring, for 5–6 minutes, or until the mushrooms are soft.

6 Add the flour to the pan and stir for 1 minute. Pour in the wine and reserved mushroom soaking liquid and bring to the boil for 1 minute, then pour in the stock and cook for 4–5 minutes, or until the liquid has reduced. Stir in the cream and cook for 1–2 minutes, or until thickened. Stir in the thyme and season. Cool.

7 Divide the pastry into two portions. Roll out one portion between two sheets of baking paper to 2.5 mm (¹/8 inch) thick to line the base and side of the pie dish. Line the pie dish, then spoon in the cooled mushroom filling. Lightly brush the edges of the pastry with egg.

8 Roll out the remaining pastry between the baking paper until about 2 mm (¹/8 inch) thick and cover the pie. Pinch the edges together and pierce the top three times with a fork. Trim the edges. Roll the trimmings and cut into mushroom shapes. Arrange over the pie and lightly brush the top with more egg. Place on the hot tray and bake for 35–40 minutes, or until the pastry is golden brown. Set aside for 5 minutes before slicing.

Mix in the cream, using a cutting action, until the mixture comes together in beads.

Add all of the mushrooms to the pan and cook them until they are soft.

Spoon the cooled mushroom filling into the pastry-lined dish.

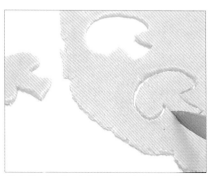

Cut the pastry trimmings into mushroom shapes to decorate the pie.

COCKTAIL LEEK PIES

Preparation time: 20 minutes + cooling
Cooking time: 35 minutes
Makes 32

60 g (2 oz) butter
2 tablespoons olive oil
1 onion, finely chopped
3 leeks, finely sliced
1 clove garlic, chopped
1 tablespoon plain flour
2 tablespoons sour cream
1 cup (100 g/3¹/2 oz) grated
    Parmesan cheese
1 teaspoon chopped fresh thyme
4 sheets frozen puff pastry,
    thawed
1 egg, lightly beaten

1 Heat the butter and oil in a large frying pan over medium heat. Add the onion and cook, stirring occasionally, for 2 minutes. Add the leek and garlic and cook for 5 minutes, or until the leek is softened and lightly coloured. Add the flour and stir into the mixture for 1 minute. Add the sour cream and stir until slightly thickened. Transfer to a bowl and add the Parmesan and thyme. Season with salt and freshly ground black pepper and allow to cool.
2 Preheat the oven to moderately hot 200°C (400°F/Gas 6). Place a lightly greased baking tray in the oven to heat. Using a 6 cm (2¹/2 inch) cutter, cut the pastry into 64 circles. Place 2 heaped teaspoons of filling on half the pastry circles, leaving a small border. Lightly brush the edges with

egg, then place a pastry circle on top of each. Seal the edges well with a fork. Lightly brush the tops with egg. Place the pies on the heated tray and bake for 25 minutes, or until the pies are puffed and golden.

Stir the sour cream through the leek mixture until slightly thickened.

Place 2 heaped teaspoons of filling on half of the pastry circles.

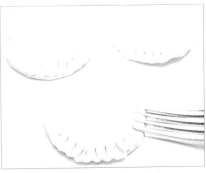

Place the remaining pastry circles on top of the filling and seal the edges well.

VEAL PIE WITH JERUSALEM ARTICHOKE AND POTATO TOPPING

Preparation time: 30 minutes
 + 10 minutes standing
Cooking time: 1 hour 15 minutes
Serves 4–6

1 tablespoon olive oil
500 g (1 lb) lean veal mince
2 onions, finely chopped
3 cloves garlic, crushed
150 g (5 oz) bacon, diced
1/2 teaspoon dried rosemary
2 tablespoons plain flour
pinch of cayenne pepper
1/2 cup (125 ml/4 fl oz) dry
    white wine
150 ml (5 fl oz) cream
1 egg, lightly beaten
2 hard-boiled eggs,
    roughly chopped

Topping
500 g (1 lb) Jerusalem
    artichokes, peeled
400 g potatoes, cut into large
    cubes
100 g (31/2 oz) butter,
    chopped

1 To make the filling, heat the oil in a large frying pan over medium heat and add the mince, onion, garlic, bacon and rosemary. Cook, stirring often, for 10 minutes, or until the veal changes colour. Stir in the flour and cayenne pepper and cook for 1 minute. Pour in the wine and 1/2 cup (125 ml/4 fl oz) water. Season well. Simmer for 5 minutes, or until the sauce is very thick, then stir in the cream, beaten egg and chopped egg.

2 Preheat the oven to hot 210°C (415°F/Gas 6–7). Lightly grease a 21 cm (81/2 inch) springform tin. To make the topping, boil the artichokes and potato together for 12–15 minutes, or until tender. Drain, return to the

pan, add the butter, then mash until smooth. Season, to taste.

3 Spoon the filling into the tin and level the surface. Spread the topping over the veal. Bake for 15 minutes, then reduce the heat to moderate 180°C (350°F/Gas 4) and bake for another 30 minutes, or until the topping is set and golden. Rest in the tin for 10 minutes before serving.

When the sauce has thickened, stir in the cream, beaten egg and chopped egg.

Mash the potato and artichoke mixture until smooth.

POTATO AND CHEESE PIE

Preparation time: 40 minutes
 + 20 minutes cooling
Cooking time: 1 hour 35 minutes
Serves 6–8

1 cup (250 ml/8 fl oz) cream
1 bay leaf
1 kg waxy potatoes (e.g.
    desiree), thinly sliced
1 teaspoon chopped fresh chives
1 teaspoon chopped fresh thyme
500 g (1 lb) home-made or
    bought puff pastry
1 clove garlic, finely chopped
1 cup (125 g/4 oz) grated
    Cheddar cheese
1 egg, lightly beaten

1 Grease a 23 cm (9 inch) top, 18 cm (7 inch) base, 3 cm (1¼ inch) metal pie dish. Pour the cream into a large saucepan. Add the bay leaf, ¼ teaspoon salt and some freshly ground black pepper. Bring the cream to the boil very slowly over low heat and when it comes to the boil, remove it from the heat.

2 Add the potato slices to the cream mixture and stir well so that they are covered in the cream. Return the saucepan to high heat until the cream comes back to the boil. Reduce the heat and simmer for 10 minutes,

stirring occasionally. Remove the bay leaf. Fold in the herbs and set aside to cool for at least 20 minutes.

3 Preheat the oven to moderately hot 200°C (400°F/Gas 6). Divide the pastry into two portions. Roll out one portion between two sheets of baking paper until it is a circle large enough to fit the base and side of the dish. Line the pie dish with the pastry. Lay half the potato slices in the pie, sprinkle with the chopped garlic and half the cheese and season. Add the remaining potato slices and season again. Top with the remaining cheese.

4 Roll out the remaining portion of dough between two pieces of baking paper to a circle large enough to cover the top of the pie tin. Brush the rim of the bottom piece of pastry with the beaten egg and cover with the pastry. Trim the edges. Make a small hole in

the centre of the pastry. Re-roll the pastry scraps and cut into shapes with which to decorate the pie. Brush the pie with beaten egg and bake for 10 minutes.

5 Reduce the oven to moderate 180°C (350°F/Gas 4) and bake for about 1 hour 5 minutes. Cover the pie with foil halfway through baking if the pastry begins to brown. Insert a skewer through the hole in the pie to test if the potatoes are tender.

Gently fold the fresh herbs into the creamy potato slices.

Sprinkle the remaining grated Cheddar over the potato slices.

MEDITERRANEAN PIE

Preparation time: 25 minutes
  + 20 minutes refrigeration
Cooking time: 35 minutes
Serves 4

Pastry
**3 cups (375 g/12 oz) plain
  flour**
1 egg, lightly beaten
**1/2 cup (125 ml/4 fl oz)
  buttermilk**
100 ml (31/2 fl oz) olive oil

2 tablespoons olive oil
**100 g (31/2 oz) button
  mushrooms, sliced**
**400 g (13 oz) can whole peeled
  tomatoes, drained and
  roughly chopped**
100 g (31/2 oz) sliced salami
**170 g (51/2 oz) jar artichokes,
  drained**
**4 tablespoons fresh basil leaves,
  torn**
**2/3 cup (100 g/31/2 oz) grated
  mozzarella cheese**
**1/4 cup (25 g/3/4 oz) grated
  Parmesan cheese**
milk, to brush

1 Preheat the oven to hot 210°C (415°F/Gas 6–7). Grease a large baking tray and place in the oven to heat up. Sift the flour into a large bowl and add the egg and buttermilk. Add the oil and mix with a large metal spoon until the mixture comes together and forms a soft dough. You may need to add a little water if the mixture is too dry. Turn onto a lightly floured surface and gather together into a smooth ball. Cover with plastic wrap and refrigerate for 20 minutes.

2 Heat the oil in a large frying pan, add the button mushrooms and cook over medium heat for 5 minutes, or until they have softened and browned a little.

3 Divide the pastry in half and roll each portion, between two sheets of baking paper, into a 30 cm (12 inch) round. Layer the chopped tomato, salami, mushrooms, artichokes, basil leaves, mozzarella and Parmesan on one of the pastry rounds, leaving a 2 cm (3/4 inch) border. Season with salt and freshly ground black pepper.

4 Brush the border with milk. Top with the remaining pastry circle to enclose the filling, then pinch and seal the edges together. Make three slits in the top. Brush the top with milk. Place on the preheated tray and bake for 30 minutes, or until golden.

Gently gather the dough together into a smooth ball.

Brush the border of the pastry round with a little milk.

149

ROSEMARY LAMB COBBLER

Preparation time: 30 minutes
Cooking time: 2 hours
Serves 4–6

600 g (1¼ lb) boned lamb leg,
    cut into 2 cm (¾ inch) chunks
¼ cup (30 g/1 oz) plain flour,
    well seasoned with salt and
    black pepper
20 g (¾ oz) butter
2 tablespoons olive oil
8 spring onions, chopped
3 cloves garlic, crushed
2 cups (500 ml/16 fl oz)
    beef stock
1 cup (250 ml/8 fl oz) dry white
    wine
2 teaspoons wholegrain mustard
2 teaspoons finely chopped
    fresh rosemary
2 celery sticks, sliced
1 teaspoon grated lemon rind
1 teaspoon lemon juice
½ cup (125 g/4 oz) sour cream

Cobbler topping
¾ cup (185 ml/6 fl oz) milk
1 egg
40 g (1¼ oz) butter, melted
1½ cups (185 g/6 oz) plain flour
2 teaspoons baking powder
1 teaspoon finely chopped
    fresh rosemary
2 tablespoons finely chopped
    fresh flat-leaf parsley

1 Put the lamb pieces and flour in a plastic bag and shake well to evenly coat the lamb. Shake off any excess.
2 Heat the butter and 1 tablespoon of the olive oil in a large saucepan over high heat, then cook half the lamb for 5 minutes, or until well browned. Remove from the pan. Add the remaining oil if needed and cook the remaining lamb.
3 Add half the spring onion to the pan with the garlic and cook for 30 seconds, or until the spring onion is softened. Return the lamb to the pan with the stock, wine, mustard, rosemary, celery, lemon rind and juice and bring to the boil. Reduce the heat and simmer, stirring occasionally, for 1¼ hours, or until the lamb is tender and the sauce has thickened.
4 Remove from the heat and stir a little of the sauce into the sour cream, then stir it all back into the lamb mixture with the remaining spring onion. Leave to cool while you make the topping.
5 Preheat the oven to 190°C (375°F/ Gas 5). To make the topping, combine the milk, egg and melted butter in a large bowl. Add the combined sifted flour and baking powder with the herbs, 1 teaspoon salt and freshly ground black pepper and stir until you have a thick, sticky batter—you may need to add a little more flour if it is too wet, or milk if it is too dry.
6 Spoon the lamb into a deep 23 cm (9 inch) top, 18 cm (7 inch) base, 3.5 cm (1½ inch) deep pie dish and, using two spoons, cover the top with small dollops of the batter, leaving a little gap between each dollop because the cobbler mix will spread. Cook for 30 minutes, or until the topping is risen and golden.

Put the lamb and flour in a plastic bag and shake until the meat is lightly covered.

Cook the lamb in a large saucepan until it is nicely browned.

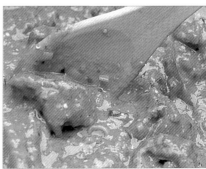

Simmer the mixture until the meat is tender and the sauce has thickened.

Stir a little of the meaty sauce into the sour cream.

Stir the batter thoroughly until it is thick and sticky.

Add spoonfuls of the batter to the top of the pie, leaving a small gap between each

BEEF AND CARAMELISED ONION PIE

Preparation time: 40 minutes
  + 20 minutes cooling
Cooking time: 2 hours 20 minutes
Serves 6–8

1/3 cup (80 ml/2¾ fl oz) oil
2 large red onions, thinly sliced
1 teaspoon dark brown sugar
1 kg (2 lb) lean rump steak, cut
    into 2 cm (¾ inch) cubes
¼ cup (30 g/1 oz) plain flour,
    seasoned
2 cloves garlic, crushed
225 g (7 oz) button mushrooms,
    sliced
1 cup (250 ml/8 fl oz) beef stock
150 ml (5 fl oz) stout
1 tablespoon Worcestershire
    sauce
1 tablespoon tomato paste
1 tablespoon chopped fresh
    thyme
350 g (11 oz) potatoes, cut into
    1.5 cm (5/8 inch) pieces
2 carrots, cut into 1.5 cm
    (5/8 inch) pieces
600 g (1¼ lb) quick flaky pastry
1 egg, lightly beaten

1 Heat 2 tablespoons of the oil in a frying pan over medium heat and cook the onion for 5 minutes, or until light brown, then add the sugar and cook for 7–8 minutes, or until the onion caramelises. Remove from the pan. Wipe the pan clean.
2 Toss the beef in flour and shake off the excess. Heat the remaining oil in the same pan and cook the meat in batches over high heat until browned. Return all the meat to the pan, add the garlic and mushrooms and cook for 2 minutes. Add the stock, stout, Worcestershire sauce, tomato paste and thyme. Bring to the boil, then reduce the heat and simmer, covered, for 1 hour. Add the potato and carrot and simmer for 30 minutes. Remove from the heat and set aside to cool.
3 Preheat the oven to 190°C (375°F/ Gas 5). Grease a 5 cup (1.25 litre) pie dish. Pour in the filling, then top with the onion. Roll the pastry out between two sheets of baking paper until it is 3 cm (1¾ inch) wider than the pie dish. Cut a 2 cm (¾ inch) strip around the edge of the pastry circle, brush with water and place damp-side-down on the rim of the dish. Cover with the remaining pastry, pressing down on the edges to join the two pastries. Knock up the edges by using the back of a knife to make small slashes in the edges of the pastry. Re-roll any pastry scraps and use them to decorate the pie. Brush with egg and bake for 25 minutes, or until golden.

Spoon the caramelised onion over the filling in the pie dish.

Place the strip of pastry damp-side-down on the rim of the dish.

HAM, CHEESE AND POTATO PIE

Preparation time: 25 minutes
 + cooling + 10 minutes standing
Cooking time: 1 hour 45 minutes
Serves 6–8

1/4 cup (60 ml/2 fl oz) olive oil
3 onions, finely chopped
1 clove garlic, finely chopped
300 g (10 oz) ham, chopped
430 g (14 oz) desiree potatoes,
    diced
2 cups (250 g/8 oz) grated
    Cheddar cheese
2 eggs
1/3 cup (80 ml/2 3/4 fl oz) cream
2 teaspoons chopped fresh
    chives
4 sheets ready-rolled frozen
    puff pastry, thawed
1 egg, lightly beaten

1 Heat the oil in a frying pan over medium heat. Add the onion and garlic and cook, stirring, for 5 minutes, or until the onion softens. Add the ham and potato and cook, stirring occasionally, for 5–7 minutes, or until the potatoes soften slightly. Transfer to a bowl and stir in the cheese.

2 Mix together the eggs and cream and pour into the bowl. Add the chives and mix thoroughly. Season well with salt and freshly ground black pepper. Allow to cool.

3 Preheat the oven to moderately hot 200°C (400°F/Gas 6). Grease a 23 cm (9 inch) top, 18 cm (7 inch) base, 3 cm (1 1/4 inch) deep pie dish. Line the pie dish with 2 sheets of puff pastry, and brush the edge with beaten egg. Spoon the filling into the pie dish.

4 Cut the remaining sheets of pastry into quarters, and each quarter into three equal lengths. Place the strips, overlapping, around the top of the pie, leaving the centre open. Press down the edges with your fingers so that the top and bottom layers stick

together, then trim the edges of the pastry with a sharp knife.

5 Brush the top of the pie with the beaten egg, and bake in the oven for 30 minutes. Reduce the temperature to moderate 180°C (350°F/Gas 4) and cook the pie for another hour, covering the top with foil if it is browning too much. Leave for 10 minutes before serving.

Pour the creamy egg mixture into the bowl with the ham and cheese.

Overlap the pastry strips around the pie, leaving a gap in the middle.

CHEESE AND ONION PIE

Preparation time: 25 minutes
  + 10 minutes cooling
Cooking time: 45 minutes
Serves 4

2 tablespoons olive oil
2 onions, chopped
1¹/2 cups (185 g/6 oz) grated
    Cheddar
1 tablespoon chopped fresh flat-
    leaf parsley
1 teaspoon English mustard
2 teaspoons Worcestershire
    sauce
2 eggs, beaten
2 sheets frozen ready-rolled
    puff pastry, thawed

1 Preheat the oven to moderately hot 190°C (375°F/Gas 5). Heat the oil in a large frying pan over medium heat, add the onion and cook for 5–7 minutes, or until soft and golden. Transfer to a bowl and allow to cool for 10 minutes.
2 Add the cheese, parsley, mustard and Worcestershire sauce to the onion and mix well. Add half the egg to the bowl and season well with salt and freshly ground black pepper.
3 Cut each sheet of pastry into a 23 cm (9 inch) circle. Lay one sheet of pastry on a lined baking tray. Spread the filling over the pastry base, piling it higher in the middle and leaving a 2 cm (³/4 inch) border. Lightly brush the border with some of the beaten egg and place the second sheet on top,

stretching it slightly to neatly fit the bottom. Press and seal the edges well and brush the top with the remaining beaten egg. Cut two slits in the top for steam to escape.
4 Bake for 10 minutes, then reduce the heat to moderate 180°C (350°F/Gas 4). Cook for another 20–25 minutes, or until the pastry is crisp and golden.

Mix the cheese, parsley, mustard and Worcestershire sauce through the onion.

Brush the border of the pastry with some of the beaten egg.

Lift the second pastry circle over the cheese and onion filling.

WELSH LAMB PIE

Preparation time: 20 minutes
+ cooling
Cooking time: 2 hours 35 minutes
Serves 6

750 g (1½ lb) boned lamb
   shoulder, cubed
¾ cup (90 g/3 oz) plain flour,
   seasoned
2 tablespoons olive oil
200 g (6½ oz) bacon rashers,
   finely chopped
2 cloves garlic, chopped
4 large leeks, sliced
1 large carrot, chopped
2 large potatoes, cut into 1 cm
   (½ inch) cubes
1¼ cups (315 ml/10 oz) beef
   stock
1 bay leaf
2 teaspoons chopped fresh
   flat-leaf parsley
375 g (12 oz) quick flaky pastry
1 egg, lightly beaten

1 Toss the meat in the seasoned flour and shake off the excess. Heat the oil in a large frying pan over medium heat. Cook the meat in batches for 4–5 minutes, or until well browned, then remove from the pan. Add the bacon to the pan and cook for 3 minutes. Add the garlic and leek and cook for about 5 minutes, until the leek is soft.

2 Put the meat in a large saucepan, add the leek and bacon, carrot, potato, stock and bay leaf and bring to the boil, then reduce the heat, cover and simmer for 30 minutes. Uncover and simmer for 1 hour, or until the meat is cooked and the liquid has thickened. Season to taste. Remove the bay leaf, stir in the parsley and set aside to cool.

3 Preheat the oven to moderately hot 200°C (400°F/Gas 6). Place the filling into a 23 cm (9 inch) top, 18 cm (7 inch) base, 3 cm (1¼ inch) deep pie dish. Roll out the pastry between two sheets of baking paper until large enough to cover the pie. Remove the top sheet of paper and invert over the filling.

4 Trim the edges and pinch to seal. Re-roll the scraps and cut out shapes to decorate the pie. Cut two slits in the top for steam to escape. Brush with egg and bake for 45 minutes, or until the pastry is crisp and golden.

Season the meat mixture and remove the bay leaf.

Cut out shapes from the pastry scraps to decorate the pie.

CHINESE BARBECUED PORK PIES

Preparation time: 35 minutes
 + 1 hour refrigeration
Cooking time: 45 minutes
Makes 4

2 tablespoons cornflour
1/4 cup (60 ml/2 fl oz) oyster
  sauce
1/4 cup (60 ml/2 fl oz) rice wine
2 tablespoons kecap manis
2 tablespoons lime juice
1 tablespoon grated fresh ginger
1/2 teaspoon ground white pepper
400 g (13 oz) Chinese barbecued
  pork, diced
150 g (5 oz) snowpeas, sliced
2 cups (100 g/3 1/2 oz) thinly
  sliced Chinese cabbage
375 g (12 oz) home-made or
  bought shortcrust pastry
375 g (12 oz) home-made or
  bought puff pastry
milk, for brushing
1 teaspoon sesame seeds

1 Preheat the oven to moderate 180°C (350°F/Gas 4). Grease four 11 cm (4 1/2 inch) top, 9 cm (3 1/2 inch) base and 3 cm (1 1/4 inch) deep metal pie dishes. Mix the cornflour with 2 tablespoons water. Heat a large frying pan over low heat and add the oyster sauce, rice wine, kecap manis, lime juice, ginger, white pepper and the cornflour mixture. Simmer for 2 minutes, or until very thick. Add the pork, snowpeas and cabbage. Cook, stirring, for 5 minutes. Cool, then refrigerate for 1 hour, or until cold.

2 Meanwhile, roll out the shortcrust pastry between two sheets of baking paper until it is 3 mm (1/8 inch) thick. Using a saucer as a guide, cut out four

16 cm (6 1/2 inch) rounds. Line the pie dishes with the pastry, then refrigerate.

3 When the filling is cold, fill the pastry shells. Roll out the puff pastry between the baking paper to 3 mm (1/8 inch) thick and cut out four rounds large enough to cover the tops of the pie dishes. Cover the pies with the puff pastry rounds and trim any excess. Use a fork to seal the edges and prick a few holes in the top. Brush the lids

with milk, sprinkle with sesame seeds, and bake for 35 minutes, or until lightly golden.

Add the pork, snow peas and cabbage and cook, stirring, for 5 minutes.

Cut four rounds of shortcrust pastry and use them to line the pie dishes.

Cut rounds from the puff pastry and cover the tops of the pies.

COTTAGE PIE

Preparation time: 30 minutes
Cooking time: 1 hour 30 minutes
Serves 6–8

2 tablespoons olive oil
2 onions, chopped
2 carrots, diced
1 celery stick, diced
1 kg (2 lb) beef mince
2 tablespoons plain flour
1¹/2 cups (375 ml/12 fl oz) beef
   stock
1 tablespoon soy sauce
1 tablespoon Worcestershire
   sauce
2 tablespoons tomato sauce
1 tablespoon tomato paste
2 bay leaves
2 teaspoons chopped fresh
   flat-leaf parsley

Topping
800 g (1 lb 10 oz) potatoes, cut
   into 2 cm (3/4 inch) cubes
400 g (13 oz) parsnips, cut into
   2 cm (3/4 inch) cubes
30 g (1 oz) butter
¹/2 cup (125 ml/4 fl oz) milk

1 Heat the oil in a large frying pan over medium heat and cook the onion, carrot and celery, stirring occasionally, for 5 minutes, or until the onion has softened and is lightly coloured. Add the mince and cook for 7 minutes, then stir in the flour and cook for 2 minutes. Add the stock, soy sauce, Worcestershire sauce, tomato sauce, tomato paste, and the bay leaves and simmer over low heat for 30 minutes, stirring occasionally. Remove from the heat and leave to cool while you make the topping. Remove the bay leaves and stir in the parsley.

2 To make the topping, place the potato and parsnip in a large saucepan with ¹/2 teaspoon salt, cover with water, bring to the boil and cook over medium heat for 15–20 minutes, or until softened and cooked through. Drain, return to the pan and add the butter. Mash with a potato masher or push through a coarse sieve. Fold in enough of the milk to make a firm mash.

3 Preheat the oven to moderate 180°C (350°F/Gas 4) and lightly grease a 2.5 litre (10 cup) ovenproof dish. Spoon the filling into the dish and spread the topping over it. Fluff it up with a fork. Bake for 25 minutes, or until the topping is lightly golden.

Mash the potato and parsnip together with a potato masher.

Spoon the cooled meat filling into the ovenproof dish.

MINI OYSTER PIES

Preparation time: 30 minutes
 + 20 minutes cooling
Cooking time: 45 minutes
Makes 30

2 cups (500 ml/16 fl oz) fish
  stock
1 tablespoon olive oil
2 leeks, chopped
30 g (1 oz) butter
1 tablespoon plain flour
1 teaspoon lemon juice
1 teaspoon chopped fresh chives
8 sheets frozen puff pastry,
  thawed
30 fresh oysters
1 egg, lightly beaten

1 Pour the stock into a saucepan and simmer over medium heat for 15 minutes, or until reduced by half — you will need 1 cup (250 ml/8 fl oz).
2 Heat the oil in a saucepan over medium heat. Add the leek and cook, stirring well, for 5 minutes, or until soft and lightly coloured. Transfer to a small bowl to cool slightly.
3 Melt the butter in a small saucepan

over low heat. Add the flour and cook, stirring well, for 2 minutes, or until the flour is golden. Remove from the heat and gradually add the fish stock, stirring well. Return to the heat and bring to the boil, stirring constantly for 2 minutes, or until the mixture has thickened. Add the lemon juice, chives and leek and season well with salt and freshly ground black pepper. Set aside to cool for 20 minutes. Preheat the oven to moderately hot 200°C (400°F/ Gas 6) and grease two baking trays.
4 Using a 6 cm (2½ inch) round cutter, cut out thirty circles of pastry and put 1 oyster and a heaped teaspoon of the filling on top of each, leaving a 5 mm

(¼ inch) border. Lightly brush the edges with beaten egg.
5 Cut thirty 8 cm (3 inch) circles from the remaining sheets of pastry. Cover the filling with these rounds and press the edges with a fork to seal. Brush the tops with the remaining beaten egg, place on the baking trays and bake for 15–20 minutes, or until golden and well puffed.

Gradually add the fish stock and boil, stirring constantly, until thickened.

Place an oyster and a heaped teaspoon of filling on each pastry round.

CHICKEN, POTATO AND PRESERVED LEMON PIE

Preparation time: 40 minutes
 + 20 minutes refrigeration + cooling
Cooking time: 1 hour 15 minutes
Serves 4–6

2 tablespoons olive oil
2 leeks, thinly sliced
3/4 preserved lemon, pulp
     removed, rind washed
     and cut into thin strips
1 kg (2 lb) chicken thigh fillets,
     cut into bite-size pieces
2 tablespoons plain flour
1 cup (250 ml/8 fl oz) chicken
     stock
250 g (8 oz) kipfler potatoes,
     thinly sliced
2 tablespoons chopped fresh
     flat-leaf parsley
1 egg, lightly beaten

Pastry
100 g (3¹/2 oz) self-raising
     flour
150 g (5 oz) plain flour
60 g (2 oz) butter, chilled
     and cubed
60 g (2 oz) lard, chilled
     and cubed
3–4 tablespoons iced water
1 egg, lightly beaten

1 Heat the oil in a large frying pan, add the leek and cook over medium heat for 2–3 minutes, or until golden. Add the preserved lemon and cook for 3 minutes, or until the lemon is fragrant. Remove from the pan.
2 Add a little extra oil to the pan if needed, add the chicken in batches and cook, stirring, for 5 minutes, or until browned. Return all the chicken to the pan along with the leek and lemon. Sprinkle with flour and cook, stirring, for 2 minutes, or until the flour is mixed through.
3 Gradually stir in the chicken stock, then add the potato. Bring to the boil, then reduce the heat and simmer for 7 minutes, or until thickened slightly. Stir in the parsley. Transfer to a bowl and allow to cool completely.
4 To make the pastry, sift the flours and a pinch of salt into a large bowl and rub in the chopped butter and lard with your fingertips until the mixture resembles fine breadcrumbs. Make a well, add almost all the water and mix with a flat-bladed knife, using a cutting action, until the mixture comes together in beads, adding more water if necessary.
5 Turn out the dough onto a lightly floured surface, gather into a ball, cover in plastic wrap and refrigerate for 20 minutes. Preheat the oven to moderately hot 200°C (400°F/Gas 6). Heat a baking tray in the oven.

6 Spoon the filling into a 26 cm (10¹/2 inch) top, 16 cm (6¹/2 inch) base, 4 cm (1¹/2 inch) deep pie plate. Roll out the dough between two sheets of baking paper until large enough to cover the pie. Remove the top sheet and invert the pastry onto the pie, allowing any excess to hang over the sides. Use a small sharp knife to trim any excess pastry, then press to seal on the rim. Cut a few steam holes in the top and decorate the pie with any remaining pastry. Brush with the egg, place on the hot tray and bake for 35–40 minutes, or until the crust is crisp and golden.

When the chicken mixture has thickened slightly, stir in the parsley.

159

CHILLI CON CARNE PIE

Preparation time: 25 minutes
  + 20 minutes refrigeration
Cooking time: 2 hours 15 minutes
Serves 6–8

Pastry
1½ cups (185 g/6 oz) plain flour
100 g (3½ oz) butter, chilled
    and cubed
¾ cup (90 g/3 oz) grated
    Cheddar
1–2 tablespoons iced water

2 tablespoons olive oil
1 onion, chopped
2 cloves garlic, chopped
¼ teaspoon chilli powder
2 teaspoons ground cumin
1 teaspoon ground coriander
¼ teaspoon cayenne pepper
1 teaspoon paprika
1 teaspoon dried oregano
750 g (1½ lb) beef mince
2 tablespoons tomato paste
½ cup (125 ml/4 fl oz) dry red
    wine
425 g (14 oz) can crushed
    tomatoes
1 tablespoon wholegrain
    mustard
290 g (10 oz) can red kidney
    beans, drained and rinsed
2 tablespoons chopped fresh
    flat-leaf parsley
1 tablespoon chopped fresh
    oregano
⅔ cup (160 g/5½ oz) sour cream

1 Sift the flour into a bowl and rub in the butter with your fingertips until the mixture resembles fine breadcrumbs. Stir in the cheese. Make a well and add almost all the water. Mix with a flat-bladed knife, using a cutting action, until the dough comes together, adding more water if necessary.

2 Gather the dough together and lift out onto a lightly floured surface. Press it into a ball and flatten slightly into a disc. Cover in plastic wrap and refrigerate for at least 20 minutes.

3 Heat the oil in a large saucepan over medium heat and cook the onion for 5 minutes, or until softened. Add the garlic, spices and dried oregano and cook for 2 minutes. Add the mince and cook over high heat for 5 minutes, or until brown. Stir in the tomato paste

and cook for 1 minute. Pour in the wine and simmer for 3 minutes. Add the tomato and mustard, bring to the boil, then reduce the heat and simmer for 30 minutes.

4 Add the kidney beans to the beef and cook for 30 minutes, or until any excess moisture has evaporated. Stir in the fresh herbs. Season, to taste.

5 Preheat the oven to moderately hot 200°C (400°F/Gas 6). Lightly grease a 23 cm (9 inch) top, 18 cm (7 inch) base, 3 cm (1½ inch) deep pie dish, then fill with beef mixture. Roll out the pastry

to fit the top of the dish, then place over the top and trim and crimp the edges. Make two or three steam vents, bake for 10 minutes, then reduce the oven to moderate 180°C (350°F/Gas 4) and cook for 40–45 minutes, or until the top is golden. Cover the top with foil if it is browning too much. Serve with sour cream.

Simmer the mixture until the excess liquid has evaporated.

Use a rolling pin to help you roll the pastry over the filling.

CHICKEN AND CORN PIES

Preparation time: 25 minutes
  + 2 hours refrigeration
Cooking time: 50 minutes
Makes 6

1 tablespoon olive oil
650 g (1 lb 5 oz) chicken thigh
   fillets, trimmed and cut into
   1 cm (1/2 inch) pieces
1 tablespoon grated fresh ginger
400 g (13 oz) oyster mushrooms,
   halved
3 corn cobs, kernels removed
1/2 cup (125 ml/4 fl oz) chicken
   stock
2 tablespoons kecap manis
2 tablespoons cornflour
90 g (3 oz) fresh coriander
   leaves, chopped
6 sheets ready-rolled shortcrust
   pastry
milk, to glaze

1 Grease six 12.5 cm (5¼ inch) top,
9.5 cm (3¾ inch) base, 3 cm (1¼ inch)
deep metal pie tins. Heat the oil in a
large frying pan over high heat and
add the chicken. Cook for 5 minutes,
or until golden. Add the ginger,
mushrooms and corn and cook for
5–6 minutes, or until the chicken is
just cooked through. Add the stock
and kecap manis. Mix the cornflour
with 2 tablespoons water in a small
bowl or jug, then stir into the pan. Boil
for 2 minutes before adding the
coriander. Transfer to a bowl, cool a
little then refrigerate for 2 hours, or
until cold.
2 Preheat the oven to moderate 180°C
(350°F/Gas 4). Using a saucer to guide
you, cut a 15 cm (6 inch) round from
each sheet of shortcrust pastry and

line the six pie tins. Fill the shells with
the cooled filling, then cut out another
six rounds large enough to make the
lids. Top the pies with the lids, cut
away any extra pastry and seal the
edges with a fork. Decorate the pies
with shapes cut from pastry scraps.
Prick a few holes in the top of each
pie, brush with a little milk and bake
for 35 minutes, or until golden.

*Boil the chicken and corn mixture for
2 minutes.*

*Cut out six rounds of pastry to fit the
tops of the tins, then cover the filling.*

161

TOURTIERE

Preparation time: 40 minutes
  + 20 minutes refrigeration
  + cooling
Cooking time: 1 hour
Serves 6

Pastry
2¼ cups (280 g/9 oz) plain flour
½ teaspoon baking powder
120 g (4 oz) butter, chilled and
  cubed
½ teaspoon finely chopped
  fresh thyme
1 teaspoon lemon juice
1 egg, lightly beaten
1–2 tablespoons iced water

1 small carrot
1 baby fennel bulb, thick outer
  leaves removed
4 French shallots
20 g (¾ oz) butter
200 g (6½ oz) bacon, chopped
3 cloves garlic, crushed
500 g (1 lb) pork mince
1 teaspoon finely chopped fresh
  thyme
1 teaspoon finely chopped fresh
  sage
¼ teaspoon ground nutmeg
¾ cup (185 ml) chicken stock
250 g (8 oz) potatoes, cut into
  2 cm (¾ inch) cubes
1 egg, lightly beaten

1 To make the pastry, sift the flour, baking powder and ¼ teaspoon salt into a large bowl and rub in the chilled butter with your fingertips until the mixture resembles fine breadcrumbs. Stir in the thyme, then make a well in the centre and add the lemon juice, egg and a little of the water. Mix with a flat-bladed knife, using a cutting action, until the mixture comes together in beads, adding more water if necessary.

2 Gently gather the dough together and lift out onto a lightly floured work surface. Press together into a ball and flatten slightly into a disc, wrap in plastic wrap and refrigerate for at least 20 minutes.

3 Finely chop the carrot, fennel and shallots in a food processor. Heat the butter in a large frying pan over medium heat and add the chopped vegetables, bacon, garlic and mince.

Cook, stirring often, for 10 minutes, or until the pork changes colour, then stir in the thyme, sage and nutmeg. Season well with salt and freshly ground black pepper. Add ¼ cup (60 ml/2 fl oz) of the stock and simmer for 10 minutes, or until it is absorbed. Set aside to cool.

4 Preheat the oven to moderately hot 200°C (400°F/Gas 6) and heat a baking tray. Grease a 23 cm (10 inch) top, 18 cm (7 inch) base, 3 cm (1¼ inch) deep pie dish. Place the remaining stock in a saucepan with the potato and simmer for about 10 minutes, or until tender. Do not drain. Mash coarsely, then stir into the pork mixture.

5 Divide the dough into two portions, one slightly larger than the other. Roll out the larger portion between two sheets of baking paper until large enough to fit the base and side of the prepared dish. Line the dish. Spoon in the filling, levelling the surface. Brush the exposed pastry with beaten egg.

6 Roll out the remaining dough between the sheets of baking paper until large enough to cover the dish. Carefully cover the filling, trim the edges and crimp to seal. Brush the surface with egg and make 6–8 small slits over the surface. Bake on the hot baking tray on the centre shelf of the oven for about 30 minutes, or until golden.

COOK'S FILE

Note: The flavour of a tourtière improves over 24 hours and it is excellent served cold.

Use your fingers to remove the thick outer leaves from the baby fennel.

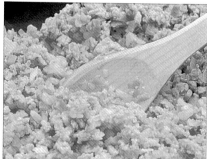

Cook the pork mixture, stirring often, until the pork changes colour.

Mash the potato and stock together, then stir into the pork mixture.

Trim the edges of the pastry and crimp them to seal.

MINI SPINACH PIES

Preparation time: 45 minutes
  + 30 minutes cooling
Cooking time: 35 minutes
Makes 24

1/3 cup (80 ml/2³/4 fl oz) olive oil
2 onions, finely chopped
2 cloves garlic, finely
    chopped
150 g (5 oz) small button
    mushrooms, roughly chopped
200 g (6¹/2 oz) English spinach,
    chopped
¹/2 teaspoon chopped fresh
    thyme
100 g (3¹/2 oz) feta, crumbled
750 g (1¹/2 lb) home-made or
    bought shortcrust pastry
milk, to glaze

1 Heat 2 tablespoons of the oil in a frying pan over medium heat, add the onion and garlic and cook for 5 minutes, or until soft and lightly coloured. Add the mushrooms and cook for another 4 minutes, or until softened. Transfer to a bowl.

2 Heat 1 tablespoon of the oil in the same pan over medium heat, add half the spinach and cook, stirring well, for 2–3 minutes, or until the spinach has softened. Add to the bowl with the onion. Repeat with the remaining oil and spinach. Add the thyme and feta to the bowl and mix. Season with salt and freshly ground black pepper and set aside to cool.

3 Preheat the oven to moderately hot 200°C (400°F/Gas 6) and grease two 12-hole round-based patty tins. Roll out half the pastry between two sheets of baking paper and cut out 24 rounds using a 7.5 cm (3 inch) cutter. Use these to line the patty tins,

then divide the spinach mixture among the holes. Roll out the remaining pastry between the baking paper and cut into 24 x 7 cm (2³/4 inch) rounds to fit the tops of the pies. Cover the pies with the lids and press the edges with a fork to seal. Prick the tops once with a fork, brush with milk

and bake for 15–20 minutes, or until golden. Serve immediately or cool on a wire rack.

Cook the spinach in the oil until the spinach has softened.

Spoon the spinach mixture into the pastry-lined patty tins.

Seal the edges of the pies with a fork, then prick the tops once.

BRAISED LAMB SHANK PIE

Preparation time: 30 minutes
 + 2 hours refrigeration
Cooking time: 3 hours 10 minutes
Serves 6

8 lamb shanks
plain flour seasoned with salt
    and black pepper
2 tablespoons olive oil
4 red onions, quartered
8 cloves garlic, peeled
1 cup (250 ml/8 fl oz)
    full-bodied red wine
4 cups (1 litre) beef stock
2 tablespoons finely chopped
    fresh rosemary
6 whole black peppercorns
1/4 cup (30 g/1 oz) cornflour
375 g (12 oz) home-made or
    bought puff pastry
1 egg, lightly beaten

1 Preheat the oven to hot 220°C (425°F/Gas 7). Lightly dust the shanks in the seasoned flour, shaking off any excess. Heat the oil over medium heat in a large frying pan and cook the shanks for 2 minutes each side, or until well browned. Transfer to a deep roasting tin and add the onion, garlic, wine, stock, rosemary and peppercorns. Cover with foil and bake for 1 hour.

2 Remove the foil, stir the mixture and return to the oven for 1 hour 10 minutes, stirring occasionally, until the meat falls off the bones.

3 Remove the lamb bones from the tin with tongs. Combine the cornflour with 2 tablespoons water, then stir into the tin. Return to the oven for 10 minutes, or until thickened. Transfer to a large bowl, allow to cool, then refrigerate for at least 2 hours, or overnight.

4 Preheat the oven to moderate 180°C (350°F/Gas 4). Grease a warm 23 cm (9 inch) pie plate with a rim, then fill with the meat mixture. Roll the pastry out between two sheets of baking paper until 3 cm (1¼ inch) wider than the plate. Cut a 2 cm (3/4 inch) strip around the edge of the pastry, brush with water and place damp-side-down on the rim. Cover with the pastry circle, pressing down on the edges. Use the back of a knife to make small slashes around the edge. Trim, then re-roll the scraps to decorate. Brush with egg and bake for 45 minutes, or until the pastry is golden and has risen.

Cook the lamb shanks until the meat falls off the bones.

Stir the cornflour mixture into the tin and continue cooking until the sauce thickens.

ITALIAN EASTER PIE

Preparation time: 40 minutes
 + 20 minutes cooling
Cooking time: 1 hour 5 minutes
Serves 6–8

450 g (14 oz) silverbeet, stalks
 removed
1 cup (80 g/2^3/$_4$ oz) fresh white
 breadcrumbs
1 cup (250 ml/8 fl oz) milk
550 g (1 lb 1^1/$_2$ oz) ricotta
 cheese (see Note)
2 cups (200 g/7 oz) coarsely
 grated Parmesan cheese
8 eggs
pinch of ground nutmeg
pinch of cayenne pepper
10 small fresh marjoram
 leaves
150 g (5 oz) butter
20 sheets filo pastry

1 Bring 2 cups (500 ml/16 fl oz) salted water to the boil in a large saucepan. Add the silverbeet, cover and cook for 5 minutes, or until wilted. Drain well.

When cool, wring out all the liquid in a clean tea towel. Chop well.
2 Preheat the oven to moderate 180°C (350°F/Gas 4). In a large bowl, put the breadcrumbs and milk, leave for 5 minutes, then add the ricotta, half the Parmesan, 4 eggs, the nutmeg, cayenne, marjoram and the chopped silverbeet. Season well and mix.
3 Melt the butter, then lightly brush a 23 cm (9 inch) springform tin with it. Line the base and the side with a sheet of filo pastry. Brush with melted butter and place another filo sheet on top, positioned so that any exposed wall of the tin is covered. Continue in this way, using a total of ten sheets of filo. Don't worry about the filo forming folds on the tin walls, just push them flat as you brush with butter.
4 Spoon the filling into the tin. Make four deep indentations in the surface around the edge of the pie, then break an egg into each. Season and sprinkle with the remaining Parmesan. Fold over any overhanging pastry. Cover with the remaining filo, buttering each layer.

5 Bake for 40 minutes, cover with foil, then bake for another 20 minutes. Cool in the tin for 20 minutes. Serve warm or at room temperature.

COOK'S FILE

Note: Use ricotta from a wheel, not pre-packaged ricotta as this tends to be very moist.

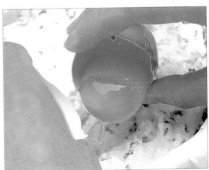

Gently break an egg into each of the four indentations you have made.

CHUNKY VEAL AND CAPSICUM PIE

Preparation time: 40 minutes
+ 10 minutes resting + cooling
Cooking time: 2 hours
Serves 6

¹/₃ cup (80 ml/2³/₄ fl oz) olive oil
3 capsicums, cored, seeded and
    cut into 2.5 cm (1 inch) pieces
2 cloves garlic, crushed
1 kg (2 lb) neck, shoulder or
    breast of veal, trimmed and
    cut into 2.5 cm (1 inch) pieces
plain flour, seasoned with salt
    and black pepper
40 g (1¹/₄ oz) butter
2 onions, finely chopped
8 French shallots, peeled
¹/₄ teaspoon cayenne pepper
2 teaspoons red wine vinegar
³/₄ cup (185 ml/6 fl oz) chicken
    stock
2 tablespoons chopped fresh
    flat-leaf parsley
375 g (12 oz) home-made or
    bought shortcrust pastry
1 egg, lightly beaten

1 Heat half the oil in a large saucepan. Sauté the capsicum over medium heat for 2–3 minutes. Add the garlic, cover the pan and reduce the heat to low. Cook gently for 5 minutes, then remove from the pan.

2 Put the veal and flour in a plastic bag and shake until the veal is evenly coated, shaking off any excess. Heat the butter and the remaining oil over high heat in the same saucepan and cook the veal in batches until evenly browned. Return all the veal to the pan, add the onion, shallots and cayenne and reduce the heat to low. Cook, covered, for 10 minutes. Stir in the vinegar, cover and turn off the heat. Leave for 10 minutes.

3 Add the capsicum, stock and parsley to the meat, bring to the boil, then reduce the heat to low. Cover and simmer for 20 minutes, or until the meat is tender.

4 Uncover and cook for another 30–40 minutes to reduce the liquid until it thickens and darkens. Season to taste and cool slightly. Preheat the oven to moderately hot 200°C (400°F/ Gas 6) and preheat a baking tray. Lightly grease a 23 cm (9 inch) top, 18 cm (7 inch) base, 3 cm (1¹/₄ inch) deep pie dish.

5 Spoon the filling into the pie dish, levelling the surface. Roll the dough out between two sheets of baking paper to a size slightly larger than the top of the pie dish. Carefully cover the filling and press the pastry over the edge to seal. Neatly trim the edges with a sharp knife. Brush the surface with egg.

6 Roll out the pastry scraps and cut out three cows using a biscuit cutter. Arrange on the pie surface and brush with egg. With the point of a knife, make cuts at the front and back feet of the cows to resemble grass. Place on the hot tray and bake for 30 minutes, or until golden.

Spoon the filling into the pie dish, then level the surface.

FAMILY-STYLE MEAT PIE

Preparation time: 30 minutes + cooling
+ 20 minutes refrigeration
Cooking time: 1 hour 45 minutes
Serves 6

1 tablespoon oil
1 onion, chopped
1 clove garlic, crushed
750 g (1½ lb) beef mince
1 cup (250 ml/8 fl oz) beef stock
1 cup (250 ml/8 fl oz) beer
1 tablespoon tomato paste
1 tablespoon vegetable yeast
    extract
1 tablespoon Worcestershire
    sauce
2 teaspoons cornflour
375 g (12 oz) home-made or
    bought shortcrust pastry
375 g (12 oz) home-made or
    bought puff pastry
1 egg, lightly beaten

1 Heat the oil in a large saucepan over medium heat, add the onion and cook for 5 minutes, or until golden. Increase the heat to high, add the garlic and mince and cook, breaking up any lumps, for about 5 minutes, or until the mince changes colour.
2 Add the stock, beer, tomato paste, yeast extract, Worcestershire sauce and ½ cup (125 ml/4 fl oz) water. Reduce the heat to medium and cook

for 1 hour, or until there is little liquid left. Combine the cornflour with 1 tablespoon water, then stir into the mince and cook for 5 minutes, or until thick and glossy. Remove from the heat and cool completely.
3 Lightly grease a 23 cm (9 inch) top, 18 cm (7 inch) base, 3 cm (1¼ inch) pie tin. Roll the shortcrust pastry out between two sheets of baking paper until large enough to line the base and side of the tin. Remove the top sheet of paper and invert the pastry into the tin, then remove the remaining sheet of paper. Use a small ball of pastry to help press the pastry into the tin, allowing any excess to hang over.
4 Roll out the puff pastry between two sheets of baking paper to a 24 cm (9½ inch) circle. Spoon the filling into the pastry shell and smooth it down. Brush the pastry edges with beaten egg, then place the puff pastry over

the top. Cut off any overhang with a sharp knife. Press the top and bottom pastries together, then scallop the edges with a fork or your fingers, and refrigerate for 20 minutes. Preheat the oven to moderately hot 200°C (400°F/ Gas 6) and heat a baking tray.
5 Brush the remaining egg over the top of the pie, place on the hot tray on the bottom shelf of the oven (this helps make a crisp crust for this pie) and bake for 25–30 minutes, or until golden and well puffed

Spoon the cooled meat filling into the pastry shell.

Trim the edges of the puff pastry with a sharp knife.

PUMPKIN, LEEK AND CORN PIE

Preparation time: 30 minutes
  + cooling
Cooking time: 1 hour 15 minutes
Serves 6

1/3 cup (80 ml/2³/4 fl oz) olive oil
2 leeks, thinly sliced
2 large cloves garlic, chopped
1 butternut pumpkin (1.7 kg/
    3lb 6 oz), peeled, seeded and
    cut into 1 cm (1/2 inch) cubes
3 corn cobs
1¹/2 cups (185 g/6 oz) grated
    Cheddar
1 teaspoon chopped fresh
    rosemary
1/2 cup (15 g/¹/2 oz) chopped
    fresh flat-leaf parsley
12 sheets filo pastry
5 eggs, lightly beaten

1 Preheat the oven to moderate 180°C (350°F/Gas 4). Grease a 32 cm (13 inch) long, 24 cm (9¹/2 inch) wide and 6 cm (2¹/2 inch) deep, ovenproof dish.
2 Heat 1 tablespoon of the oil in a small saucepan and cook the leek and garlic over medium heat for 10 minutes, stirring occasionally, until soft and lightly golden. Transfer to a large bowl and allow to cool.
3 Meanwhile, cook the pumpkin in boiling water for 5 minutes, or until just tender. Drain well and cool. Cook the corn in a saucepan of boiling water for 7–8 minutes, or until tender. Drain, leave until cool enough to handle, then cut away the kernels. Add to the bowl with the cheese, pumpkin, rosemary and parsley, season generously and mix gently but thoroughly.
4 Place the filo pastry on a clean workbench and cover with a damp tea towel to prevent the pastry drying out.

Lightly brush one sheet of filo with oil and place in the dish. Layer five more sheets in the dish, brushing all but the last sheet with oil.
5 Gently stir the eggs into the pumpkin mixture, then spoon into the dish. Cover with the remaining filo pastry, again brushing each layer with oil, and tuck in the edges. Bake for 1 hour, or until the pastry is golden brown and the filling has set. Serve immediately.

Spoon the pumpkin and corn mixture into the ovenproof dish.

Tuck the edges of the filo pastry into the side of the dish.

SAUSAGE AND ONION PIE

Preparation time: 30 minutes
Cooking time: 55 minutes
Serves 6–8

1 tablespoon olive oil
2 onions, chopped
1 clove garlic, chopped
1 kg (2 lb) English-style pork
   sausages
1 tablespoon chopped fresh
   chives
1 teaspoon chopped fresh
   flat-leaf parsley
1¹/₂ teaspoons English mustard
1 egg, lightly beaten
600 g (1¹/₄ lb) home-made or
   bought shortcrust pastry
1 egg, lightly beaten, extra

1 Preheat the oven to moderately hot 200°C (400°F/Gas 6) and grease a 23 cm (9 inch) top, 18 cm (7 inch) base, 3 cm (1¹/₄ inch) metal pie dish. Heat the oil in a frying pan over medium heat, add the onion and garlic and cook for 5 minutes, or until soft and lightly golden. Transfer to a large bowl.
2 Remove the sausage meat from the casings, crumble slightly and add to the onion. Add the chives, parsley and

mustard. Season well with salt and freshly ground black pepper. Mix well, then stir in the beaten egg.
3 Roll out two-thirds of the pastry between two sheets of baking paper to make a round large enough to fit the base and side of the pie tin. Line the tin with the pastry and trim the edges. Fill with the sausage mixture.
4 Roll out the remaining dough between two pieces of baking paper to a round large enough to cover the pie. Brush the rim of the first piece of pastry with the extra egg, then cover the top with the pastry and press the edges to seal. Make a small hole in the centre. Re-roll the scraps, cut into shapes and decorate the pie. Brush the pie with beaten egg and bake

for 10 minutes. Reduce the oven to moderate 180°C (350°F/Gas 4) and bake for 40 minutes. Serve hot.

COOK'S FILE

Note: It's important to use lean, English-style pork sausages as they contain grains which soak up any excess liquid. Other sausages will make the pie too wet.

Using your fingers, remove the sausage meat from the casings.

Fill the pastry-lined pie dish with the sausage mixture.

PRAWN POT PIES

Preparation time: 30 minutes
Cooking time: 40 minutes
Makes 4

2 tablespoons peanut oil
5 cm (2 inch) piece fresh ginger,
    peeled and grated
3 cloves garlic, chopped
1.5 kg (3 lb) raw medium
    prawns, peeled and deveined
1/4 cup (60 ml/2 fl oz) sweet
    chilli sauce
1/3 cup (80 ml/2³/4 fl oz) lime
    juice
1¹/2 teaspoons fish sauce
1/3 cup (80 ml/2³/4 fl oz) cream
4 tablespoons chopped fresh
    coriander leaves
375 g (12 oz) home-made or
    bought shortcrust pastry
1 egg, lightly beaten
milk, for brushing

1 Preheat the oven to moderately hot 200°C (400°F/Gas 6). Grease a baking tray and put it in the oven to heat up. Heat the peanut oil in a large frying pan or wok over medium–high heat and stir-fry the ginger, garlic and prawns for 2–3 minutes. Remove the prawns from the pan. Add the chilli sauce, lime juice, fish sauce and cream and simmer over medium heat for about 5 minutes, or until the sauce has reduced by about one-third. Return the prawns to the pan and stir in the coriander leaves.

2 Roll out the pastry between two sheets of baking paper to 2.5 mm (1/8 inch) thick, and cut out four circles large enough to cover the tops of four 1¹/2 cup (375 ml/12 fl oz) ramekins. Divide the filling among the ramekins, moisten the rims with milk and attach

the lids. Cut a steam hole in each lid. Brush with the egg. Bake for 30 minutes, or until the pastry is lightly browned.

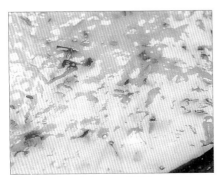

Simmer the mixture until it has thickened and reduced by about one-third.

Add the prawns and chopped coriander to the mixture.

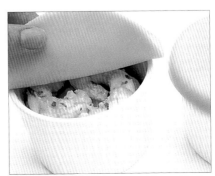

Cover the tops of the ramekins with the pastry rounds.

More than a basic meat pie

For pie lovers, nothing surpasses a plain meat pie. Quick variations of the basic pie can be made by adding a few extra ingredients such as chopped mushrooms or bacon, as well as spices. Toppings can also be varied—mashed potato, for instance, is a popular choice.

MEAT PIE

Preparation time: 25 minutes + cooling
Total cooking time: 55 minutes
Makes 4

1 tablespoon olive oil
1 onion, finely chopped
1 clove garlic, crushed
500 g (1 lb) beef mince
2 tablespoons plain flour
3/4 cup (185 ml/6 fl oz) beef stock
2 tablespoons tomato paste
1 tablespoon Worcestershire
   sauce
4 sheets frozen shortcrust
   pastry, thawed
beaten egg, to glaze

1 Heat the oil in a frying pan, add the onion and cook for 5 minutes, or until softened. Add the garlic and cook for another minute. Add the beef mince and cook over medium heat for 5–7 minutes, or until the mince is browned, carefully breaking up any lumps with a fork.

2 Sprinkle the flour over the meat and stir to combine. Cook for 1 minute, then add the stock, tomato paste, Worcestershire sauce, 1/4 teaspoon salt and some freshly ground black pepper and stir for 2 minutes. Bring to the boil, then reduce the heat slightly and simmer for 10 minutes, or until the mixture has thickened. Cool completely.

3 Preheat the oven to hot 210°C (415°F/Gas 6–7). Place a large baking

tray into the oven to heat. Grease four 11 cm (4½ inch) pie tins. Cut out four 14 cm (5½ inch) rounds from the pastry, line the pie tins, then cut four 11.5 cm (4¾ inch) rounds as lids. Spoon the filling into the pastry cases, put the lids on and seal with beaten egg. Pinch the pastry cases and lids together. Decorate with pastry scraps, brush with the egg and pierce the tops with a fork.

4 Bake on the hot baking tray for 30 minutes, or until the pastry is crisp and brown.

CURRY PIE

Add 1 teaspoon Madras curry powder and, from a can, 2 whole, peeled tomatoes, crushed, to the basic meat mixture and then simply proceed with the recipe.

POTATO PIE

Make the basic meat recipe. Line the pastry cases with pastry. You will only need 2 sheets of frozen pastry. Roughly chop 5 large potatoes and cook in a saucepan of boiling water for 10–15 minutes, or until the potatoes are soft. Drain thoroughly and mash the potatoes with a potato masher. Add ¼ cup (60 ml/2 fl oz) milk and 45 g (1½ oz) butter to the potato and beat in with a wooden spoon until smooth and creamy. Fill the pastry bases with the meat mixture and top the pies with the potato mixture— you can either spread it evenly or, for an attractive effect, pipe it on. Bake for 20–25 minutes, or until the potato topping is lightly golden. This much-loved topping is a delicious variation on pastry.

BACON PIE

Cook 200 g (6½ oz) chopped bacon with the onion as in the original recipe. Don't add any extra salt as the bacon will make the filling salty enough. Follow the recipe as described above.

MUSHROOM PIE

Roughly chop 150 g (5 oz) button mushrooms. Heat 2 tablespoons oil in a frying pan, add the mushrooms and cook for 5 minutes, or until they are golden. Add to the meat mixture before filling the pies, then proceed with the recipe.

Clockwise from back: Curry pie; Potato pie; Basic meat pie; Bacon pie; Mushroom pie

MASHES & SIDES

ROAST VEGETABLE MASH

Preparation time: 30 minutes
Total cooking time: 1 hour 30 minutes
Serves 4–6

2 large pontiac or sebago
   potatoes
400 g (13 oz) pumpkin
400 g (13 oz) orange sweet
   potato
2 large parsnips
1 large onion, chopped
2 tomatoes, quartered
6 cloves garlic
2 tablespoons olive oil
30 g (1 oz) butter,
   chopped

1 Preheat the oven to moderate 180°C (375°F/Gas 4). Peel the potatoes, pumpkin, orange sweet potato and parsnip, then cut into large pieces and place in a large baking dish with the onion, tomato and garlic. Drizzle with the oil and sprinkle with salt and freshly ground black pepper.
2 Roast the vegetables for 1½ hours, or until soft and starting to brown, stirring every 30 minutes.
3 Transfer the vegetables to a bowl, add the butter and mash roughly with a fork. Season to taste with salt and freshly ground pepper and serve.

Peel the potatoes, pumpkin, orange sweet potato and parsnip.

Place the cut vegetables in a large baking dish and drizzle with the oil.

Roast until the vegetables are soft and starting to brown.

Place the vegetables in a bowl, add the butter and mash roughly with a fork.

JERUSALEM ARTICHOKE PUREE

Preparation time: 20 minutes
Total cooking time: 12 minutes
Serve 4–6

rind and juice from 1 lemon
1 kg (2 lb) Jerusalem artichokes
20 g (3/4 oz) butter
2 tablespoons olive oil

1 Add half the lemon juice to a large bowl of water. Peel and slice the artichokes, placing them in the lemon-water as you work to prevent them discolouring. Cook them in a large pot of boiling salted water for 12 minutes, or until tender. Drain well.

2 In a food processor, purée the artichokes, butter, 1 tablespoon of the reserved lemon juice and 1 teaspoon of the lemon rind, adding more juice and rind to taste. With the motor still running, gradually pour in the oil, mixing until it is incorporated. Season to taste and serve hot.

COOK'S FILE

Note: Jerusalem artichokes have a white, sweet, nutty flesh. Buy tubers that look firm and fresh.

Peel and slice the artichokes, placing them in the lemon-water to stop browning.

In a food processor, purée the artichokes, butter, and some rind and lemon juice.

With the motor still running, gradually add the oil and process until incorporated.

CUMIN, MAPLE AND ORANGE SWEET POTATO MASH

Preparation time: 30 minutes
Total cooking time: 15 minutes
Serves 4

750 g (1½ lb) floury potatoes, such as pontiac or spunta
850 g (1 lb 12 oz) orange sweet potato
70 g (2¼ oz) butter
1 onion, very finely chopped
2 teaspoons ground cumin
1 teaspoon ground coriander
1–2 tablespoons maple syrup
⅓ cup (80 ml/2¾ fl oz) cream or milk

1 Peel and chop the potatoes and orange sweet potatoes, then cook them in separate pans of lightly salted boiling water until very tender.

2 While the potato and sweet potato are cooking, melt 40 g (1¼ oz) of the butter in a small frying pan. When the butter is foaming, add the onion and cook over medium heat for 3–4 minutes, or until soft and lightly golden. Stir in the cumin and coriander and cook for 1 minute. Add 1 tablespoon of maple syrup, and half the cream or milk; simmer for about 1 minute. Remove from the heat.

3 Drain the potato and sweet potato and mash separately until smooth and creamy, seasoning to taste. Add the remaining butter and the cream or milk to the potato, beating until creamy. Add the onion mixture to the sweet potato, adding more maple syrup to taste, and beating until smooth.

4 Using a large metal spoon, carefully fold the potato mash with the sweet potato mash, being careful not to overmix—the colours should be quite separate for a marbled effect.

Peel the potatoes and orange sweet potatoes. Chop into evenly sized pieces.

Add some maple syrup and half the cream or milk to the fried onion and spices.

Gently fold the potato and orange sweet potato mashes together.

ORANGE SWEET POTATO MASH WITH CORIANDER

Preparation time: 15 minutes
Total cooking time: 20 minutes
Serves 4

750 g (1¹/₂ lb) orange sweet
  potato
45 g (1¹/₂ oz) butter, chopped
1 clove garlic, crushed
2 teaspoons grated fresh ginger
2 teaspoons soy sauce

1¹/₂ tablespoons chopped
  coriander
sprigs of coriander, to garnish

1 Peel the sweet potato, chop into evenly sized pieces, then cook in a pot of lightly salted boiling water for 10–15 minutes, or until tender. Drain.
2 Melt the butter in a small pan and add the garlic and ginger. Cook over low heat, stirring, for 1 minute.
3 Mash the hot sweet potato until almost smooth. Stir through the garlic mixture, soy sauce and coriander.

Garnish with coriander sprigs and serve immediately.

COOK'S FILE

Serving suggestion: This mash is lovely with pork, chicken, beef or lamb.
Note: Orange sweet potato is sweeter than regular potatoes, with a texture between a potato and a pumpkin.

Peel the sweet potato, and cut into evenly sized pieces.

Fry the garlic and ginger in the melted butter over low heat.

Mash the hot sweet potato and stir in the garlic mixture, coriander and soy sauce.

CELERIAC, POTATO AND ROASTED GARLIC MASH

Preparation time: 20 minutes
Total cooking time: 45 minutes
Serves 4–6

juice of 1 lemon
1 kg (2 lb) celeriac
500 g (1 lb) sebago or pontiac
  potatoes, peeled and chopped
4 large cloves garlic,
  unpeeled
50 g (1³/₄ oz) butter
2 tablespoons cream

1 Preheat the oven to hot 200°C (400°F/ Gas 6). Add the lemon juice to a large bowl of water. Peel and chop the celeriac, placing it in the lemon-water to prevent browning.
2 Cook the celeriac and potatoes in separate pans of lightly salted boiling water. Cook the potatoes for about 15 minutes, or until tender; cook the celeriac for 25 minutes, or until tender. Drain them both well.
3 Meanwhile, place the garlic on a baking tray and bake for 20 minutes, or until softened. Allow to cool a little, then peel away the skins.
4 While the drained potato is still

hot, mash it with the butter and cream. Make sure you use a potato masher as the mixture will become gluggy in a food processor.
5 Process the drained celeriac with the roasted garlic in a food processor until smooth, then beat it into the potato mixture using a wooden spoon. Season to taste with salt and freshly ground black pepper and serve hot.

Add the lemon juice to a large bowl of water. Add the peeled, chopped celeriac.

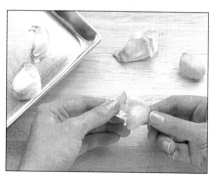

Remove the skins from the cooled cloves of roasted garlic.

Beat the celeriac and garlic mixture into the mashed potato.

FRUITY RICE

Preparation time: 20 minutes
Total cooking time: 25 minutes
Serves 4–6

1/3 cup (80 ml/2³/4 fl oz) olive oil
1¼ cups (250 g/8 oz) basmati rice
1 large onion, finely chopped
2 cloves garlic, crushed
1/3 cup (55 g/2 oz) raisins
1/3 cup (55 g/2 oz) pine nuts
1/3 cup (55 g/2 oz) currants
3 tomatoes, peeled, seeded and
    chopped

1/2 cup (15 g/1/2 oz) chopped
    parsley
1/2 cup (15 g/1/2 oz) chopped mint
plain yoghurt or sour cream,
    to serve

1 Heat half the oil in a large pan, add the rice and stir over medium heat for 2–3 minutes, or until well coated, but not browned. Add 6 cups (2.5 litres) boiling water and bring back to the boil. Boil for 10–12 minutes, or until just cooked. Drain and keep warm.
2 Meanwhile, heat the remaining oil in a frying pan. Add the onion and garlic and cook, stirring, for 3–4 minutes or until soft. Add the raisins, pine nuts and currants; stir for 2–3 minutes. Mix in the tomatoes and herbs.
3 Add the rice and stir until heated through. Season with salt and freshly ground pepper and serve topped with plain yoghurt or sour cream.

COOK'S FILE

Note: This dish is best cooked just before serving, although it may be reheated in a microwave.

Heat half the oil in a large pan. Add the rice and stir until well coated with oil.

When the onion and garlic are soft, stir in the raisins, pine nuts and currants.

Add the cooked rice to the pan and stir until heated through.

SPICED MUSHY PEAS

Preparation time: 15 minutes
Total cooking time: 25 minutes
Serves 4–6

2 tablespoons vegetable oil
1 onion, diced
1/2 teaspoon salt
1/2 teaspoon ground cumin
good pinch of chilli powder
1/2 teaspoon ground cinnamon
1 teaspoon garam masala
500 g (1 lb) fresh or frozen peas
1 cup (250 ml/8 fl oz) vegetable
    stock
2 tablespoons finely chopped
    mint

1 Heat the oil in a pan and cook the onion until softened. Stir in the salt and ground spices; stir-fry over medium heat for 2 minutes, or until fragrant.
2 Add the peas and stir-fry for 2 more minutes, then pour in the stock. Simmer gently for 20 minutes, or until the peas are mushy and the liquid has been absorbed.
3 Stir in the chopped mint and beat with a wooden spoon until the peas are mushy. Serve at once.

COOK'S FILE

Serving suggestion: This is a wonderful side dish for Indian curries and stews.
Note: Garam masala is a blend of up to 12 spices, including pepper, cloves, cinnamon, coriander, cumin, nutmeg and cardamom. It is easy to make, but readily available in supermarkets.

Fry the onion until soft. Add the salt and spices and stir-fry for 2 minutes.

Add the peas and simmer gently until the liquid has been absorbed.

Stir in the mint and beat the peas with a wooden spoon until mushy.

ROAST PUMPKIN AND WALNUT MASH

Preparation time: 20 minutes
Total cooking time: 1 hour
Serves 4

12 walnut halves
1.5 kg (3 lb) pumpkin
olive oil, for brushing
1/3 cup (80 ml/2¾ fl oz) cream
90 g (3 oz) butter
1 tablespoon chopped parsley

1 Preheat the oven to hot 220°C (425°F/Gas 7). Place the walnuts on a baking tray, transfer to the oven and bake for 3–5 minutes, or until the walnuts are brown. Remove from the oven and leave to cool, then chop the walnuts roughly.
2 Peel the pumpkin and chop into even-sized pieces. Place on a baking tray, brush the pumpkin with olive oil, then transfer to the oven and roast for 1 hour, or until soft in the centre.
3 Gently warm the cream in a small saucepan. Place the roasted pumpkin in a food processor and blend with the pulse button until smooth. Add the cream and salt and black pepper to taste, then pulse again until well combined. Do not overprocess.
4 Melt the butter in a small pan and gently cook until nut coloured. Add the chopped parsley, then spoon the mixture over the mash. Garnish with the chopped walnuts to serve.

When the roasted walnuts have cooled, chop them roughly.

Place the peeled pumpkin pieces on a baking tray and brush with olive oil.

Blend the roasted pumpkin in a food processor until smooth. Add the cream.

YELLOW SPLIT PEA AND GARLIC MASH

Preparation time: 10 minutes +
  15 minutes standing
Total cooking time: 1 hour 15 minutes
Serves 4–6

500 g (1 lb) packet dried yellow
  split peas
2–3 cloves garlic, crushed
1 onion, finely diced
6 cups (1.5 litres) chicken
  stock
1 teaspoon salt
2 tablespoons extra virgin olive
  oil
2 tablespoons finely chopped
  parsley

1 Rinse the split peas well, then place them in a large pan with the garlic, diced onion, chicken stock and salt. Bring to the boil and skim off any froth. Reduce the heat, then cover and simmer for 1 hour without stirring, or until the split peas are of a thick, puréed consistency.
2 If the mixture is too wet, remove the lid and simmer for 10–15 minutes, or until thick.
3 Remove the pan from the heat and leave the peas to stand for 15 minutes, or until mash-like. Add the olive oil and chopped parsley and beat with a wooden spoon. Season to taste with salt and freshly ground black pepper and serve.

COOK'S FILE

Serving suggestion: This mash is lovely with roast chicken and warm pitta bread.

Bring the peas, garlic, onion, stock and salt to the boil, skimming off any froth.

Cover and simmer the split pea mixture until thick and of a puréed consistency.

When the peas have cooled and thickened, beat in the olive oil and parsley.

CREAMY MUSHROOM AND POTATO BAKE

Preparation time: 25 minutes
Total cooking time: 50 minutes
Serves 4–6

1 kg (2 lb) potatoes
1 tablespoon cream
20 g (³/₄ oz) butter
1 egg yolk
¹/₄ teaspoon nutmeg

Mushroom Filling
40 g (1¹/₄ oz) butter
125 g (4 oz) mushrooms, finely
    chopped
2 spring onions, finely chopped
50 g (1³/₄ oz) ham, finely
    chopped
60 g (2 oz) Gruyère cheese,
    grated
1 cup (90 g/3 oz) fresh
    breadcrumbs

1 Peel the potatoes and cut them into evenly sized pieces. Cook in boiling salted water for about 15 minutes, or until tender. Drain the potatoes, then mash thoroughly. While the potatoes are still hot, gradually beat in the cream, butter, egg yolk and nutmeg. Season to taste with salt and freshly ground black pepper and set aside.
2 To make the mushroom filling, melt half the butter in a pan and cook the mushrooms and spring onions for 2–3 minutes, or until softened. Add the ham and freshly ground black pepper to taste. Stir well and set aside.
3 Preheat the oven to hot 200°C (400°F/Gas 6). Divide the mashed potato into 2 portions. Spread the first portion evenly into a well-greased 23 cm (9 inch) round ovenproof pie dish. Spread the mushroom filling over the top, sprinkle with the grated cheese, then spread the remaining mashed potato over the top.
4 Melt the remaining butter and stir it through the breadcrumbs, mixing well. Spread the breadcrumbs evenly over the mashed potato, then bake for 30 minutes, or until lightly browned. Serve at once.

Stir the cream, butter, egg yolk and nutmeg into the hot mashed potato.

Fry the mushrooms and spring onions in half the melted butter until soft.

Sprinkle the grated cheese over the mushroom filling.

SWEDE AND ORANGE MASH

Preparation time: 10 minutes
Total cooking time: 20 minutes
Serves 4

1 kg (2 lb) swedes
45 g (1¹/2 oz) butter, chopped
1 teaspoon finely grated orange
   rind
¹/3 cup (80 ml/2³/4 fl oz) orange
   juice
2 teaspoons honey
ground cinnamon, for sprinkling

1 Peel the swedes to remove the thick skin. Chop into evenly sized pieces and cook in lightly salted boiling water until tender. Drain well.

2 While the swedes are still hot, mash them with the butter, orange rind, orange juice and honey. Season to taste with salt and freshly ground black pepper. Sprinkle with cinnamon and serve immediately.

COOK'S FILE

Notes: When grating oranges, avoid the white pith as it has a bitter taste.

● Swedes are often confused with turnips. Turnips are white or pinky white and are usually sold with the green stems attached; swedes are generally bigger with a more yellow flesh. If the swedes are young, you will only need to peel them thinly. Older swedes develop a hard woody stem, best removed by peeling thickly.

Serving suggestion: This mash is lovely with pork, chicken or lamb.

Using a vegetable peeler, peel the swedes to remove the thick skin.

Cook the swedes in boiling water until tender and drain well.

While the swedes are still hot, mash them with the butter, rind, juice and honey.

QUICK ORANGE AND RAISIN COUSCOUS

Preparation time: 10 minutes
Total cooking time: 10 minutes
Serves 4

2 oranges
1½ cups (375 ml/12 fl oz) vegetable stock
2¼ cups (315 g/10 oz) instant couscous

Remove the rind from an orange using a zester or vegetable peeler.

2 cloves garlic, crushed
¼ cup (30 g/1 oz) raisins
60 g (2 oz) butter

1 Remove the rind from 1 of the oranges using a zester—or peel off thin strips using a vegetable peeler, avoiding the bitter white pith, and cut them into fine shreds. Set aside. (You will need 2 tablespoons of zest.)
2 Squeeze the oranges to obtain 1 cup (250 ml/8 fl oz) of juice. Place in a pan with the stock and bring to the boil.

Add the couscous to the boiling orange juice and stock.

Add the couscous, garlic and raisins and stir well. Cover the pan, reduce the heat to low and cook for about 5 minutes, stirring now and then.
3 Remove from the heat and add the butter and orange zest. Mix together well, then cover and set aside for 5 minutes. Separate the grains of couscous with a fork before serving.

Fluff up the cooked grains of couscous using a fork.

ORANGE SWEET POTATO AND SAFFRON MASH

Preparation time: 5 minutes
Total cooking time: 1 hour 50 minutes
Serves 2

1 large floury potato (about 300 g/10 oz), unpeeled
1 orange sweet potato (about 650 g/1 lb 5 oz), unpeeled
¼ cup (60 ml/2 fl oz) milk
pinch of saffron powder (see Note)
30 g (1 oz) butter

1 Preheat the oven to moderate 180°C (350°F/Gas 4). Place the whole potato and sweet potato on a baking dish and bake for 1 hour 45 minutes, or until tender. Check the potato after 1 hour, as it may cook more quickly. Allow to cool enough to handle.
2 Meanwhile, put the milk and saffron in a small saucepan and bring briefly to the boil. Remove from the heat and cover with a lid to prevent a skin forming.
3 Remove the skins from the potato and sweet potato and cut into pieces. Mash with a mouli, ricer or potato masher, but not a food processor or the mash will be gluggy.

4 Add the butter and saffron milk. Transfer to a saucepan and stir over low heat until heated through. Season to taste with salt and freshly ground black pepper and serve at once.

COOK'S FILE

Serving suggestion: This is a nice accompaniment to pork dishes.
Note: Pungent and aromatic, saffron is the world's most expensive spice. If you can't locate any, use a pinch of ground turmeric in this recipe instead.

Place the milk and saffron in a small saucepan and bring to the boil.

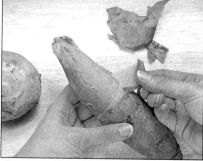

Remove the skins from the baked potatoes and cut the flesh into pieces.

Stir the butter and saffron milk into the mashed potatoes.

187

POTATO AND ZUCCHINI MASH WITH PARMESAN

Preparation time: 10 minutes
Total cooking time: 20 minutes
Serves 4

200 g (6^{1}/2 oz) zucchini
500 g (1 lb) potatoes
    (see Note)
30 g (1 oz) butter
1 clove garlic, crushed
^{1}/4 cup (60 ml/2 fl oz) cream
^{1}/4 cup (25 g/^{3}/4 oz) freshly
    grated Parmesan cheese

1 Grate the zucchini finely, then squeeze the flesh to remove as much moisture as possible. Set aside.
2 Peel the potatoes and chop them into evenly sized pieces, then cook in lightly salted boiling water for about 20 minutes, or until tender.
3 Drain the potatoes thoroughly, then return them to the pan over low heat. Add the butter, garlic and cream and mash until fluffy.
4 Add the grated zucchini and stir well with a wooden spoon until the zucchini has heated through. Remove the pan from the heat, then stir in the grated Parmesan and season to taste with salt and freshly ground black pepper.

COOK'S FILE

Note: Floury potatoes are generally good for mashing. Pontiac and sebago are good all-purpose potatoes that can be relied upon to give good results.

Squeeze the finely grated zucchini to remove as much moisture as possible.

Add the butter, garlic and cream to the potatoes and mash until fluffy.

Stir the grated zucchini into the potato mixture until heated through.

Peel the potatoes using a vegetable peeler and chop into evenly sized pieces.

Roll the potato balls in the egg, then the crushed noodles.

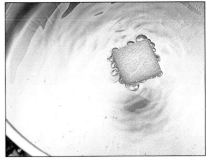

Gently drop a cube of bread into the hot oil to test the temperature.

Deep-fry the thistles in small batches for 2 minutes, or until crisp and golden.

POTATO THISTLES

Preparation time: 25 minutes
Total cooking time: 25 minutes
Makes 30

Thistles
800 g (1 lb 10 oz) potatoes
1/4 cup (25 g/3/4 oz) freshly
   grated Parmesan cheese
2 tablespoons cream
20 g (3/4 oz) butter
1 egg yolk
good pinch of ground nutmeg

Noodle coating
90 g (3 oz) thin vermicelli noodles
1/3 cup (40 g/1 1/4 oz) plain flour
1 egg, beaten with 2 teaspoons
   water
oil, for deep-frying

1 To make the thistles, peel the potatoes and chop into evenly sized pieces. Cook in lightly salted boiling water for 15 minutes, or until tender. Drain the potatoes, then mash them thoroughly. While still hot, beat in the remaining thistle ingredients. Leave to cool, then roll the mixture into small, evenly sized balls.

2 To make the noodle coating, crush the noodles finely, mix them with the flour and then spread them on a tray. Roll the potato balls in the beaten egg, then the crushed noodles.

3 Heat 5 cm (2 inches) of oil in a large, deep pan. Drop a 1 cm (1/2 inch) cube of bread into the oil: if it turns golden brown in 20 seconds, the oil is ready. Cook the thistles a few at a time for 2 minutes, or until crisp and golden—do not overcook, or they will burst. Drain on paper towels and serve hot.

PRESERVED LEMON COUSCOUS

Preparation time: 5 minutes
Total cooking time: Nil
Serves 4

1½ cups (280 g/9 oz) instant
    couscous
1½ cups (375 ml/12 fl oz)
    boiling chicken stock
1½ tablespoons finely chopped
    mint
½ preserved lemon
45 g (1½ oz) butter

1 Place the couscous in a large heatproof bowl. Add the chicken stock and mint and stir to combine. Leave the couscous to stand for 3–4 minutes.
2 Remove and discard the salty flesh from the preserved lemon and rinse the rind thoroughly under running water. Chop the rind finely: you will need 1–2 tablespoons, to taste.
3 Stir the butter and preserved lemon through the couscous with a fork to fluff up the grains. Serve hot.

COOK'S FILE

Notes: If possible, use a low-salt chicken stock or a home-made stock, as preserved lemons are very salty.
● Preserved lemons are sold in some speciality shops. You can make your own by cutting fresh lemons into quarters, then firmly packing them in a jar with salt and lemon juice and leaving them to stand for 4 weeks.
Serving suggestion: Lovely with lamb, beef, veal, chicken or fish.

Place the couscous and mint in a large heatproof bowl. Pour in the boiling stock.

Remove the salty flesh from the preserved lemon using a sharp knife.

Stir the butter and preserved lemon through the couscous with a fork.

PEA PUREE WITH CHIVES AND SOUR CREAM

Preparation time: 30 minutes
Total cooking time: 15 minutes
Serves 4

30 g (1 oz) butter
1 large leek, finely chopped
1 tablespoon finely chopped
   mint
1 chicken stock cube, crumbled
1 kg (2 lb) fresh peas, shelled
1 large lettuce leaf, shredded

2 tablespoons sour cream
1 tablespoon chopped chives
1–2 whole chives, to garnish

1 Melt the butter in a saucepan and gently fry the leek for 5 minutes, or until softened but not browned.
2 Stir in the mint, stock cube, peas and lettuce and just enough water to cover the peas. Bring to the boil, then reduce the heat to low and simmer for 8–10 minutes, or until the peas are tender. Do not overcook or the peas will lose their bright colour.
3 Drain thoroughly, transfer to a food processor and blend until smooth. Season to taste with salt and white pepper, stir in the sour cream and chopped chives, and serve at once, garnished with whole chives.

COOK'S FILE

Note: Instead of fresh peas, you could use 3 cups (450 g/14 oz) frozen peas. Reduce the cooking time to 3–4 minutes.

Fry the finely chopped leek in the butter until soft but not browned.

Stir in the mint, stock cube, peas, lettuce and enough water to cover.

Drain the pea mixture well, then blend in a food processor until smooth.

191

PUMPKIN AND WHITE BEAN PUREE

Preparation time: 25 minutes
Total cooking time: 1 hour 20 minutes
Serves 4

1 kg (2 lb) pumpkin
1 tablespoon olive oil
1 small onion, chopped
1–2 cloves garlic,
 chopped
1 stick celery, chopped
1 carrot, chopped
300 g (10 oz) can butter beans,
 drained and rinsed
1/3 cup (35 g/1 1/4 oz) freshly
 grated Parmesan cheese

1 Preheat the oven to moderate 180°C (350°F/Gas 4). Peel the pumpkin, chop into evenly sized pieces and set aside. Heat the oil in a large flameproof dish on the stove top. Add the onion, garlic, celery and carrot and cook, stirring often, for about 5 minutes, or until the vegetables are softened but not browned. Add the pumpkin and stir thoroughly.

2 Cover the dish with baking paper and bake in the oven for 45 minutes, or until the vegetables are cooked but not browned, stirring the mixture about 3 times during cooking. Allow the vegetables to cool slightly, then transfer to a food processor. Add the drained beans and half the Parmesan and blend to a purée.

3 Spoon the purée into 4 oiled 1-cup (250 ml/8 fl oz) ovenproof ramekins. Smooth the surface and sprinkle with the remaining Parmesan. Bake for about 30 minutes, or until the purée is hot, bubbling and browned.

COOK'S FILE

Note: Dried beans can be used in this recipe. Soak them in a large bowl of water overnight, drain well, then boil in a large pot of water for 1 hour, or until tender. Drain well. You will need to cook about 1/2 cup (100 g/3 1/2 oz) of dried beans for this recipe.

Add the pumpkin pieces to the softened vegetables and cover with baking paper.

Blend the baked vegetables, drained beans and half the Parmesan in a food processor.

Sprinkle the ramekins with the remaining Parmesan and bake for 30 minutes.

CREAMY PARSNIP MASH

Preparation time: 10 minutes
Total cooking time: 15 minutes
Serves 4

1 kg (2 lb) parsnips
20 g (3/4 oz) butter
2 tablespoons cream
1/4 teaspoon ground nutmeg

1 tablespoon finely chopped
 parsley

1 Peel the parsnips, chop into evenly sized pieces and cook in boiling salted water for 15–20 minutes, or until tender. Drain thoroughly.

2 Mash the parsnips well using a potato masher. Using a wooden spoon, gradually beat in the butter, cream, nutmeg, and salt and freshly ground

black pepper to taste. Sprinkle with parsley to serve.

COOK'S FILE

Note: You could use a food processor to mash the parsnip and to blend in the remaining ingredients.

Peel the parsnips and chop them into evenly sized pieces.

Drain the cooked parsnips and mash them using a potato masher.

Gradually beat in the butter, cream, nutmeg, and salt and pepper to taste.

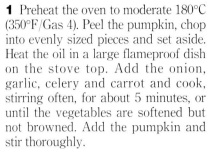
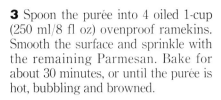

CHAMP

Preparation time: 10 minutes
Total cooking time: 25 minutes
Serves 4–6

**1 kg (2 lb) floury potatoes, such
    as sebago or pontiac
1 cup (250 ml/8 fl oz) milk
6 spring onions, finely chopped
60 g (2 oz) butter**

1 Peel the potatoes, then chop them into evenly sized pieces. Cook the potatoes in a pan of lightly salted boiling water for about 20 minutes, or until tender. Drain and mash well.
2 Meanwhile, pour the milk into a saucepan. Add two-thirds of the finely chopped spring onions and poach them over low heat for 15 minutes. Strain the milk, discarding the spring onions, and whip it into the mashed potato until creamy.

3 Melt the butter in a small pan over low heat. Add the remaining spring onions and gently cook them for about 4 minutes, or until softened.
4 Drizzle the melted butter over the mashed potato then spoon the softened spring onion over the top and serve immediately.

Cook the potatoes for about 20 minutes, or until tender.

Strain the milk into the mashed potato, discarding the poached spring onions.

Add the remaining spring onions to the melted butter and cook until softened.

ORANGE SWEET POTATO CRUMBLE

Preparation time: 25 minutes
Total cooking time: 40 minutes
Serves 4–6

1 kg (2 lb) orange sweet
   potato
50 g (1¾ oz) butter
⅓ cup (80 ml/2¾ fl oz) milk
   or cream
¼ teaspoon ground cinnamon

Crumble topping
480 g (15 oz) loaf sourdough
   bread
½ cup (55 g/2 oz) freshly
   grated Parmesan cheese
1 teaspoon dried thyme

1 Preheat the oven to moderate 180°C (350°F/Gas 4). Peel the orange sweet potato, cut it into chunks, then cook in lightly salted boiling water for about 15 minutes, or until tender. Drain well and return to the saucepan.
2 Mash with a potato masher, adding the butter, milk and cinnamon. Season to taste with salt and freshly ground black pepper, then spoon into a shallow casserole dish and smooth the top.
3 To make the crumble topping, remove the crusts from the bread. Break the bread into smaller pieces and finely chop in a food processor. Mix in the Parmesan and thyme, then scatter over the mash and bake for 20 minutes, or until the crumble is golden and crispy. Serve immediately.

Peel the orange sweet potato and cut into evenly sized chunks.

Spread the mashed potato mixture into a shallow casserole dish.

Sprinkle the crumble topping over the mixture and bake until golden and crisp.

CREAMY POTATO AND PARSNIP MASH

Preparation time: 10 minutes
Total cooking time: 20 minutes
Serves 4–6

2 large potatoes
5 large parsnips
30 g (1 oz) butter
1 tablespoon milk

2 tablespoons sour cream
chopped chives, to garnish

1 Peel the potatoes and parsnips, then chop into evenly sized pieces. Cook them in a large pan of lightly salted boiling water for about 20 minutes, or until soft.
2 Drain well, then transfer to a bowl and mash with the butter, milk and sour cream until smooth and fluffy. Season generously with salt and freshly ground black pepper. Sprinkle with chives and serve.

COOK'S FILE

Note: Sebago, bison, coliban, nicola, pontiac and Kind Edward are some good all-purpose potatoes that give successful results in this recipe.

Peel the potatoes and parsnips and chop them into evenly sized pieces.

Drain the vegetables well and transfer to a large bowl.

Add the butter, milk and sour cream and mash until smooth and fluffy.

WATERCRESS AND POTATO MASH

Preparation time: 20 minutes
Total cooking time: 25 minutes
Serves 4–6

1.5 kg (3 lb) sebago or pontiac
   potatoes
250 g (8 oz) watercress, washed
   and trimmed

1 clove garlic, crushed
1/2 cup (125 ml/4 fl oz) cream
60 g (2 oz) butter

1 Peel and chop the potatoes, then cook in lightly salted boiling water for 20 minutes, or until tender.
2 Blanch the watercress in boiling water for 2 minutes, then rinse with cold water to hold the colour. Chop the watercress finely and place in a pan. Warm gently over low heat.

3 Drain the potatoes, add the crushed garlic, cream and butter, then mash until smooth and creamy. Season to taste with salt and black pepper.
4 Stir the warmed watercress into the mashed potato mixture. Serve at once, garnished with roughly ground black peppercorns.

Drain the blanched watercress well, then chop finely.

Drain the potatoes, then add the garlic, cream and butter and mash until smooth.

Stir the warmed watercress through the mashed potato mixture.

CAULIFLOWER AND FENNEL PUREE

Preparation time: 10 minutes
Total cooking time: 25 minutes
Serves 6

1 medium fennel bulb (see Note)
1 large cauliflower, trimmed
90 g (3 oz) butter
1 tablespoon cider vinegar or
    white wine vinegar
1 teaspoon salt
1/4 teaspoon sugar

1 Reserving the fronds, trim the fennel and finely chop the bulb and thin green stems. Set the stems aside. Cut the cauliflower into florets.
2 In a large pan, melt two-thirds of the butter and gently fry the chopped fennel bulb for 5 minutes, stirring occasionally. Add the cauliflower, toss to coat and cook for 1–2 minutes, then add enough water to just cover.
3 Add the vinegar, salt and sugar and bring to the boil. Reduce the heat and simmer for 15 minutes, or until the cauliflower is very tender. Drain thoroughly, then transfer to a food processor and blend to a smooth purée. Stir in the rest of the butter and the chopped fennel stems. Season to taste and garnish with fennel fronds.

COOK'S FILE

Note: Fennel bulbs are usually sold already trimmed but, if possible, buy an untrimmed bulb for this recipe, so you can use the stalks to add flavour, and the fronds to garnish.

Trim the fennel, reserving the fronds and thin green stems. Chop the bulb finely.

Add the cauliflower florets to the fennel and add enough water to just cover.

Stir the remaining butter and finely chopped fennel stems into the purée.

CREAMY CORN AND POTATO MASH

Preparation time: 15 minutes
Cooking time: 15 minutes
Serves 4

6 fresh corn cobs
1 large pontiac potato
    (about 200 g/6¹/2 oz),
    peeled and chopped
40 g (1¹/4 oz) butter
1 onion, chopped
2 tablespoons cream

1 Remove the husks and silks from the corn. Cook the corn cobs in a large pan of lightly salted boiling water for about 5 minutes, then drain and allow to cool.
2 Cook the potato in a separate pan of lightly salted boiling water until tender, then drain well and mash.
3 Melt the butter in a small pan over low heat. Add the onion and cook, stirring, for about 5–10 minutes, or until very soft but not browned.
4 Cut the kernels from the corn with a sharp knife, then blend them with the cooked onion in a food processor until smooth, adding salt and freshly ground black pepper to taste. Stir in the mashed potato and cream, and season again with salt to taste.

COOK'S FILE

Note: When removing cobs of corn from their husks, wipe around the cob using a damp cloth: this will help remove the silks that persistently cling to the corn kernels.

Remove the husks and silks from the cobs of corn.

Using a sharp knife, cut the kernels from the cooled corn.

Stir the mashed potato and cream into the puréed corn mixture.

CREAMY POLENTA WITH PARMESAN, PAPRIKA AND GARLIC

Preparation time: 10 minutes
Total cooking time: 10 minutes
Serves 4

1 teaspoon salt
2 cloves garlic, crushed
1 cup (150 g/5 oz) instant polenta
1/2 cup (125 ml/4 fl oz) cream
40 g (1 1/4 oz) butter, chopped
1/3 cup (35 g/1 1/4 oz) freshly
   grated Parmesan cheese
1/4 teaspoon paprika, and extra
   to garnish
Parmesan cheese shavings,
   to garnish

1 In a large, heavy-based pan, bring 3 1/2 cups (875 ml/28 fl oz) water to the boil. Add the salt and garlic. Stir in the polenta with a wooden spoon, breaking up any lumps. Cook over medium heat for 4–5 minutes, or until smooth, stirring often.

2 Add half the cream and cook for 2–3 minutes, or until the polenta is thick and comes away from the pan. Stir in the butter. Remove from the heat and stir in the Parmesan, paprika and remaining cream. Transfer to a warm serving bowl and sprinkle with paprika. Garnish with Parmesan shavings and serve at once.

COOK'S FILE

Notes: Polenta must be served hot to keep its creamy, light consistency.
• Use a vegetable peeler to peel cheese shavings from a block of Parmesan.

Pour the polenta into the boiling water, stirring well with a wooden spoon.

Add half the cream to the polenta and cook for 2–3 minutes, or until thick.

Stir in the Parmesan, paprika and the rest of the cream.

POTATO AND GARLIC MASH WITH FRESH TOMATO RELISH

Preparation time: 40 minutes
Total cooking time: 25 minutes
Serves 4

1.5 kg (3 lb) floury potatoes
50 g (1³/4 oz) butter
3 cloves garlic, crushed
¹/4 cup (60 ml/2 fl oz) cream

Fresh Tomato Relish
2 tablespoons olive oil
1 onion, finely chopped
2 cloves garlic, crushed
2 teaspoons ground cumin
2 teaspoons ground coriander
3 ripe tomatoes, chopped
2 teaspoons soft brown sugar
¹/4 cup (30 g/1 oz) sultanas or
    raisins
1 teaspoon balsamic vinegar
1 tablespoon chopped oregano
1 tablespoon chopped lemon
    thyme
1 tablespoon chopped parsley

1 Peel the potatoes and cut into evenly sized pieces. Cook in lightly salted boiling water until tender.
2 While the potatoes are cooking, make the fresh tomato relish. Heat the oil in a heavy-based pan, add the onion, garlic, cumin and coriander and stir over medium heat for 2–3 minutes, or until the onion softens. Add the tomatoes and cook for 5–10 minutes. Stir in the sugar, sultanas and vinegar and simmer for 5 minutes. Stir in the herbs and keep the relish warm.
3 Drain the potatoes well. Add the butter, garlic and cream and mash until smooth and creamy. Season with

salt and freshly ground pepper. Serve topped with the tomato relish and sprinkle with fresh herbs.

Fry the onion, garlic and spices in the hot oil until the onion softens.

Add the sugar, sultanas and vinegar and simmer for 5 minutes.

Mash the potatoes, butter, garlic and cream until smooth and creamy.

COLCANNON

Preparation: 15 minutes
Cooking time: 15–20 minutes
Serves 4

800 g (1 lb 10 oz) floury potatoes
90 g (3 oz) butter, chopped
3 cups (225 g/7 oz) finely shredded green cabbage
8 spring onions, finely chopped
2/3 cup (170 ml/5½ fl oz) milk

pinch of ground nutmeg
chopped parsley, to garnish

1 Peel the potatoes and cut them into evenly sized pieces. Cook them in lightly salted boiling water for about 15 minutes, or until tender. Drain the potatoes, return them to the pan and stir over low heat until all the moisture has evaporated, then mash well.
2 Melt a third of the butter in a frying pan, add the shredded cabbage and stir-fry over high heat until softened and lightly browned. Stir in the chopped spring onions.

3 Add the remaining butter and milk to the mashed potato. Stir the cabbage mixture into the potato with the nutmeg, and salt and freshly ground black pepper to taste. Sprinkle with chopped parsley to serve.

COOK'S FILE

Note: King Edward, russet and spunta are some floury potatoes. You could also use pontiac or sebago.

Stir the drained potatoes over medium heat until the moisture has evaporated.

Fry the cabbage in a third of the butter until softened. Stir in the spring onions.

Add the remaining butter and milk to the mashed potato.

CARROT AND TURNIP MASH WITH GOLDEN APPLES

Preparation time: 30 minutes
Total cooking time: 15–20 minutes
Serves 4

3 large carrots
3 large turnips or swedes
1 green apple
1 red apple
60 g (2 oz) butter
2 teaspoons soft brown sugar
1 tablespoon golden syrup
1 teaspoon Dijon mustard
1 teaspoon mixed spice
finely chopped chives, to serve

1 Peel and chop the carrots and turnips and cook in lightly salted boiling water until very tender.
2 Meanwhile, core the apples with an apple corer, leaving the skin on, and cut into 1 cm (½ inch) slices.
3 Melt two-thirds of the butter in a large non-stick frying pan. Add the sugar, syrup, mustard and mixed spice. Stir over medium heat until the sugar starts to dissolve, then add the apple slices in a single layer. Simmer gently for 8–10 minutes over medium-low heat until the apples are tender, golden yet still firm, carefully turning once or twice during cooking.
4 Drain the turnips and carrots. Add the remaining butter and some salt and black pepper and mash until smooth. Serve with the apple slices, sprinkled with chives and freshly ground black pepper.

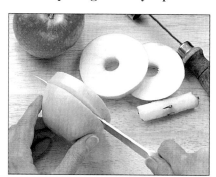

Leaving the skin on, core the apples using an apple corer, then cut into slices.

In a single layer, add the apple slices to the spiced sugar syrup.

Season the turnips and carrot, then mash with the remaining butter until smooth.

203

KALAMATA OLIVE AND POTATO MASH

Preparation time: 20 minutes
Total cooking time: 20 minutes
Serves 4–6

1 kg (2 lb) pontiac or desiree
   potatoes, chopped
2 tablespoons extra virgin olive
   oil
30 g (1 oz) butter
6 spring onions, finely sliced
1/3 cup (80 ml/2¾ fl oz) milk
16 Kalamata olives, pitted and
   roughly chopped
1 tablespoon chopped chives

1 Peel the potatoes, chop them into evenly sized pieces, then cook in lightly salted boiling water for about 20 minutes, or until tender.
2 While the potatoes are cooking, heat the olive oil and butter in a small pan and cook the spring onions over low heat for about 3 minutes, or until soft. Set aside.
3 Drain the potatoes well and return them to the saucepan. Mash the potatoes using a potato masher, adding the milk and spring onion while mashing. Season to taste with salt and freshly ground black pepper and stir with a wooden spoon until well combined.
4 Stir in two-thirds of the chopped olives. Spoon the mash into a warm serving dish and scatter with the remaining olives and chopped chives to serve.

Add the spring onions to the olive oil and melted butter and fry until soft.

Mash the potatoes, adding the milk and sautéed spring onion mixture.

Stir two-thirds of the chopped olives into the mashed potato mixture.

INDEX

A

apple(s)
    braise, Pork and, 52
    Carrot and turnip mash with golden, 203
    Chicken calvados with glazed, 39
artichoke
    and potato topping, Veal pie with Jerusalem, 147
    purée, Jerusalem, 176
    stew, Beef and globe, 58
Asparagus pie, 117

B

bacon
    pie, 173
    pie, Egg and, 137
    turkey and cider pie, 130
    and zucchini, Spring veal with, 77
baked beans, Boston, 8
beef
    in beer with capers and anchovies, 111
    bourguignon, 80
    and caramelised onion pie, 152
    carbonnade, 83
    and globe artichoke stew, 58
    olives, 40
    and peppercorn stew, 106
    pie, 118
    pie, Burgundy, 140
    potato and capsicum stew, Spicy, 9
    in red wine, 14
    sausage and mushroom stew, 43
    stew, Country, 21
    stew, Mexican, 23
    stew with pecans, 25
    stout and potato pie, 133
    see also steak
Bombay curry lamb, 62
Boston baked beans, 8
Braised chicken with chickpeas, 17
Braised lamb shank pie, 165
Burgundy beef pie, 140

C

Cajun spiced fish braise, 88

Carrot and turnip mash with golden apples, 203
Casserole of autumn vegetables, 67
Casserole of curries vegetables, 82
Cauliflower and fennel purée, 198
Celeriac, potato and roasted garlic mash, 179
Champ, 194
Chargrilled vegetable and Parmesan pie, 120
cheese
    and onion pie, 154
    pie, Potato and, 148
    and potato pie, Ham, 153
chicken
    with baby vegetables, Country-style, 98
    cacciatore, 56
    calvados with glazed apples, 39
    chasseur, 44
    with chickpeas, Braised, 17
    and coconut cream curry, 74
    and corn pies, 161
    curry, 32
    leek and mushroon pies, 116
    and leek pie, 113
    Majorcan, 107
    marsala, 38
    Mediterranean, 97
    and mushroom casserole, 15
    and noodle casserole, Vietnamese, 79
    and orange casserole, 86
    Persian, 63
    pies, Mini Thai, 135
    potato and preserved lemon pie, 159
    Roman, 18
    with sherry, raisins and pine nuts, 56
    stew, Creamy tomato and, 16
chickpea
    Braised chicken with, 17
    and vegetable curry, 76
chilli
    beans, 59
    con carne, 50
    con carne pie, 160
    Vegetarian, 11
Chinese barbecued pork pies, 156
Chunky veal and capsicum pie, 167
Cioppino, 104
Cocktail leek pies, 146
Colcannon, 202
Coq au vin, 68
Cottage pie, 157
Country beef stew, 21

Country rabbit in red wine, 45
Country-style chicken with baby vegetables, 98
couscous
    Preserved lemon, 190
    Quick orange and raisin, 187
    Vegetable stew with, 53
Creamy chicken with mushrooms, 20
Creamy corn and potato mash, 199
Creamy mushroom pie, 144
Creamy mushroon and potato bake, 184
Creamy parsnip mash, 192
Creamy polenta with Parmesan, paprika and garlic, 200
Creamy potato and parsnip mash, 196
Creamy tomato and chicken stew, 16
Cumin, maple and orange sweet potato mash, 177
Curry pie, 173

D

duck curry, Gingered, 99

E

Egg and bacon pie, 137
eggplant
    pie, Lamb and, 125
    pot, Pork and, 42

F

Family-style meat pie, 168
Famous Irish stew, 26
fennel
    casserole, Veal and, 89
    pie, Sweet potato and, 141
    pies, Mini seafood and, 132
    and potato stew, Seafood, 105
    purée, Cauliflower and, 198
fish
    braise, Cajun spiced, 88
    and broad bean pie, White, 122
    pie, 138
    Luxury fisherman's pie, 121
    stew, Lemon grass, coriander and, 46
Fruity rice, 180

Ruler markings in left margin: 1 cm through 25 cm

USEFUL INFORMATION

All our recipes are thoroughly tested. Standard metric measuring cups and spoons are used in the development of our recipes. All cup and spoon measurements are level. We have used 60 g (2 oz) eggs in all recipes. Sizes of cans vary from manufacturers to manufacturers and between countries—use the can size closest to the one suggested in the recipe.

CONVERSION GUIDE

1 cup	= 250 ml (8 fl oz)
1 teaspoon	= 5 ml
1 Australian tablespoon	= 20 ml (4 teaspoons)
1 UK/US tablespoon	= 15 ml (3 teaspoons)

Dry Measures	Liquid Measures	Linear Measures
30 g = 1 oz	30 ml = 1 fl oz	5 mm = ¼ inch
250 g = 8 oz	125 ml = 4 fl oz	1 cm = ½ inch
500 g = 1 lb	250 ml = 8 fl oz	2.5 cm = 1 inch

CUP CONVERSIONS—DRY INGREDIENTS

1 cup cheese, grated, lightly packed:

    natural Cheddar = 125 g (4 oz)

    processed cheddar = 155 g (5 oz)

    Parmesan, Romano = 125 g (4 oz)

1 cup flour = 125 g (4 oz)

1 cup minced pork or beef = 250 g (8 oz)

1 cup pasta shapes = 125 g (4 oz)

1 cup rice, shortgrain, raw = 200 g (6½ oz)

1 cup split peas = 250 g (8 oz)

1 cup instant polenta = 150 g (5 oz)

OVEN TEMPERATURES

In the following temperature ranges, the lower temperature applies to gas ovens, the higher to electric ovens. This is to allow for the fact that the flame in gas ovens generates a drier heat, which effectively cooks food faster than the moister heat of an electric oven, even if the temperature setting is the same.

Mark	°C	°F	Gas
Very slow	120	250	½
Slow	150	300	2
Warm	160	315	3
Moderate	180	350	4
Mod hot	200	400	6
Hot	210	415	6–7
Very hot	230	450	8

Note: For fan-forced ovens check your appliance manual, but as a general rule, set oven temperature to 20°C lower than the temperature indicated in the recipe.

INTERNATIONAL GLOSSARY

capsicum	red or green pepper
plain flour	all-purpose flour
cornflour	cornstarch
eggplant	aubergine
snow pea	mange tout
spring onion	scallion
zucchini	courgette

First published in 2003 by Murdoch Books Pty Limited, Erico House, 6th Floor North, 93-99 Upper Richmond Road, Putney, London SW15 2TG.

This edition published in 2007 for Index Books Ltd, Garrard Way, Kettering, Northants, NN16 8TD

ISBN-13: 1 921259 37 X
ISBN-10: 978 1 921259 37 1

Food Editors: Rebecca Clancy, David Herbert, Kathy Knudsen, Kerrie Ray, Tracy Rutherford.
Recipe Development: Alison Adams, Rebecca Clancy, Amanda Cooper, Michelle Earl, Joanne Glynn, Justine Finlay, Jo Glynn, David Herbert, Janelle Holmes, Kathy Knudsen, Valli Little, Barbara Lowery, Sally Parker, Kim Passenger, Kerrie Ray, Jo Richardson, Alison Turner and the Murdoch Test Kitchen team.
Home Economists: Renée Aiken, Anna Beaumont, Jo Forrest, Wendy Goggin, Michelle Lawton, Kerrie Mullins, Peter Oszko, Zoe Radze, Margo Smithyman, Alison Turner. **Photography:** Jon Bader, Cris Cordeiro, Luis Martin. **Step-by-step Photography:** Reg Morrison, Andy Payne.
Food Stylists: Carolyn Fienberg, Sarah O'Brien. **Food Preparation:** Jo Forrest, Justin Finlay, Valli Little.
Chief Executive: Juliet Rogers. **Publisher:** Kay Scarlett.

Printed by Sing Cheong Printing Company Ltd.
PRINTED IN CHINA